Great
BEAR

Great BEAR

A Journey Remembered

Frederick B. Watt

Outcrop Ltd.
Yellowknife, Northwest Territories

First printing 1980
Second printing 1982

ISBN 0-919315-00-3

Design: John Allerston

Editor: Rosemary Allerston

Photographs:
F. B. Watt
Unless otherwise indicated

Outcrop Ltd.
The Northern Publishers
Box 1114, Yellowknife, Northwest Territories
Canada X0E 1H0

Printed and bound in Canada

For Ernie.

Foreword

My first sight of Great Bear Lake was in 1929, when I dropped three prospectors at Hunter Bay. I was filled with astonishment at its size and the grandeur of the cliffs and fiords of the eastern shoreline.

Ted Watt is a lifelong friend. I've known him since we were boys and teenagers growing up in Edmonton some 65 years ago. He was always big for his age and became a strong, heavyset fellow– a characteristic that was to stand him in good stead when he faced the rigors of an Arctic winter on Great Bear in 1932.

This book is a true story of the adventures and misadventures of two men who, thrown together by economic necessity, became dependent on each other for survival whether they liked it or not. Neither had any real experience of the relentless winter weather they would have to cope with, or the close confinement of a small tent, or the daily chores that went with wood, water and food.

The story of their adventures in the rugged terrain of Great Bear Lake, woven with Ted's personal feelings and reactions makes *Great Bear* doubly interesting.

I share with the author and some of the men he mentions a great respect and love for the stark beauty of this, the greatest of all lakes in Canada.

C.H. "Punch" Dickins
September, 1980

1

It is a giant among the world's freshwater seas. Astride the Arctic circle, it is instantly identifiable on the smallest-scale map of Canada. It stretches in burnished beauty under the unsleeping summer sun, 12 000 square miles of liquid ice moving restlessly between its low western shore and the craggy heights that contain it to the east. With autumn comes twilight and grey turbulence. The huge swells have 150 miles in which to gather strength before they shatter against the eastern mountains. Even after winter's shield has crushed the life from them, the fury of the waves can be seen chiseled in crystal, high on the naked stone.

This is Great Bear Lake, long shrouded in mystery and superstition, as cold and pitiless as the treeless Barren Ground which lies to its north.

Until 1930, Great Bear brooded in the vast silence of the Northern wilderness, unknown to much of the world. Then, in May of that year, two prospectors trudged onto the ice of its eastern shore. They were worn with their struggle, and one of them had become helplessly snow-blind. They camped at the entrance to one of the great fiords, called Echo Bay. The healthy man struck out alone, making a skilled examination of the rocky cliffs that rose from the snow. On a hanging wall, his prospector's hammer exposed a blaze of ore. It was a spectacularly broad vein of pitchblende, black and glossy amid streaks of silver and copper. The man had dreamed of this discovery, and he knew something of its meaning. His name was Gilbert LaBine and he named his find Eldorado.

News of his strike traveled far and fast when it reached the Outside. Pitchblende, processed into radium, had vital uses in medicine. It fetched enormous prices on the world market and could be profitably mined, even in remote Great Bear.

The discovery was a beacon, a solitary ray of hope to an economy that was floundering in the darkness that followed the crash of 1929.

Great Bear became a magnet to men battered by the ravages of the Depression. Its name was magic, and they began to follow LaBine's trail north.

I was one of those men.

My journey to Great Bear, motivated by need and hope, became something more than a prospector's adventure. It was a journey into a savage land, a country for which I was unprepared. And it became a desolate struggle, a passage into the dark landscape of the self. It was, I think, the most important chapter of my life.

In that harsh environment, I encountered hardships that stretched my physical strength to its very last limits, and psychological pressures that stripped me of all pretension to civilized behavior. The journey to Great Bear took me to the edge of my world, and made me look on it with new eyes.

The cold crucible of the lake seared and shaped me. But I could not know this when my journey began.

Great Bear had been a legend for me since boyhood. I was brought to Edmonton by my parents in 1905, at the age of four. It was then the brand-new capital of the brand-new province of Alberta, with a river of mud for a main street. It surged with ox carts and dog trains, prairie schooners and buggies, water carts and drays. There were even five automobiles. Some of the buildings of the old log fort, high above the swift-running North Saskatchewan river, were still in use, and Indian tribes camped yearly on the flats below it. Citizens on the outskirts, five or six streets away, had their chicken coops raided occasionally by lynx and coyote.

My parents were newspaper people, and our little apartment in a brick building on Jasper Avenue was always filled with visitors. They flowed in and out, telling stories that stirred my boyish dreams, until the North itself seemed to surge around me like a deep sea, flowing in and out of the sluice-gate city. Names like Athabaska, Great Slave, and Mackenzie were part of my earliest vocabulary.

Northmen became my heroes, skinning rabbits before my amazed eyes, raising teepees in the front yards of my playmates, and telling wonderful tales. Three men in particular shaped my dreams, and set my imagination afire with images of Great Bear.

They were Cosmo Melvill, John Hornby and George Douglas. Though widely different in character, all three had certain things in common. None had natural roots in the North. All were well-educated. And each had a hard-won familiarity with Great Bear Lake. This put them in a select class even among Northerners. The remote monster, partially explored by Sir John Franklin in the nineteenth century, had been visited by only a scatter of white men since.

The degree of Great Bear's isolation could be measured by the fact that its largest inflowing river, the Camsell, had remained nameless until 1900 when it was traversed by a federal geologist, Dr. Mackintosh Bell, and Charles Camsell, his young assistant.

The lake's gateway was the Bear River, a steep, 90-mile rock trench which spurted its crystal waters into the brown flood of the Mackenzie at Fort Norman. Under normal conditions, when the stream was clear of its own ice and that which it sucked out of the lake, the hardy and lightly laden Indians of the area could make the voyage to Fort Norman in 10 hours. Returning against the current took at least as many days. Rare, more heavily equipped parties, running into unfavorable conditions, had measured their upward progress in weeks as they had been forced to track their boats along steep shores that frequently refused even a decent foothold.

Melvill, Hornby and Douglas, like Franklin in 1825, reached Great Bear by forcing the fiercely resisting river. There was no mechanical substitute for brutal hard work and simple determination.

Melvill, who reached the lake in 1908, was an Englishman of means who took an orderly interest in far places. He had a considerable knowledge of flora and fauna and an instinct to expand it. When he carried his personal and scientific curiosity to Great Bear, he also carried an outfit for trading with the native trappers who were its semi-nomadic inhabitants.

Hornby accompanied Melvill as one of his helpers and found in the Canadian wilderness something which both deeply satisfied him and eternally lured him. It drove him to his death, on the Barrens in 1927.

Melvill returned south in 1911 just as Douglas, an engineer setting out to explore the Barrens between the northwest corner of the lake and the mouth of the Coppermine, moved north. Hornby transferred from one party to the other. Douglas was interested in the heavy mineralization that had been reported in the Coppermine region ever since Samuel Hearne had followed that river to the Arctic in 1771.

Unconscious of a small boy on the fringes of their adult audience, these three explorers wove stories of Great Bear that filled me with dreams of its color and savagery. I marveled at their journeys and their heroism: living off the land, struggling against incredible odds, covering unimaginable distances. And I imagined, always, the monstrous lake itself. An intangible link had begun to grow within me, a link with the lonely land and the mysterious saltless sea at its heart.

I knew every word of the old stories of fur traders and explorers and massacres in the Barrens. I knew that my parents' friends were among the very few white men who had seen Great Bear in the twentieth century – that it still lay in stone-age solitude, with even its trading post at Fort Franklin, near the mouth of the Bear River, deserted most of the time.

It was my overriding ambition to one day see Great Bear for myself.

Those early years of the century, during which I grew tall enough to lie about my age and join the Navy in World War I, paved the way for sudden development in the North. The first serious tremors of change came in 1920.

Life on the long-established highway of Mackenzie's river had altered little since the years immediately following its discovery. Wood-burning paddle steamers had supplanted the big freight canoes, a few amenities had been added to the forts of the fur traders which, every 150 miles or so, marked the confluence of secondary streams with the main waterway. Even as close-in a post as Fort Chipewyan on Lake Athabaska, where Mackenzie had been based when he had set out to confirm the Indian-reported path to the Northern ocean, still remained a picturesque dot on the ancient route of the fur traders. The new railhead at Waterways had made little difference to the habits of the place.

When the beginnings of the transformation came it was with electrifying suddenness. Fifty miles downstream from where Great Bear's crystal waters met those of the tawny Mackenzie, an Imperial Oil Company crew, unobtrusively probing the dark seepages Mackenzie himself had noted, found what they were seeking. Many days passed before the word could be carried to Waterways but, once it had reached the telegraph wire there, the paddle wheelers began to have outsize passenger lists. A full-scale staking rush convulsed the season of ice-free navigation.

During the excitement below Fort Norman, Imperial Oil decided to establish a private air service between the discovery well and the Outside. Their two Junkers monoplanes were of considerable value to the newspapers, for whom they provided some magnificent stories, but the project was eventually suspended and for several years the ponderous calm of the Mackenzie basin returned. The restless airmen who flew the planes carried on, however.

They began with forays into remote mining areas farther south, chiefly in Quebec, Ontario and Manitoba. Little charter outfits began to learn as they earned. Lessons in the rudiments of bush flying came high, as did lessons in shoestring finance. In 1926, however, James Richardson of Winnipeg, a man of wealth and boldness, established a substantial service, known as Western Canada Airways. The association between the airplane and the North quickened.

The pilots were men of my own generation, with whom I had grown up in Edmonton and shared the city's transition from frontier settlement to provincial capital. Wop May, the war ace who flew the first Imperial Oil Junkers to Edmonton, and Punch Dickins, who later on was to drop Gilbert LaBine onto Great Bear's ice where his discovery was made, were both schoolmates. Their saga, from its beginnings, was an immediate experience for me.

They were young men in a hurry, charged with the dynamism of wartime air battles, which they were applying to the building of a new industry and the breaking open of a million square miles of harsh new terrain. They ranged over distant reaches of tundra and mountain in a fraction of the time it had taken the earlier explorers.

The fliers took on the style and mystique of the North's earlier explorers and trail breakers. They learned to dress and eat and sleep like bushmen, for the mechanical wonders they depended upon to tame the primeval were far from infallible. A moment's poor judgment or bad luck, a lost gamble, could put a flier down in the forest or tundra, and back into the stone age. Survival depended on wisdom and experience borrowed from the native people, plus a wide streak of courage and stubbornness.

Their exploits were the stuff of Northern legend.

When I followed my parents into newspaper work in 1920, as a reporter for the Edmonton Journal, the new North and the men who were creating it became fruitful sources of copy. By 1928 I had exchanged the routine deadlines of a staff job for the independent life of a freelance writer. The colorful adventures of my flier friends were eagerly read in the South. I shortly acquired a quadrupled income and a New York agent.

By the summer of 1929 the Northern revolution had gained momentum. Freely flowing risk capital, released by an unprecedented North American stock market boom, had enabled the planes of both charter companies and large mineral exploration concerns to crisscross the Territories. The federal government had ordered the Canadian Corps of Signals into the Mackenzie valley and five wireless stations, spaced between Fort McMurray and Aklavik, began to provide weather reports and other blessings of instant communication.

Wop May was acquainting himself with the lower reaches of the Mackenzie as chief pilot of Commercial Airways, a new company that had won the contract to establish the regular mail and passenger service from the railhead to the Arctic. Punch Dickins was making the same territory his own as flying superintendent for Western Canada Airways.

On October 23, 1929, the first paralyzing breath of the Depression reached the stock markets. Compared to it, the tundra gales were gentle.

It was a huge and numbing setback for me: the first in a 28-year life which, up until then had passed in an easy and orderly way. I had been married for nearly four years to Ernestine Mattern, whom I'd met at the Armistice Ball of 1924. She was at that time supervising the soldiers' pavilion at Edmonton's University Hospital. We shared what passed for sophistication among our postwar generation, she having nursed in China and I having served in the wartime navy. Our life was hardly complicated, we thought, by the easy credit of which we took eager advantage during the twenties. We had a son, Erik, who was three when the roof fell in.

The effects of the market crash were brutal. Within the month, the rich magazine market which had sustained my writing career dried up. Publications folded overnight, and even payment for work already published was months in coming. Nothing remained of the boomtime interlude except the bills. We cashed insurance policies, sold household goods. And still the creditors could not be paid.

Ernie, with the courage of her pioneer parents, stood up to it all bravely. I needed her self-reliance, as my hope and confidence steadily eroded.

We moved from our apartment to an old frame house on the outskirts of the city. In winter, the cold bit through its uninsulated walls, using up all our precious coal, and forcing us to live on one floor, huddling by the kitchen stove.

As our hardships increased, my self-confidence plummetted. I had always had a terror of not being able to pay my own way. Now it seemed as if I could not make a living for my family. I could not face the harsh new realities crowding in on me, and turned increasingly to the solace of the bottle. I had begun a pattern of heavy drinking in the years right after World War I. Even though I had been too idealistic to quaff the ritual tot of rum when I was at sea, I was disoriented and anxious to prove my adult masculinity when I got out of the Navy. I thought people *expected* a grizzled veteran of 18 to be a boozer.

The habit had grown to the point where I needed to drink. The 1929 crash made the need acute. Booze became my only escape. If I couldn't buy it, I scrounged it, my self-respect in tatters. And I tried, still, to make a living. My attempts became increasingly frantic and futile. But at last things took a temporary turn for the better.

I had a big news break when I flew to Aklavik on the very first mail flight. It began with a chance encounter on Jasper Avenue, one November morning. Wop May came in sight, his cloth cap pulled low against the driving snow. The wind cut right through our conversation, but he stopped long enough to ask, "How're things?"

I told him.

"Tough," he commented, almost roughly, and we resumed our separate ways. But a moment later, he was calling me back.

"If I could sell the company on your covering the Aklavik first flight would you consider it?"

"Try me," I said, attempting to keep a desperate new hope from my voice.

He was on his way to a directors' meeting but it was several days before the suspense ended. Eventually his fellow directors agreed that the publicity would justify the weight of already carefully measured cargo I would have to displace.

When it was settled the Journal agreed to pay $3 a column for whatever I filed with the new wireless stations along the route. But no advance was forthcoming. I managed to scratch up a $100 loan for imperative Arctic clothing and for subsistence during the week I expected to be away.

We set off in the Red Armada – two Bellanca monoplanes bearing the insignia of Commercial Airways – and dropped into Fort Norman on Christmas Eve, 1929. We were carrying a mountain of first covers, forwarded by stamp collectors anxious to have souvenirs of the new mail service. Until this night, there had been only one winter mail delivery to Aklavik each year by dog team: It had taken two months to carry the sacks from Fort McMurray, the end of steel, 2000 miles south. Our flight would change all that.

We were still two days away from completion of our mission, but the airmen were working in a strong undercurrent of excitement: they knew the historic job *would* get done.

I was experiencing another kind of excitement – for I knew that Norman was the gateway to Great Bear. We were only half an hour's flight from the lake, and I felt its presence, a mythic solitude in my imagination. We had seen Great Bear's waters, open even in the iron-hard winter, where they poured into the Mackenzie. The current was too violent, the force of the Bear's watershed too great, for the rivers to freeze over at their joining-point.

That night, I was filled with the cold magic of the North, as we watched the aurora borealis and traded stories. The temperature was − 55 °F. We sat together in the snug log-house quarters of Fort Norman's manager, Bill Cooke, listening to the still novel radio. We were conscious of our isolation on this holiday night. Messages came through for us, Christmas wishes from Wop May's wife, Vi; and for me, from my son Erik. We listened raptly to this tenuous link with the Outside. Then a news broadcast came on, crackling with interference from the Northern Lights.

We heard snippets of news about the Depression-ravaged nation. Then we drew closer, for a local story was next.

"Yesterday," said the announcer, "Rags Wilson was buried at Fort Norman. He was found dead in his cabin on November 29. Wilson had taken over the new post on Good Hope Bay on Great Bear after 12 years at Fort Norman. It was December 8 when four Indian dog teams brought word of his death, which appeared to have been from natural causes.

"W. F. Cooke and Constables McIntyre and Hutchison of the Mounted Police left immediately for Great Bear, reaching Good Hope Bay in six days. It was impossible to bury Wilson there, so the body was brought back the 120 miles by dog team. Fittingly, Wilson will rest above one of the most magnificent stretches of the river that has seen a parade of his adventurous breed.

"His closest companion, a cat, stood guard over his body during the days he lay alone, and traveled back with him on his last trip to Norman. It will receive a home with Bill Cooke.

"The post where Wilson died is the most isolated in the Mackenzie basin."

Static reclaimed the air shortly after and Cooke switched off the instrument. A tatter of fur launched itself from the floor and landed in his lap.

"Rags' cat?" asked Wop.

The trader nodded, stroking the animal's still-prominent ribs.

"It's a hard country," I advanced, fatuously.

"At times," agreed Cooke, noncommittal in his courtesy. "It took us three days to dynamite Rags' grave in the permafrost."

Christmas morning, with the thermometer still anchored near 60 below, was as bright and keen as whetted steel. The nearest river surface fit for landing had been two miles across the jagged-toothed floes of the main stream, and the air engineers, Tim Sims and Casey Vanderlinden, had gone back at the planes long before the reluctant dawn. By the time the rest of us arrived, gasoline blowtorches had been pouring their heat for an hour into the asbestos cowlings around the motors. Over an open wood fire, the hooded workers were also re-liquefying the oil that had been drawn from the engines immediately after the previous day's flight. When we joined them the bubbling fluid was swiftly restored to the two red Bellancas and the propellers set whirring before the frost could again immobilize the motors.

Taking off in a storm of fan-whipped snow, we watched Fort Norman drift below. Smoke was rising pencil-straight from the chimneys of the huddled log buildings. My eyes searched the Bear River, following it up the rising terrain to the east, and to Bear Rock, the imposing 1500-foot guardian of its final mile. Vapor was rising from the gaping hole in the ice of the Mackenzie, like the discharge from a subterranean furnace.

With the excellent visibility, it was possible to follow the Bear to the curve of the horizon. Steadily climbing, it was more a trail than a watercourse – a pallid track striking out purposefully between dark upheavals of rock and forest. My imagination excitedly leaped the frost-blurred skyline. I could almost have sworn I saw the long-envisioned face of Great Bear itself.

But Fort Norman was the closest I came for another two years. Gilbert LaBine made his discovery at Echo Bay the following May, and the rest of the New Year passed before I heard of it – this despite being steadily involved with the men who were giving the new development wings.

The silence LaBine threw around his discovery was supported by tight security at the site. The handful of uninvolved prospectors and airmen in a position to have wind of it were close-mouthed in the extreme. The prospectors wanted no additions to their numbers until they had staked what they wanted for themselves. The professional code of the bush pilots kept them tight-lipped about their customers' business.

Eldorado was a well-kept secret until the summer of 1931, when Gilbert LaBine's brother Charlie began to move a substantial amount of mining equipment down the Mackenzie and up the Bear. Awareness that something big was happening at Echo Bay was reflected in mining exchanges across the land. A flurry of new claims was registered in the weeks before freezeup; then most of the stakers retreated south. With them came heightened waves of excitement. The search for new capital to develop ground near the LaBine find encouraged extravagant claims and high-pressure promotion.

Spud Arsenault, one of the prospectors fresh from Great Bear, reached Edmonton after the 1931 open season. Our friendship dated from the 1930 Christmas Day disappearance of Commercial Airways pilot Idris Glyn-Roberts while on a mercy flight along the Arctic coast. In the week he was overdue, news interest had been high and, when he finally was found, I was able to beat my way to Fort McMurray for an exclusive interview when he arrived there. As usual, there was the promise of $3 a column after publication but no advance. My personal fortune on reaching McMurray was critically low.

When bad weather delayed Glyn's return, greater crisis was at hand. Arsenault, whom I had just met, solved it. As general handyman around the Canadian Airways shack, which served as a mess for en route pilots, Spud drew attention to the empty bunks there and to the fact that he hated eating alone. The food and shelter were welcome but no more than the companionship of the stocky, boyishly gregarious Prince Edward Islander. Though still new to the North, he had already developed a zest for it and an acquaintance with practically everyone who moved in and out through the bottleneck of McMurray.

A crowning generosity, after my story on Glyn had finally been filed, was his gift of a 12-pound cut of moose meat. I had no difficulty imagining the effect at home when this solid food arrived. Suddenly, the vision faded. Wop May, blowing in from the North, offered me what I badly needed – a lift to Edmonton. There was one proviso, though. He was loaded to the limit and if I was to travel with him there couldn't be a single pound of added weight beyond the Arctic gear I stood in.

Spud, with whom I shared my dilemma, agreed it would be unwise to raise the question of the moose meat with Wop, but argued that what the flier didn't know wouldn't bother him. Then he demonstrated how it would be possible to hang the great roast on a cord around my neck, concealed inside my billowing parka.

Though I occupied the co-pilot's seat all the way to Edmonton, Wop remained unaware of my treachery. This was slim comfort, however, when a blizzard overtook us 50 miles out of McMurray. Using the meandering railway line below as a guide through the driving, white curtain, Wop held the plane at slightly more than treetop level for the remainder of the journey. As we burned up fuel, the excess 12 pounds around my neck felt like a ton. I had never been so grateful to land as I was when we finally touched down at Edmonton airport.

What we all remembered, though, when Spud paid us his visit in late 1931, was how the moose meat had lasted for days, tasting better as it diminished. The temperature of our leaky old house seemed to go up the moment Arsenault's grinning face came through the door.

He had, he announced, just returned from spending the open season with one of LaBine's field parties. While giving away nothing specific about Eldorado, his enthusiasm for Great Bear itself was without qualification.

"What a country!" he exulted. "Great, long bays running 15, 20 miles deep into the mountains! Rock faces dropping straight into water so clear you can see the lake trout swimming 70 feet down! And what fish! Thirty-pounders aren't worth mentioning. And the meat! They don't breed any soft steaks in that water!

"It's perfect prospecting country. Clean rock, with plenty of it stuck on end hundreds of feet in the air so you can see the formation. No overburden except in the draws and, even there, you've only to scratch and the rock starts biting back at your pick. And all day to do it – 24 hours of light without a break – if you really want to go to work. Man, oh man!"

Spud brought something for each of us, including Erik. He had our four-year old wide-eyed with his tales of the Indians and the wildlife, particularly the fierce Barren Lands grizzly. When Erik suggested he would like to have such a pet, he was given instant assurance it would be forthcoming if Spud should again encounter one on the trail.

With the spell of the visit still fresh, other events followed in quick succession. John Sydie, whose investment and insurance office had been a haven of liquid hospitality on such occasions as he had made a good business deal, invited me to drop in. "How would you like to go to Great Bear Lake?" he asked.

I blinked. "When?"

"Before the in-between."

"Nobody goes in until after the breakup," I told him, "or, at earliest, just before it."

"That's the point," explained John confidentially. "There's going to be a king-sized rush with open water. Right now, though, there's a market for ground that hasn't even been prospected. Anything close to Echo Bay is worth, at rock bottom, $1000 a claim. Anyone who staked all his licenses – even if he didn't hit anything – would be in the chips."

"Go on," I said cautiously.

"Some of us have formed a small syndicate," said John, "and we've got a first-rate prospector. We've gone over the staking maps with him and, despite the claims that were put in last summer, he's satisfied there's still open ground not too far from Eldorado. The area has never been properly surveyed, so there's still nothing to go on except the jigsaw that's been put together from the staking maps. Between the blocks of record-ed claims there's bound to be plenty of fractions – some of them big ones.''

He stroked the ends of his moustache. "Two men can go in there some time after the New Year and, with their own licenses and proxies, put in 36 claims before the staking year ends on March 31. Then they can start all over again with their 1932 licenses.''

"But the country doesn't clear for prospecting until late in May at the earliest," I pointed out.

"Exactly," John agreed. "There's nothing wrong with snowshoe claims, though. They're a legitimate gamble, par-ticularly if they tie on to ground that already looks good. We'll put those first 36 claims for quick sale on the strength of their location. That will finance the serious staking and prospecting we do after the snow is gone. What's more, we'll be on the ground, with our 1932 licenses to fill, weeks before the rush ar-rives from the Outside. It will be well into June before the first planes can land on floats after the in-between – July, at least, before anything can get through by water.''

"I'm no prospector," I warned.

"Our man can teach you. You can learn as you earn.''

"How much would it be worth?''

John became slightly less relaxed.

"You'd be paid in syndicate shares. With air freight at $14 a pound from McMurray it's going to take all we can raise to buy an outfit and land our party at the lake. Of course," – his confidence returned quickly – "it'll be different after we have that first batch of snowshoe claims to cash in on.''

"What does your prospector get?" I asked tentatively.

"He'll get shares, too. That's the way he wants it. He's not interested in a salary when there's this gamble to cut in on.''

"I don't know," I said. "Ernie's pregnant and we're worse than broke.''

John was honestly sympathetic.

"I know how it is. If we could possibly do something about a salary, too, you'd have it in a minute. The town's full of experienced men, though, ready to jump at the chance – if only for something to do.''

"I could make something out of the newspaper stories, of course," I mused. "There would be planes going in until March and plenty to write about in my spare time."

John was quick to agree. "That's been one of the considerations," he admitted. "It wouldn't do the field any harm to have a newspaperman on the ground. If you wanted, you could be free to cut loose and give all your time to writing once you'd filled all your licenses for the syndicate."

I asked for 24 hours to ponder the offer, but orderly thought was almost impossible in the cross-sea of excitement and anxiety that was breaking over me. There was a powerful attraction in the prospect of making my long-dreamed-of trip to Great Bear. And I'd be taking on regular work again. From this crest, I descended into a trough of realism. John's offer rated scant consideration. I didn't want to leave Ernie to fend for herself through the unsparing winter. If she hadn't been pregnant, if there'd been even a little money to leave with her, even if there was someone who would stay with her, it might have been different.

She listened quietly that night when I told her what had happened. The longer I talked, the more I felt her reading me as she sometimes did when I was offering a well-thought-out explanation for arriving home at daybreak.

When I had finished she said, "If you want to know what I think, I think you should go with John's syndicate."

"But – " I protested.

"We'll get along all right," she promised. "I'll find someone to stay with us, you'll be able to sell the Journal enough stories to keep us fed, and after John cashes in on those snowshoe claims we can all move into the royal suite at the Macdonald Hotel."

Ernie knew better than I did how important it was to settle on an immediate target for my disorganized energies and staggering spirit.

The hard light of morning did nothing to change her mind. She had already thought of an unattached woman who might readily move in with her, providing not only company but financial assistance. In fact, she made her end of the situation sound so simple that it exposed my own indecisiveness. Self-doubt had overtaken me in the night as I realized that my previous experience of the North – moving from fort to fort in a plane's cabin – hadn't altogether equipped me to be dropped on the naked face of Great Bear in midwinter.

At last I convinced myself that the one way to eliminate uncertainty was to defy it. That afternoon I told Sydie I was his man. The gambler's chance of reversing our financial fortunes was terribly important.

Then, too, Great Bear's inaccessibility was now a promise of sanctuary. For months I would be beyond the reach of telephones, creditors, and impossible responsibilities.

On February 16, in a whirling blizzard, Eric Beck, prospector for the new syndicate, left Edmonton on the weekly "Muskeg Express" for Fort McMurray. With him went his new assistant, Frederick B. Watt.

2

John Sydie's prospector was something of a surprise. I had known Eric Beck as an official in the mining section of a now-defunct stockbroking firm. During the time of preparation for our winter odyssey there had been little opportunity to weigh our compatibility for such a venture. Getting equipment and money together had been more important. On the 24-hour trip to the end of steel, however, we had an uninterrupted chance to size one another up. We were the lone passengers in the sleeping car, and the falling snow blotted out whatever diversion the increasingly wild landscape might have provided.

Eric Beck would not have been my choice as the man with whom to share a desert island. I had never found him very communicative, but this hadn't mattered much one way or the other in our former casual acquaintance. Moving closer to the moment when I would have him as sole companion for long periods and under comfortless conditions, however, it suddenly mattered a good deal. I had heard too many stories about men who had become "bushed".

I was sure, too, that I was under the same sidelong scrutiny.

About my own age – in his early thirties – Beck appeared older. He was spare and of medium height, his dark hair already in retreat across his forehead. His voice had a high-noted huskiness and his laughter came when you least expected it. He was unmarried, apparently self-sufficient. I had a few memories of him at parties – of a man whose character changed drastically when he had been drinking and who then became as eagerly gregarious as he was normally reserved.

The one point on which Beck was outspoken during the rail trip was his low opinion of snowshoe claims. Adequate mineralization was the only real justification for putting in corner posts, he insisted. However, if the syndicate needed wildcats with which to prime the pump, he'd get them the best he could.

Waterways, the little town at the end of the line, was still the Outside. Its buildings were new and the train looked at home among them. Three miles farther along the Athabaska River, however, Fort McMurray was definitely "down North". It had its planes on the frozen waterfront, and some new shacks among the poplars, but these had scarcely altered the community created by generations of voyageurs and fur men. The old, whitewashed log cabins had a comfortable look of permanence. Indians and dog trains traveled the rambling main street. The infrequent howl of the train whistle, drifting down the valley from Waterways, had a dreamlike sound.

Our outfit had arrived by the previous week's train and was waiting at the McMurray snye, the island-protected channel at the confluence of the Clearwater and the Athabaska Rivers which provided a natural harbor for the planes. Hod Torrie, the quietly efficient engineer in charge of the Canadian Airways base, had bad news for us, however. Our cargo was a good deal heavier than could normally be carried in the one charter flight credited to our syndicate. Moreover, conditions were not normal.

"We've been having the devil's own time with our landings," Hod explained. "Last winter we could make them almost anywhere there was ice but there's been so much damage lately the boys are under orders to put down only at specified points. It's the heavy drifting that's doing it. There are bits of ski and undercarriage scattered all across the Territories and we've had to reduce the maximum planeload by 200 pounds."

"But we need all our stuff!" protested Beck.

"Better repack what you can get by on until open water," advised the engineer. "We can ferry in the rest later."

This was only one of our trials at McMurray. Our hope for a quick getaway was frustrated by bad weather, then by the failure of Archie McMullen, our assigned pilot, to show up from another charter flight.

An advance party of John Michael's winter crew headed by his mining engineer, George Mooney, boomed in with Andy Cruickshank and paused only long enough to exchange greetings before continuing on to Great Bear. Their word that a pre-breakup rush seemed to be developing Outside did nothing to raise our morale or patience.

That same evening two trappers drove in by dog from Fort Chipewyan. Half the North Country, they reported, was converging on Great Bear. Many parties had headed down the Mackenzie the previous autumn but had been held up at Fort Franklin, across the lake from Echo Bay, by the freeze-up. For some weeks, though, the invasion had been under way again.

"I'll bet," said one of our informants, "there's more people on Echo and Hunter bays than anywhere else in the Territories. Two, three hundred, probably. The claim stakes will be sticking out like quills on a porcupine."

The atmosphere at the little hotel became intolerable. We were growing restless with the urge to get going. Then I thought of a diversion.

"Let's call on Vi May," I suggested. "She's panic-proof and maybe some of it will rub off." The pilot's wife was a famous hostess in McMurray.

We knew that Wop May wasn't home, as did just about everybody else that winter of 1932. For days the press and radio had been flashing out fragmentary wireless reports from Aklavik about a dramatic manhunt in which the flying ace was taking a colorful part. In the shadow of the Rockies, west of the Mackenzie Delta, May was doing double duty with a posse in pursuit of one Albert Johnson, the Mad Trapper of Rat River.

Where Johnson came from before he appeared in the Delta as a bad-tempered loner has never been established. He had terrorized the Indian trappers in his district – and killed a Mounted Policeman, Constable Spike Millen, after a series of desperate gun battles. The chase that followed covered hundreds of miles and took 49 days. Retreating with the cunning of a hunted wolf, Johnson was tracking towards the Yukon. The supply lines of the posse were stretched to the limit. Without Wop's hastily organized airlift, the chase would have been lost.

Once involved, the flier hadn't confined himself to ferrying supplies. Reverting to his old hedge-hopping skills, he was scouting ahead of the posse in an attempt to locate the fugitive. At last word, however, Johnson was managing to merge with the sheltering bush. His shrewdly confused trail was still keeping him ahead of the ground party.

That night, as on most nights, the May home on Franklin Avenue was filled with airmen and their wives. It was a one-story frame building, converted from a small store, and its hostess had made the most of such potential as it had for attractiveness and comfort.

Violet Bode May was as completely natural in this setting as she had been on the Outside. Thoroughbred horses had been the love of her life up to the time Wop had filled it with planes, frontier living and oversized dogs.

Vi shared Wop's facility for direct and unvarnished statement, warmed by freely-flowing humor. Her sensitivity was something never forgotten by those who experienced it, especially the airmen's wives to whom she brought the first word of their widowhood.

Having had previous experience of the May establishment, I allowed Beck to enter first. He was immediately greeted by the canine members of the family. Tim, a Great Dane, jarred the scales at 135 pounds and Togo, an Arctic-coast Husky which Wop had brought home as a pup, was now large even for his breed. The paws Tim invariably planted on the chest of a new arrival were friendly enough but, for the unprepared, they had an upsetting force. Beck, picking himself from the floor, was clearly impressed.

The room was filled with chatter and the radio-relayed strains of an Edmonton dance band. It provided just the right antidote for our impatience and depression. Most talk centered on the manhunt. There had been word that the posse was now close on the heels of its quarry.

At one point Hod Torrie burst through the door to announce that a discouraging wireless message had just come in. Johnson, he reported, had sneaked out of the woods the previous evening, climbed on board Wop's parked plane, then disappeared in the general direction of Alaska. He told the tale with a straight enough face to fool most of us. Vi, however, was smiling tolerantly even as he spoke. Hod was Wop's closest friend and she knew all about his solemn banter.

A few minutes later, we learned the real story. The brassy rhythms of "I Want to be Loved by You" died abruptly in the throat of the loudspeaker and the following silence sent a hush through us all. Then came the excited voice of the announcer.

"The hunt for the Mad Trapper of Rat River is over. Albert Johnson was killed this afternoon in a furious battle with the posse which finally overtook him. Word of the successful conclusion to the long and hazardous pursuit reached Aklavik with pilot Wop May when he flew in to hospitalize dangerously wounded Staff Sergeant Hershey of the Canadian Corps of Signals."

The music resumed, but Hod cut it off with a flick of the switch. Everyone's eyes were on Vi. She was sitting quietly on the arm of a chair, thinking her own thoughts. Then she sighed and said, "Well, that will put an end to all the reporters. They've been wiring constantly, for word on my emotions as the wife of a man-hunting pilot."

I didn't ask about her emotions, but suggested I could use information for the story I proposed to file that night.

"You know as much as I do," she responded. "I've only heard from Wop once since he left. He wired from Lapierre House and said the weather was bad and the landings worse. That was all."

It was probably just as well that Vi had been spared greater detail. One of the landings Wop had referred to had been on a 6000-foot plateau, with a sheer dropoff at the end of the section he had used as an impromptu runway. He was forced to depend on the generous void for gathering flying speed, after completing his takeoff run.

Later, when he was racing to Aklavik with the desperately wounded Hershey, there was another squeaker. Minutes were precious if he was to get the patient to an operating table in time, so Wop used a previously unflown pass through the mountains. There was a draft through the gorge which, while it added substantially to his speed, proved a mixed blessing.

"I guess I wasn't really flying the machine then," he told me a couple of years later. "I just sat back and let the current suck us through the pass. It wasn't bad except at the turns."

The successful conclusion of Operation Mad Trapper seemed to us to be an omen. Maybe our own operation would now come on better days. This hope glowed brighter on February 18 when Archie McMullen landed in the snye, his previous charter completed. He was a very large young man with a round, cherubic face – one of the few pilots who had qualified for the bush without previous wartime experience.

He announced that his plane would require some extra servicing before he could continue north with us. Frustration gripped us harder on the 19th when the weather proved a washout. On the 20th we actually took off, but were driven back 10 minutes later by a blizzard which came boiling up the Athabaska valley.

We rolled in that night with a feeling of having been eternally damned, but the sky turned clear and cold as we slept. The long delay was over.

On February 21, the hotel thermometer read $-50°F$ when we checked it at 6:30 A.M. We started to taxi down the snye at eight o'clock but an air strut collapsed and we had to shift our load to another machine. We actually got away at 9:30. It was a cold trip to Fitzgerald. After we gassed up there, I went to sleep and woke just as Fort Resolution hove in sight.

If we had not had the trouble with the strut, we would have been able to make it to Fort Rae, 150 miles across Great Slave Lake. As it was, Resolution was the safe outer limit of our flight. But I was prepared to accept the delay. Resolution was an old stamping ground of mine – a pleasant post, with the handsome lake on its doorstep and a cluster of picturesque offshore islands. It was also the home of Carl Murdoff, manager for Northern Traders and one of the North's most sophisticated characters. With him was Bobby Porritt, his assistant, who later was elected to the Territorial Council.

Two other pilots, Walter Gilbert and Ronnie George, had already parked their planes close to the shore – and Carl's house was crowded. Among the visitors were Henry Camsell and Henry Jones, two prospectors for a Fort Resolution syndicate. They had an interesting story to tell.

They were just in from Great Bear, having been the first men in the field that year. For the past month they had been staking the Mac and Hen groups on Echo Bay, putting in 54 claims. They testified to the richness of the new strike.

Just two days ago, they told us, they were present when Heb Jackson, a Fort Norman trapper, dislodged a chunk of glittering ore while driving in a claim post at his stakings on Great Bear Lake. The sample was the size of a pigeon's egg. They accompanied him to camp, where he laid the ore on the red-hot stove. Almost immediately, molten silver trickled across the stove lid, leaving only a small portion of slag. Two-thirds of the sample was pure metal.

My imagination locked immediately on this scene, and my excitement rose. Naturally, the extent of the ore body would remain unknown until the disappearance of the snow in the late spring. The discovery, I knew, would bring the already simmering field to the boiling point. Jackson's claims were 10 miles from LaBine Point, in territory that had seen staking only during the past week.

The gathering in Murdoff's living room ran late while we pumped Camsell and Jones for all the information they were prepared to offer. When we finally rolled in, I was taut with combined jubilation and apprehension. Lying among the rows of humped sleeping bags on the spartan second floor, I whispered to Beck, "If they've staked 54 claims on Echo Bay it's almost certain they've picked up those fractions you were sure were there."

"It just proves my theory," Eric yawned. "If there was open ground waiting for them, there'll be some for us, too. This strike of Jackson's will work in our favor. Everyone who's in there now will be dashing off to the new centers of excitement and leaving Echo Bay alone."

Takeoff next morning had an electric quality. Ours was the only plane going North and this was the beginning of our leap into the unknown. Resolution was the last wireless station. From now on communication would depend on the few planes we encountered during the next month. After that would come the complete break of the in-between season, when no planes flew.

With our early takeoff, the prospect of making Great Bear that day was excellent. But difficulties began over the pale mass of Great Slave Lake. Wedges of fog closed in from different levels and threatened to force us back to Resolution. Later, strong air currents tore the mist apart and scattered it astern, but the wind itself presented a problem. It was blowing from directly ahead, driving down the long funnel of Rae Arm. Every mile became a laboring effort as the icy blasts penetrated the fuselage.

More than two hours passed before the plane banked and, below our dipped right wing, we saw Fort Rae. The thought of warming ourselves in the post while Archie refueled for the next leg of the journey lifted our spirits.

Uncertainty hit when we realized how cautiously the pilot was selecting his landing area. When, at long last, he did touch down, we were far away from the fort and the pleasant promise of its chimneys. It was, in fact, six miles distant. We had to trudge across Marian Lake's unsheltered face to reach it.

When we started walking towards the fort, our sleeping bags on our shoulders, Archie explained. "The landing in front of the place has been bad all winter – but passable. I decided it was no *longer* passable when I noticed Andy Cruickshank's plane sitting there with a broken undercarriage."

My face was frost-bitten before we reached the fort, but it had seemed much colder in the plane.

That night we slept behind wooden walls and in consistent warmth for what we knew would be the last time in several months. The next day, we picked up caribou hides at the Hudson's Bay Company post to use as added insulation against the permafrost which would lie under our beds from now on. Fort Rae was close enough to the Barrens and the still unlimited armies of caribou that we were able to buy hides for a dollar apiece.

The route to Great Bear followed the long, linked trenches of two rivers – the Marian, flowing south to Great Slave – then, across the height of land, the Camsell, forging north. Along their lengths and to either side lay the myriad lakes and the veining of streams which fed them.

It was impossible, jammed in with our cargo, to determine when we had left the Marian and picked up the Camsell. Seen through biting mist, the jigsaw puzzle of frozen waterways seemed endless and unchangeable. Yet, at a certain point I realized with mounting excitement that it *was* changing. The terrain was becoming wilder and more mountainous.

My niche in the piled-up supplies was on the left-hand side of the cabin, the favored position for getting the first glimpse of the lake itself. Beck, as the mining expert, was entitled to the right side from which the geological features of the land were visible for future reference.

The sea of low mountains that had been rising beneath us became more turbulent. Black cliff-faces slashed across the otherwise bone white upheavals of snow-buried rock. One stone giant, sitting some distance from its nearest companions, impassively contemplated a small lake held high on its lap. Whether the winding waterways at the feet of the mountains were rivers, smaller lakes or arms of Great Bear itself, I couldn't decide.

Then the lake was there. Perhaps the lifting of the gauzy mist had done it, perhaps it had been in view for minutes – unrecognized because its hugeness so closely shared the immensity of the sky. Whatever the explanation, one moment it was a vision of the mind, heightened by years of anticipation; the next it was reality. It was inverse landfall – the development of space out of substance. Featureless, impersonal as time, Great Bear stretched to the pale infinity of the western horizon.

3

We had gone over the map with Archie that morning, deciding where he should land when we reached our destination. There were three choices. The first, LaBine Point, at the entrance to Echo Bay's 15-mile-deep fiord, was the most southerly. Here there were men living behind wooden walls at Eldorado. Just around the corner, in Glacier Bay, there was at least a watchman at the Consolidated Mining and Smelting camp.

Thirty-five miles farther north, just short of the Arctic Circle, another possibility offered itself. Hunter Bay and the surrounding area had been a center of exploration and other activity before the LaBine strike. There were still men working there, and a modest wireless station.

Between Echo and Hunter bays was the third break in the iron coastline, the 15-mile-wide mouth of Lindsley Bay. Dotted with craggy islands, it ran inland on a course roughly paralleling Echo Bay. At its southeast corner it edged over closer to Echo and there appeared to be a possible portage between the two inlets. Deep coves stabbed inward from each of the large bays. Three small lakes, lying like an uneven necklace across the throat of intervening land, gave some promise that these might be linked by a passable valley. After some discussion, Archie picked a cove on the map and said, "If it's to be Lindsley Bay this is the one landing I can guarantee." We were all satisfied.

For half an hour after the first sighting of the lake my view from the port side of the cabin was confined to the flat, marbled surface of the icebound lake. Beck, from the other side, shouted from time to time that we were following the coastline closely and that it looked like a prospector's paradise. Finally he yelled, "There it is – Echo Bay! Eldorado should be just down there. Yes, by God, it is. I can see the bunkhouse."

I tried to squirm out of my straitjacket of heaped supplies but my attempt to share the landward view was fruitless until the plane tipped gently to starboard. As it straightened out again land became visible from my own window. It was, if anything, more grimly beautiful than it had been farther south – and as cold as the mountains of the moon. I could identify our course from my memory of the map. We were cutting diagonally across from the Echo Bay entrance towards the inner reaches of Lindsley Bay.

"That's where the cove should be," I told myself, as tense as a child on a treasure hunt. And, a moment later, there it was, like an axe-cut on the southern rim of the bay. Framed by ponderous rock shoulders, it formed the threshold to a long, steep valley leading in an almost straight line to the south. In the distance, the gap could be seen opening into a long indent in the Echo Bay shoreline. The three small lakes were stepping stones along its length.

McMullen had been gradually losing altitude and, circling the cove, he checked the landing conditions. Even since the last heavy snow there had obviously been activity here. The surface was marked by ski and sled tracks, all of which converged at the cove's apex. Here there was a growth of spruce, taller and more closely grouped than the scraggly parade on the slope above. From it drifted a single sign of life, a thin spiral of smoke hanging, ghostly, above the trees.

There were no spruce markers on the ice to identify an established runway, but ski tracks from earlier planes suggested the best landing. McMullen felt his way down on a course that carried us across the face of the cove. As the plane touched it jarred heavily on a drift, and we skidded to a halt.

Coming about, Archie headed cautiously for shore. The aircraft waddled over the gently rolling snow contours, the motor humming where the surface was smooth and growling angrily where extra power was required to climb a drift. A hundred feet offshore from the spruce grove the pilot throttled down, then cut his engine.

The silence was profound. It was always so, when a plane's motor died after unbroken hours of clamor. Normally something else would quickly claim the senses, taking over from the sound and motion of the plane itself. There would be howling sleigh dogs, welcoming human voices, other aircraft. Here the stillness was unrelieved for several minutes as we unfolded ourselves from the cramped cabin and felt the bite of the outer air.

Then a single figure detached itself from the shore and walked towards us. The man's moccasins creaked on the hard snow surface like footsteps in an alley, making the place seem even more lonesome.

"Welcome," he said.

His voice was strange, with a sandpaperish quality. There was a proprietorial tone to it, though it was not unfriendly. His face was red and rough-hewn, with small, bright eyes, and a bristling sandy beard.

McMullen introduced us. The welcomer's name was Ed De Melt.

The pilot told us there was no rush to unload our outfit. He intended to remain at Lindsley Bay for the night, so there would be plenty of time for us to locate a camp site and pack cargo directly to it from the plane rather than dumping it hurriedly on the lake ice. He went off with De Melt, towards a tent which was now visible among the spruces. His engineer began draining the oil from the engine, to prepare the aircraft for night.

Beck and I moved with urgency. The sun was already past the zenith of its brief venture over the horizon. The light breeze was stabbing home the $-30^{\circ}F$ air and there was every encouragement to establish our shelter before dark. Since we had brand-new, untried equipment, we could expect to be slowed down while becoming acquainted with it.

Selecting a campsite was simple, if only because the grove offered limited ground to choose from. A stream entered the cove here and on either bank was a small, comparatively level bench which gave the spruces good rootage. De Melt's 10 by 12 tent, heavily marked by weather, wear and smoke, was pitched 50 feet back from the creek, on the right bank. It had ready access to the lake but was deep enough in the spruces for shelter.

A spot 25 feet from Ed's front door looked suitable. It was on the edge of a well-beaten sled track that followed the stream up the valley and enough traffic had paused here to tramp down the snow over a small area. We were able to work without snowshoes, and to use them instead as shovels for clearing the site on which our tent would rise.

McMullen and De Melt emerged from the tent, waved us their encouragement and, picking up Archie's engineer as they went, tramped out into the bay. They carried their snowshoes but, as long as they remained in sight, managed without them, following a discernable sled trail. They were striking a strong pace as they vanished around the western shoulder of the cove.

"What's that all about?" I asked.

"I'd guess," Eric answered, "it's all about some ground that fellow has located and laid out by pre-arrangement. If Archie isn't signing claim posts before the daylight's gone, his trip down the bay won't make much sense."

We pressed our own race against the coming darkness. The path on the ice between the plane and the shore had become sharply defined by the time we had backpacked 1500 pounds of boxes, bundles and bags to the campsite. In our hurry they were deposited without any sense of order in an ever-widening circle.

Disentangling this mound brought our first serious difficulty. The search for immediately required articles resulted in a good deal of fruitless unpacking. This, in turn, further extended the perimeter of our dump. Items, once found, had a way of disappearing in the surrounding snow if they were laid aside. It was as though a white, silent sea moved in on the little island of ground we had cleared and, while our backs were turned, kept washing away our precious equipment.

Beck's prospecting in the past had been in friendlier places and seasons. It had been several years since he had been in the bush and he was rusty on camp organization. For me, camping out had been a boyhood adventure, overnight stuff at the most pleasant periods of the year. It was quite inadequate preparation for setting up a six-month camp, with the night and the dropping temperature closing in and with our equipment in an ever-worsening jumble.

The tent was our first priority. It was a small one – eight by ten, with a three-foot wall – but the heavy canvas was brand new. Further stiffened by the frost, it was increasingly hard to handle as we stretched it out in preparation for raising. It resisted like something alive as we fumbled with gloved fingers that became steadily more inflexible from the cold. But at last it was laid out, ready for the triangular framework of poles, which had yet to be cut.

There were three axes, small ones useful to men who would be traveling light and blazing more trees than they would be felling. I took one of them and waded off into the bush. As I swung at what seemed like a suitable spruce, the warm sweat I had started to work up suddenly turned to a cold one. Chips were flying merrily where the axe-blade was biting the tree – but some of them had a strange, metallic glint.

A hurried examination of the blade confirmed the worst: several flakes of metal were missing from the cutting edge. The soft Swedish steel, colliding with wood that had been tempered to an iron toughness by months of sub-freezing weather, had suffered almost as much as the tree. The mutilated blade was a serious – even a dangerous – problem: we could eventually find ourselves axeless. In such a country that would endanger our lives.

I decided there was no stopping now. Steel chips continued to fly, but I worked doggedly on. The tree was brought down and trimmed. The blade was looking worse than ever but at least it was still functional.

We raised the tent at last, but the place would not be habitable without a further fight, this one with our collapsible sheet-metal stove. The heating-cooking unit was a simple enough device but with our attempts to assemble it into a square box, it took on the maddening qualities of a puzzle. Pieces which should have fitted together easily refused to cooperate. I left Beck wrestling with it while I went collecting firewood but when I returned it was no nearer to being put together.

My own attack was equally fruitless. The dying light and the inexorable descent of the temperature added desperation to our efforts. From time to time we shed our gauntlets in brief, bare-handed rallies but at the slightest touch, our fingers were seared with frost-burn – as painful and scarring as if the stove were already lit, and white-hot.

Swearing no longer helped. We strained silently in the half-darkness. Our fingers were past the point of all feeling – our arms seemed to end at the wrists. We were too deeply involved with our struggle to be aware of a man who had come towards us from the bay. Only when a voice sounded from a few feet away in the twilight did we realize we were no longer alone.

"Having trouble?"

We made no reply, beyond a grunt or two.

The newcomer moved closer. His fur-trimmed parka hood was thrown back and the cloth cap underneath was neat and clean. He had classic Indian features, and he moved with graceful agility.

"Let me look," he said.

If it wasn't a command it was at least an instruction. I thought I detected a note of contempt. We were in no position to ignore help, however, and allowed him to examine the pieces of sheet metal.

In a minute – or perhaps two at the most – he had the stove together. Then, barely acknowledging our thanks, he walked off towards De Melt's tent. A lighted candle set it aglow and we heard its fire being re-stoked.

With a sense of having experienced black magic, we moved our own stove inside, collected the sections of pipe, clumsily forced them together and completed the rigging of our heating plant. The roar of tinder-like spruce twigs responding to a match, followed by the crackle of heavier wood taking hold, was a wind from heaven.

The tent, its double fly sealing the entrance, heated quickly. How long we would have simply hunkered there thawing out we never knew, for a fresh crisis developed. In the darkened interior of our new home pinpoints of light began to twinkle through the canvas above the stove.

"Look," I remarked. "The stars are out – showing clean through the roof."

Beck bellowed, "Stars be damned! We're on fire!"

We were seeing falling sparks on the outer canvas roof, and some of them were burning through. The glowing rims of the holes steadily widened. While I stumbled outside to throw snow on them, Beck methodically snuffed out the red circles from within. By the time the alarm was over, the front end of the tent appeared to have absorbed a scatter of buckshot.

"That's the one thing I forgot," Beck groaned. "A bit of wire mesh to go over the stack."

"What do we do – let the fire go out?" I chattered.

"Not on your life – not if we burn the damn place down," declared Beck. "I'll think of something."

The lid of a lard pail, perforated by a series of short jabs from his hunting knife, was the answer. Fitted over the top of the stack, it allowed only the small and harmless sparks to escape while still permitting an adequate draft. We settled back again to complete our interrupted thawing-out. The outfit was still scattered beyond the tent; there might be animal raiders near at hand with greedy intent towards our food supply, but for the moment we had to have a breather. The candles had not yet been unpacked and we already had sensed the need for economical use of our flashlights, so we sat silent in the darkness, as close to the red-hot stove as we could get without frying.

The sound of voices and the darting beam of a flashlight announced the return of Archie and his companions. When we emerged to meet them, De Melt was surveying our scattered equipment. In the darkness it was impossible to see the expression on his face, but his voice was tolerant.

"You still seem to have plenty to do," he said. "Better come over for dinner. I'll yell when it's ready."

"I notice you don't have a cache," Beck said. "Does that mean there's no wolverines or other animals to worry about?"

"Nothing's bothered me – yet," answered the Northman. "Let's say it's a calculated risk."

Calculated risk or no, we were in no condition to start building a cache that evening. We cleared a hole in the snow alongside the tent, and roughly stacked our supplies there, covering everything hurriedly with a tarpaulin.

We were still sorting and stacking when De Melt bellowed, "Come and get it!"

The six of us filled his tent almost to capacity and put strain on his supply of tablewear even after Beck and I had dug out our own shiny new tin plates, cups and cutlery. The social niceties adjusted themselves as we squatted in a semicircle in the inner half of the tent. De Melt, presiding over the stove near the door, passed out bacon, bannock and tea in heart-filling quantities.

The warmth and the food brought back my first awareness of time. It seemed impossible that the last meal we had sat down to had been in the comparative luxury of the Hudson's Bay post 15 hours before – and that Fort Rae now lay hundreds of miles behind us.

This was our life now – the candle-lit ring of faces turned towards the Northern high priest at his fire-reddened altar; the airmen who would return to the world I had fled; the Indian whose world we were about to enter.

We came to know De Melt intimately in subsequent days, but his forceful character was amply impressed on us during our first meal together. He was the traditional Yankee trader with strong sub-Arctic overtones. Originally from the middle west, he had found his way to Great Slave Lake and had settled in Hay River, developing a fishing business there. The North suited him fine. It was 14 years since he had last been south of Fort Smith. Hay River Fisheries provided him with a basic industry but he was always alert to new opportunities.

As part of the previous year's waterborne invasion, he had come down the Mackenzie, up the Bear, then across the lake ice. He had neither boat nor dogs of his own this side of Hay River but he had apparently not required them to get here and, without them, he was already definitely in business.

His activity centered on his office as Acting Mining Recorder. There being no regular government official in the area, the law allowed the men on the ground to elect someone until Ottawa provided a regular functionary. Ed had been the people's choice. As Recorder, he had become a central intelligence agency. As soon as a man staked his claims he moved at speed to register them with De Melt. This not only provided

Ed with unique maps of newer sections of the field, drawn by the prospectors as they staked, but kept him well informed on what many of them were encountering.

Accustomed to doing business with the Indians in his own part of the Territories, he had become guide, philosopher and friend to many of the Bear Lake People – the Loucheux and Hareskins – who had joined in the exciting but somewhat bewildering business of putting up claim stakes on the land that had been theirs from the beginning of time. The men who normally safeguarded their interests – the RCMP and the Indian agents – were based on the Mackenzie. As advisor *pro tem* to the native people, Ed was also in touch with the best dog trains on the eastern shore of Great Bear. White men in need of transportation usually found him a natural business agent.

While noncommittal about his own ground, he let it be known he was well acquainted with those areas where there were still fractions to be picked up or where substantial blocks had been overlooked in the early rush. If a man didn't have time or inclination to go looking for himself, De Melt was available to go looking for him. In fact, he was prepared to spare a potential staker any effort other than that of moving on the ground long enough to meet the letter of the law by putting his signature on already erected corner posts.

As Beck had guessed, this was what was in the wind when Ed headed off with our flying companions. Archie and his engineer returned from their walk as claim owners.

We never discovered the yardstick by which De Melt set his fee for such services, but it was probably on a sliding scale which allowed for both the labor involved and the financial status of the staker.

Obviously Archie's new claims lay within reasonable walking distance of the cove, which meant that Lindsley Bay hadn't been as solidly staked as we'd been told at Resolution. No one volunteered their location and, had I been alone, I undoubtedly would have asked. I was learning, however, to take my cue from Beck, who was at home in the language of the prospector. It was, I discovered, a tongue in which unbridled enthusiasm, utter reticence and cautious reservation were maintained in a state of delicate balance.

At one point Beck threw in a careless question about Echo Bay. It was, he assumed, staked solid. De Melt sniffed as though the question were unworthy of consideration.

"That was gone long before any of us arrived," he said. "If there were any small fractions left they went last summer. A guy looking for open ground needs to head north – and fast."

The Indian magician who had exorcised the evil spirit from our stove had just come down from Hunter Bay. He was vague about how many men were on the move in that territory but clear about the richness of the six claims he himself had put in. From his prospector's grab-bag he displayed several samples which, he said, he had broken off with the heel of his axe from an exposed cliff-face on his property. To my uneducated eye the golden-flecked quartz was tremendously impressive. Beck was less stirred.

"Chalcopyrite," he said, after a cursory examination. "Copper. It's mineralization, of course. Where there's base metal, precious metal is always a possibility."

It was a letdown. I had hoped to see something like Heb Jackson's legendary sample, capable of spilling molten silver over a red-hot stove top.

The warmth and companionship of De Melt's tent became more and more attractive the longer we stayed. The occasional crack of the frost biting into a tree outside was a sharp reminder that we must return to our own still-unfurnished dwelling. Beck seemed no more eager to make the break than I. Had there been room, we might even have hung around in the hope of being asked to stay the night. The place, though, was obviously going to be a tight enough fit with even four sleeping bags to accommodate. With a final round of steaming tea in us, we reluctantly said goodnight.

A hard, unblinking moon illuminated the bay when we emerged, and its light, caught up by the blue-shadowed snow, was adequate for the outside work we had yet to do. This consisted chiefly of cutting spruce boughs for our beds, banking the outside walls with snow for anchorage and to reduce floor draft, and, finally, sorting out the supplies and gear we would keep inside. We located the candles and set one burning. The warm glow from within the tent challenged the cold moon-glow and the smoke from our chimney rose defiantly to the stars.

Before we could finally bed down, one more unforeseen problem had to be solved: we needed drinking water. The most sparkling water in the world lay within a stone's-throw – 12 000 square miles of it – but it was locked beneath a glassy vault door, several feet thick, which winter had slammed on it. Snow was our only alternative, but unless it was first reduced to water, it seemed to increase rather than quench our thirst.

An enameled water pail was placed on the stove and filled with snow. It was remarkable how much was required to provide even a cupful of water. When we had melted and cooled enough to meet our immediate needs, I suggested it would be a good idea to continue the operation until we had enough water for the morning as well. Beck agreed and we melted half a pailful before calling it a night.

The first half-hour or so, lying in my bag while the fire burned itself out, had me feeling wonderfully at peace with the world. The Arctic sleeping bag was snug, and the caribou hide between the down of the bag and the spruce-bough mattress was softer than my bed at home in Edmonton. At least, that was how it seemed, in my weariness. It had been a long day, but Beck Syndicate was now fully in business. I seemed to be lying on a luxurious pink cloud.

Very soon my cloud began to lose some of its fluffiness. The knobs and elbows of the hastily cut spruce boughs jutted up everywhere, joined by rocks and roots that had been over-looked in the clearing of the campsite.

It was still warm in the bag itself, but my head protruded and I learned how quickly a fireless tent takes on the outside temperature. At $-35\,°F$ to $-40\,°F$, a nose or an ear responds to the frost with equal sensitivity on either side of an unheated canvas wall.

I had kept the woolen toque I wore under my parka hood close at hand for such an eventuality and it protected the top of my head. But there was no alternative to pulling my face, turtle-like, well into the bag. I had a claustrophobic first lesson in how to breath while submerged. Somehow, I dozed off.

During the night I was startled awake by a deliberate crackling noise, quite close at hand. It had a metallic ring and I immediately thought about the tins of food stacked outside the tent. Beck stirred in his bag alongside me.

"Did you hear that?" I whispered.

"Uh huh."

"D'you think it's an animal at our stuff?"

"No, I don't think so."

"What is it, then?"

"Damned if I know, and damned if I'm getting out of my bag to find out. It'll go away."

The ghostly crackling continued. Every so often there was a pinging noise, like the ricochet of a tiny bullet. It was very distinct in the otherwise silent night – and very close. But I was tired enough to go to sleep in the middle of it.

In the morning the mystery was solved. Our half-pail of water was solidly frozen. On the surface of the ice was a litter of enamel flakes, the spent "bullets" of the ghostly fusilade in the night. Water, expanding under frost, is not good for enamel pails.

4

We were on the move early. The temperature and the rough ground made further sleeping impossible. In any case, today was zero-hour, the real beginning of our work. We had decided before turning in that no more time would be spent on improving the camp until the field had been scouted.

We had slept stretched across the width of the tent, with Beck occupying the berth nearest the stove. As long as there was heat, his was the best spot. Distance from the stove had a bearing on one's comfort: Beck lay within the tropics, while three feet farther on, my territory began at the Arctic Circle. Morning, however, brought its compensations. As the man handiest to the dead firebox, Eric was the obvious one to restore it to life.

Our breath, rising steam-like from the caverns of our sleeping bags and whitening the roof overhead, made it apparent that the temperature hadn't moderated in the night. Beck reached out a cautious arm for the kindling he had prepared the evening before and, still swathed in his bag, tried to shove it inside the stove. Three times his exposed hand encountered the sheet metal and three times he sharply withdrew it, frost-burned, to the shelter of his bag. On the fourth try he succeeded. The chimney began to roar and within a few minutes we were able to emerge for breakfast.

Though there had been no previous discussions of domestic duties, we seemed to fall into them automatically. Beck presided at the cook stove and I made myself responsible for the wood supply and the washup.

Breakfast was to consist of oatmeal, bacon, bannock and tea. It took time to prepare. Everything except the flour and cereal had to be thawed first. The water supply had to be strained to remove the enamel flakes. The bacon, butter and milk were all canned, and we had yet to learn how to thaw them properly. Exposing them, can and all, to the direct heat of the stove resulted in the thawing process moving right on to the cooking stage. This did the contents no good, and also brought about the risk of internal pressure and explosion. We weathered the various crises, however, and ate a memorable first breakfast at Great Bear.

Having planned an all-day expedition, Beck filled a small packsack with food for a couple of meals and added the necessary cooking gear. With this shouldered and our axes, .22 rifle and snowshoes in hand, we were able to step clear of the tent by nine o'clock. It was not yet full daylight, but down on the ice, Archie and his engineer were warming up their engine. We exchanged waves and struck out along the portage trail leading to Echo Bay.

The going was almost perfect. There had been a number of carioles over the track that winter and the surface was firm beneath our mukluks. In the wooded sections between the little lakes the path took advantage of the natural contours of the valley floor, looping sinuously over heights and down through the intervening gullies, but on the three bodies of water it cut from shore to shore with geometrical precision. Some drifting had occurred on the lakes, but it was not serious enough to cause us to lose the track or to check the excellent speed we were making.

It was a fascinating three miles, particularly when we were clear of the woods. Pale, pink light began to wash the ramparts to the west, filtering slowly down over rock face and scrub timber until the entire valley was luminous. Previously blurred by the pallor of the snow and the grayness of the morning, conifers and rocky sheer now came to life in strong, clearly delineated slashes of color.

One cliff face dropping into the second lake was covered

with the blues and greens of copper oxidization. It had a brief magnetic effect on Beck. Once drawn from the track, however, he floundered in deep snow and had second thoughts.

"It doesn't take much of a showing to take my mind off my work," he grunted, returning to the trail and the course for Echo Bay. "We've got better things to do than moon over someone else's ground."

"It might be on one of those fractions," I suggested, with all the professional assurance of my first day on the job.

"Not a chance," said Beck. "You can see the witness posts even from here."

As I searched more closely, the signs of staking became apparent. Along the shoreline of each lake the squared, white faces of spruce posts appeared at regular intervals, peering out from among the sombre trunks around them. A witness post, Beck explained, was cut where the boundary of a claim encountered the water. It proclaimed that so far inland and so far out under the water the ground belonged to the man whose name was on the stake. At every 1500 feet (a claim was 1500 feet square) pairs of posts were visible on our entire passage across the three lakes of the portage. The area was staked solid.

This didn't diminish the lift that came when we emerged at the Echo Bay end of the trail. Beyond the narrow mouth of the small inlet before us stretched the pale expanse of the main fiord and, beyond that again, mountains blue with distance and promise.

The trail ran straight down the center of the little arm and we followed it for about half the distance to the main bay. Here Beck called a halt and produced the uncertain staking blueprint which was our only map.

"If my hunch is worth anything," he said, "the open ground is over there to the southeast."

I followed his outstretched arm, which had a skyward angle of about 45 degrees. The eastern shore was more heavily wooded than the valley through which we had passed. While its slopes were not so steep, they made up for that in height.

"Assuming that the map is even half accurate," Beck continued, "another bay reaches in a couple of miles beyond those hills. It's this big point in between that interests me. I think we'll learn more by cutting across its base than by following it around the shoreline. It may be hard climbing but we'll save work in the long run. How are you on snowshoes?''

"I'll tell you tonight," I said. "I've never had my foot on one before."

The first thing I needed to learn was how to secure the long trail shoes. A length of lamp-wick, threaded into the babiche thongs of the shoe, was looped into a toe-latch. With the point of the foot thrust into this, the wick was then strung around the heel and tied just above the Achilles tendon – tightly enough to keep the foot and shoe together but loosely enough to allow flexibility of movement. The only difficulty was that the knotting and adjustment called for bare hands. The air, I discovered, still had teeth.

Snowshoeing itself was fairly simple, I decided. All you did was walk. The shoes went along with you as long as you didn't trip over them. With Beck in the lead and breaking trail, we reached the eastern shore without difficulty. The wind-hardened snow had sufficient crust to give support and by the time we had reached land I was convinced this was one form of transportation for which I had a natural flair.

Beck had headed for a pair of witness posts like those we had been seeing at a distance while crossing the portage. It was my first close-up of such markers. One of this pair was simply the lower section of a still-rooted spruce that grew at the water's edge. It had been lopped off five feet above the ground and the top two feet of the stump squared by an obviously experienced axeman. On one of the white faces a carpenter's pencil had inscribed the information that would lease the claim to the staker for 12 months once his fee had been paid and registered. Propped against the stump was a second, similar stake, carved from the severed upper part of the same tree. It, too, proclaimed that the ground so many hundred feet to the east and so many hundred feet out in the bay had been claimed by the owner of the license number.

"Claims," explained Beck, "are plotted with the borders running true to the cardinal points of the compass. The four posts are numbered, with Number One at the northeast corner and the others following clockwise. The line from post to post is supposed to be well enough blazed that a man can pick up one mark from the next without straining his eyes. Technically these two stakes you're looking at are supposed to be 300 feet out in the lake – at the corner of the claims. That's what they're witnessing to. Got it?''

"I follow you," I said.

"OK, follow me some more," grinned Beck, and started up the slope.

I realized that he was following the east-west line of blazes leading inland from the witness posts. This interested me – but I was distracted by the problem of my snowshoes once they were committed to the sharp grade and the deeper, fluffier snow that lay within the shelter of the trees. Not only did they sink to a surprising depth, but they showed a frequent inclination to set off on independent courses when they were lifted free. I found myself losing some of the enthusiasm I had worked up during the opening canter on the ice. Beck, breaking trail, was doing much better. Although the first burst of the uphill journey was brief, he had to pause and allow me to overtake him.

"If we follow this line," he explained, "we may well find it marching over the mountain and down into the other inlet without a break. It's as good a way to get the lay of the land as any, though. And there's no saying what we may stumble on."

I stumbled on a good deal in the first half mile. The hillside, which had appeared friendly at a distance, revealed itself on closer inspection to be well scored with small, deep gullies. Some had sheer walls which visually warned of their existence but others, completely drifted in, were blank-faced but steep pits. The deep snow also concealed a variety of small trees, rocks and windfalls, set like snares just below the surface where they could best snag the curved prow of a snowshoe. The uphill effort was demanding enough without their malevolence, and I tripped on them frequently and violently.

We arrived at last at the limit of the claim we were following. There was a clump of four stakes, the junction of as many claims. The sight of them, with the blazed lines reaching out in four directions, somehow restored my spirits. I heard myself saying, "How about letting me break trail for awhile?"

"Fair enough," Beck agreed. "You might as well take the packsack, too, and let me carry the rifle."

Following the line of blazes became a fascinating game, something like a slow-motion paper-chase. I soon forgot my weariness in the effort. Whoever had cut this line had done well. Almost invariably on arriving at one marker we could visually pick up the next, the blazes being large and the trees bearing them well-separated from their companions.

The higher we climbed, however, the sparser the trees became. High winds had sheathed them with sleet and I found myself searching vainly for the next blaze ahead.

All I could do was move forward, casting about for a sight of the missing marker or the one beyond it. My concentration on the hunt distracted me from what was developing underfoot. I took no notice of an innocent dip in the surface of the slope, and stepped over its edge. The next instant I was pitching headlong down a smother of the driest, most powdery snow I had ever experienced. When I came to a stop I was on my back, tilted feet-up at the bottom of a short 50-degree chute. There was nothing solid within 10 feet in any direction – no rocks, no trees – nothing but snow.

I was glad the snow had cushioned my fall, but I realized that the fluffy stuff was in itself a problem when I tried to stand up. The slope was against me, the weight of the packsack pinned my shoulders down, my snowshoes jutted out at angles that added to my helplessness, and there was nothing solid to offer leverage. In earlier tumbles I had learned to thrust my axe down through the snow until it touched solid ground but here, even at the end of my fully extended arm, it sank into white nothingness.

I attempted to roll over, figuring that if I could manage a face-down position I could do better, but the harder I struggled the more helpless I became.

"If I were you," came Beck's amused voice, "I'd try to slip off my snowshoes."

He was no more than a dozen feet above on the lip of the slide. His advice was practical. After several wild contortions I freed my feet and was able to squirm out of the powdery trap.

Relashing the snowshoes to my feet was torture. Once my

weight was on them they sank deep beneath the surface and the adjustment of the lamp-wick harness had to be done by touch, with my unprotected hands up to their wrists in snow. The bindings had turned stiff, making matters worse.

When I was finally mobile again Beck asked if I would like him to break trail for a while.

I realized Beck was being neither critical nor patronizing. It was simply being left to my own judgment whether I could sustain the trail-breaking to our next objective – the cluster of corner posts that lay somewhere ahead.

"Thanks," I said, "I'm all right."

We located the missing blaze, half-concealed by frozen sleet. The one beyond it was easier to find. The steepness of the climb became our major difficulty. By the time we had reached the next corner posts, even Beck was showing signs of needing a rest.

The worst, however, was behind us. The upward angle became less formidable and, after Beck had taken the lead again, it leveled off in a plateau. There was an almost dead white world up here. The snow was unusually deep, and the scattered trees were so heavily laden that, except for the shadows under the branches, they had little shape or line. Jagged islands of rock occasionally thrust themselves through the colorless mantle.

We stopped for lunch in the lee of one of these outcroppings. It was a difficult meal to prepare. A good deal of snow had to be shifted before we exposed enough flat rock for a fireplace. Dry wood was hard to locate in the sparse growth. During both cooking and eating we had to remain on our snowshoes.

The hot food was welcome but we ate in a hurry. We were sharply aware that the pause was consuming nearly an hour of precious daylight.

When we got under way again, Beck took the lead. The ground resumed its rise, but more gradually. This and the thinning ranks of the trees made it possible to steer a comparatively straight course. We simply kept lined up with the back trail, now visible for a good way behind us.

We needed that added advantage, for the heavily shrouded spruces effectively hid the next blazes. The only way to locate a marker was to bang the most likely trunk with an axe. When its snowy cloak had roared to earth, one could discover whether it was the blaze-bearer or not. Adding excitement to the game, quick footwork was required to spring clear before the sagging branches dropped their burden. Hesitation meant digging oneself out of a small avalanche.

But because of the more favorable terrain, we sighted the next posts at a considerable distance, making it possible to ignore the intervening blazes. The stakes stood out sharply on an upjutting tongue of rock. I was determined to take my turn as trail-breaker after we had reached them but even the thought made my muscles ache. I fell farther and farther behind and Beck reached the corner well ahead of me.

When he waved his axe like a tomahawk and yelled, "Come here!" my weariness vanished and I hurried to the posts. But the cause of his elation escaped me. The stakes were exactly like the ones we had left behind; and the view from the outcrop on which they were sited offered nothing new.

Suddenly I realized what the difference was: where there had been four corner posts in the clusters astern, here there were only two!

"Maybe a couple of them have blown down," I suggested.

"They haven't blown down," grinned Eric. "I've already poked around in the snow to make sure of that." He threw his arm in a sweeping motion to the ground rising gradually to the east. "My friend, what you're looking at over there is wide open. Welcome to Beck Syndicate!"

For the next few minutes we simply sat in the snow, our legs dangling over the edge of the outcrop, and gazed at the physically cheerless but spiritually uplifting prospect before us. Our pipes came out and Beck got his going. I had not yet learned to blow the stem free of saliva after use, and found mine frozen solid. The limited means for celebration were, however, incidental.

Whether there was a mine or the world's most barren rock lying beneath the sweep of snow before us, we were about to become holders of Echo Bay ground.

"There's at least two claims," said Beck, surveying the land with a general's eye. "If only we had a couple more hours of daylight we could block them in now. Got to be down on the ice before dark, though, if we're to find our way home."

"Shouldn't we put in *something?*" I cried.

"Sure," said Beck, grinning at my agitation. "We can cut our posts here, then work south along the line these other fellows have run. The ground slopes off in that direction and I'm all for going downhill again. If we're lucky I think we'll find it lets down gradually towards Echo Bay. It'll give us a chance to see if there's more open ground to the southeast as well. Now, how about cutting yourself your first corner post?"

I sought a suitably sized spruce and enthusiastically began to fell it.

"Take it easy," advised Beck, already at work on his own marker, "If you don't want some more wrestling in the snow you'd better shape it while it's standing firm. Like so."

He squared the slender trunk before him at a height of five feet or so, lopped off everything above, pyramided the crown, then severed the completed stake where its base disappeared under snow. It was the logical way to go about it and I was grateful for being shown before I had further demonstrated my greenhorn's ignorance.

Even after approaching my stake in the approved fashion I made a sadly mutilated job. The blunted axe and the frost-hardened wood showed a mutual contempt for my craftsmanship. The squared faces of the post were gouged and uneven by the time I was through, and the crown, supposed to form a neat point, looked as though it had been gnawed rather than cut. Beck, who had stacked his marker against the two already in position, moved over to examine my handiwork.

"I'd better start over again," I muttered disgustedly. "No one who saw this thing would believe it had been cut by anybody serious."

"It'll do," said Beck easily. "The inspectors make allowances for winter staking. By rights every post should be mounded at the base as well, but where would anyone find the rocks or dirt to do it at this time of year? Come summer we'll be getting metal tags from the Recorder at Fort Smith for everything we register. They'll have all the information on them that we're putting on in pencil now. After they arrive we'll have to come around and tack them to our stakes. That's when we'll do the mounding and put the finishing touches on anything that isn't a woodcarver's pride. Stick her up as she is. You can compare it to the sort of stakes you'll be cutting a week from now."

Relieved, I carried the post to the other trees and leaned it against them. Beck began to inscribe it with his carpenter's pencil, allowing me time to read what he already had printed on the one he had cut himself. Post No. 2, Watt No. 1! Passing over his own right as the senior partner, he had put my name to our first group of claims.

Even the best surface on the stake I had squared was scarred and uneven but somehow Eric managed to make legible the fact that this was Post No. 4, Watt No. 2.

"There we are," Beck said with satisfaction, driving it through the snow until it touched rock and wedging it in among its companions. "Now for the next corner. I'd better take the lead. With the down grade, breaking trail will be easier."

The weariness I had felt half an hour before was gone now. I would be quite capable, I was sure, of forerunning – even if the trail still led uphill. But I had increasing respect for Beck's unforced authority and followed obediently as he moved along the blazed line marking the outer limit of the earlier staking.

This was the easiest ground we had traversed since leaving the ice. It had a downhill slope, widely separated trees and a minimum of hidden pitfalls. We moved steadily, the silence broken only by the swishing of our snowshoes. Suddenly I was startled by a metallic chatter and a whirr of wings. A burst of large-sized snowballs whizzed over a ridge and plummetted into some low bush a hundred feet beyond us.

"Ptarmigan," announced Beck. "A bonus with the claims."

Being the gunbearer, I angled off cautiously towards the pure white birds. They were ghost-like against the colorless background, drifting ahead without haste and showing no immediate tendency to again take wing. Even when I had opened fire with the .22 they continued to run in little spurts, glancing back curiously from time to time until my third victim lay kicking. When they did take off it was only for a short distance. With fresh meat assured for the pot, I pursued them no farther.

Beck continued on course and when I caught up to him he had reached the next corner posts. Again, there were only two stakes. The ground to the east was still open and we now seemed assured of at least three claims. Again we set to with our axes and the first post of Watt No. 3 was raised. We worked quickly in the fading light. For some time, a chill overcast had been settling on the heights and now even its diffused glow was dying.

"This isn't my idea of a place to spend the night," said Beck. "Do you feel up to a cross-country run?"

"Try me," I answered.

We made no attempt to plot our course. It was impossible to obtain a clear view of our position in relation to the lake, so we followed the instinct of water, letting the slope carry us downhill towards the east. As the gloom deepened, our pace increased beyond the limit of safety and we took some hard falls. Branches clawed at us as we plunged past.

We were close to panic. The woods were becoming desperately dark. We were breathing fitfully when the ghostly expanse of Echo Bay at last came into view.

5

"All we have to do now," said Beck, "is hold the shore to our right and keep walking."

Fortunately the surface was good once we had moved out from the band of broken ice pressing the land. There were a few pressure ridges and the snow was well packed. I slipped off my snowshoes, and had an immediate sensation of buoyancy: I hadn't realized how leaden they had become until I was free of them.

The light was now so far gone that the distant shore was only a blacker element of the darkness to the south. The loom of land on our right was the edge of our world, along whose narrow rim we felt our way. Though walking was better a hundred yards out, we kept instinctively easing over toward the shore, struggling over stretches of rougher ice rather than abandon the comfort of the land's proximity.

It was the safest course, at that. The first break in the shoreline was likely to be the narrow entrance to the inlet from which we had started our climb this morning. Should we miss that gap in the darkness we would find ourselves staggering into the broadening outer reaches of Echo Bay – possibly into the vastness of Great Bear itself.

Our ability to judge distance was diminishing with our other physical and mental resources. We stopped from time to time, probing the shoreward shadows, increasingly haunted by the possibility of having already passed the gap we were seeking. There was danger in the intensifying cold and the blindness of the night. A single star, finding a break in the overcast, would have made a huge difference. The gunmetal sky, however, was blank and unreadable.

Then our anxiety was unexpectedly relieved. The solid wall of shoreline to our right was broken by a pale blur. We had come across the inlet that would soon be christened Cameron Bay. It was nameless that night when we rounded its abrupt eastern point. A mile away, at the far end of the inlet, was the portage, and at the far end of the portage was shelter!

There was a further trial to come, though. The funnel formed by the high ground on either side carried us unerringly to the head of the bay and the low-lying entrance to the valley, but we had strayed from the narrow trail packed by the dog sleds. This wasn't serious while we were on the ice: the surface on either side of the track was as firm as the path itself. But when we reached the 200-yard front of alders where the ice ended, the snow was hopelessly deep and soft. We simply had to find the portage track.

There were breaks in the trees in a dozen places, each of which looked like the natural starting point, but each time we probed, we found ourselves thigh-deep at the dead end of an alder-tangle. We realized how serious it was that we had overlooked one item of equipment for the day's journey – a flashlight. A single sweep of it across the face of the alder bush would probably have revealed the missing trail. As it was, we had to resort to feeling for it, crossing and recrossing the end of the bay in the hope that our moccasined feet would locate the ribbon of hard snow which, in the darkness, was impossible to see.

I fell upon the trail – literally – while floundering down one of the false leads between trees. Something struck me at knee level and I sprawled across the solid, yard-wide track. It was simple to trace it the short distance back to the bay. There we discovered the reason for our difficulties: just before it reached the ice, the trail took a sharp jog around a dense, obstructing clump of bush. Approached from Cameron Bay, it was perfectly masked from any wanderer in the darkness.

There was no problem maintaining our course for Lindsley from here on. But the gutter-like trail was quite a different highway from that which we had crossed in the morning light. The hills between the lakes were steeper, the distances unbelievably greater, the track itself incredibly more crooked. In the darkness its abrupt changes of direction were booby-trapped. The man in the lead, particularly if he was moving at any speed, discovered each invisible turn by charging past it and plunging headlong into deep snow. The one advantage of these upsets was that they solved the problem of choosing the forerunner. When the current one pitched on his face the other automatically took his place and carried on until it was his turn to discover the next sharp bend the hard way.

The last lake and the final tramp down the draw to Lindsley Bay passed in a haze of utter weariness. The valley was pitch-black and its walls pressed in with a physical oppressiveness. Here the trail followed the stream bed as it sought the cove. When it seemed that the watercourse, too, had lost its way, the black curtain ahead miraculously thinned and through it filtered a dull spot of light: De Melt's tent.

Ed heard us as we fumbled at the entrance to our own dwelling and a sudden triangle of light framed him in his doorway.

"Come over and have a mug while your stove's warming up," he called. "My kettle's boiling."

The hot tea was a transfusion. Stretched out on Ed's sleeping-bag, I wondered whether I could ever muster the strength or ambition to rise again. To sprawl on snowless, solid ground, to know that if sleep came there would still be an awakening, to be part of the little pocket of light, warmth and life caught between the walls of De Melt's tent, was heaven.

Ed's eyes were on us speculatively. "Quite a country back there, eh?"

"It sure is," agreed Beck.

"You need to be in shape for it – especially when you take to the high ground."

"High or low," Beck answered, "the best part is coming home to find a cup of tea waiting for you. Thanks, Ed. We'll see you tomorrow." We returned to our own tent.

Dinner, when it finally was ready, was a king's feast. With our footgear and parkas off and the candle flame steady in the still air, the harshness of the setting faded into a glow of well-being.

"I hate to think what we're going to feel like when we've had a chance to stiffen up," yawned Beck. "Was that really your first go on snowshoes?"

"Unbelievable but true," I answered.

"Twelve hours straight of that sort of going is a fair start. You must be ready for the sack."

"Not yet," I said, and dug into the small, personal pack-sack at the head of my bed.

In it was a box of cigars. They were the most expensive brand produced by a well-known tobacco company and there had been a time – long ago – when I had smoked them at my own expense. These, however, were a gift, a token earned for writing a testimonial.

This was their unveiling. Beck, as heavy-lidded as I, picked one delicately from the proffered box and said, "I think maybe I'll keep it till tomorrow."

"Whenever you like," I returned, "but I'm having mine before the candle is snuffed."

Eric gave a tired chuckle. "Maybe that's an idea."

We lit up and lounged beside the stove. Outside the frost crackled in the trees. I could sense the cliffs looking down in grim amusement on our ridiculous little display of luxury. But the smoke continued to rise – blue, gentle, aromatic – and somehow we remained awake, if silent, until the slow-burning victory beacons lay in little gray heaps on the stove top.

We woke to the moaning of the wind. Amplified by the funnel of the draw, it was accompanied by the hiss and slither of drifting snow. Inside the canvas it was warmer than it had been the previous morning but our breath curdled heavily enough to indicate that the day, with its wind, would be a washout for any lengthy work in the open.

A brief visit outside before breakfast confirmed our estimate. The wind was bitter, pressing without letup, and there was a haze of blown snow on Lindsley Bay that blotted out the far shore.

"It's just as well," said Beck philosophically. "We need to dig in properly – and two successive days like yesterday might be pushing our luck." We knew too, that few others would be willing to tackle the heights of Echo Bay.

By morning's end he had sorted our supplies, organizing the grub box so that it would be possible to carry on for a week or more without having to further disturb the dump. This, in turn, allowed us to secure the tarpaulin covering of the dump more thoroughly. I turned my own efforts to the woodpile. While the close-in dry trees had already fallen to the axes of Ed and others who had camped in the cove, there was still useful timber standing within a hundred feet of the tent. The morning's work left us with enough fuel for several days. I was forced to do it in half-hour spurts. The wind was cruel and it was a relief to be able to duck into the tent periodically.

The noonday break was a feast. Beck cooked up our three ptarmigan. The breasts emerged, brown and flavorful, from the frying pan. But the legs were tough: the ptarmigan is a runner rather than a flier.

We had begun to encounter a very special problem at mealtimes: no matter how appetizing food was as it emerged from the pan, a few minutes on a tin plate in the cool tent left unpalatable fat congealing around it. We found that by letting the fire subside somewhat after cooking, it was possible to use the stove top as a sort of steam-table. We left our plates on it as we ate and the food stayed warm and edible.

I set out in the afternoon to solve our water problem. I had noticed an ice chisel in Ed's tent and I borrowed it. Twenty-five feet out from shore I went to work.

My past experience of ice carving had been strictly limited to chipping slivers for those who liked it in their scotch. But making a hole in the surface of the cove appeared to be a simple enough job, the more so when I had cleared away a patch of snow and exposed what lay beneath. The ice was almost as transparent as the water itself. It was as unclouded as plate glass. One good thrust of the chisel, it seemed, should be sufficient to shatter it. When the chips began to fly, however, they were disappointingly small. The glass was of the bullet-proof variety.

I persisted until the wind drove me back to the tent. By this time I had a hole almost a foot deep and was beginning to hope. Ed, who had come up for air briefly, was standing outside his door looking critically at the weather.

"Howya doing?" he asked.

I told him.

"That's too bad," he remarked. "I always hoped someone would put down a waterhole here but you sure are going to have to hurry if you're going to do it today. Some of the Indians borrowed my chisel to cut fishing holes farther out on the bay and they tell me the ice is six, seven feet thick. Of course, it's probably thinner around here – maybe not more than five feet."

I did some rapid calculation of how long it had taken to make my modest indentation, then multiplied it by the distance yet to go and the difficulties that increased in proportion to the depth. The answer was that there must be an easier way of providing a water supply. Ed read my mind. "I've got in the way of cutting myself a few chunks of ice and keeping them handy to the tent," he said. "They're better than snow when you want to melt yourself some water."

After that, I maintained a collection of good-sized ice-cubes adjacent to the woodpile as our fresh water supply until the spring breakup. The hole out on the cove at least supplied a quarry for mining it.

Meanwhile Beck had turned his attention to our mutilated axe-blades. By vigorous filing he had smoothed the saw-toothed gouges in the steel, then restored the edges with a whetstone. In their next encounters with the tough, frost-hardened trees the new cutting edges still suffered but, as they were repeatedly filed down, they became acclimatized. Before spring they were cutting clean and true, without giving up a single steel chip.

That evening, with wood and water guaranteed and the tent more habitable, I turned to my secondary profession. My portable typewriter on my knees, I wrote my first dispatch for what I hoped was a waiting world. It was datelined, "Lindsley Bay, Great Bear Lake, February 25 (By Air Mail)". Since our plane's departure there had been no sound of a motor – which probably meant bad weather to the south – but the optimistic dateline gave me a lift, anyway.

There was not yet a great deal to add to what I had written from Fort Resolution. There was, of course, the open ground that had been discovered near Echo Bay but reporting on that would, obviously, be premature. Time enough to write of it when its full extent had been established – and staked.

I had written a good column and a half when Ed dropped over to invite us in for a few hands of bridge. This was to be the first of many such games, all of them unforgettable.

The age of De Melt's deck could probably have been determined as one establishes the age of a tree by counting the rings in the wood. The cards were a dull brown, with the grease and grime of many fingers overlying their original glossiness. One picked them apart rather than dealt them and this, combined with shuffling, took almost more time than it did to play the game.

It was necessary to light two candles in order to ascertain the values of some which had become unusually stained. The pack had survived at full strength only by enlisting the joker as the two of clubs and labeling a blank card as the ten of diamonds.

A gunny-sack spread on the dirt floor served as the playing surface and it was plain from the practiced way in which he laid it out that Ed had nothing to learn from any Outside hostess in the setting of a bridge table.

"The best way to play this time of year," he announced, "is to pivot every other hand. That puts each of us alongside the stove two out of every six hands. If it's really cold that's the only way to keep the game going properly. You notice it when you're farthest from the stove. I once played with a fella – a sort of thin-blooded guy – who was forever dropping his cards before he was out of the cool corner."

There were no stakes and three-handed bridge doesn't encourage a man's best skills, but if we had been playing for a dollar a point in a masters' tournament Ed could not have taken the game more seriously. Normally there was a suggestion of shrewd humor back of his eyes but none of it came through once the grubby cards were fanned in his paw. He was completely in earnest.

Halfway through the fifth or sixth hand he picked up the last trick, examined it closely, then turned gimlet eyes on me. "Didn't you play a heart on the third round?" he asked, suspiciously.

I assured him it had been a club. I felt it was important he should be convinced.

"You're sure?" Ed's tone was still flat.

"Why not check back?" Beck suggested.

De Melt glared at the tricks lying face-down on the gunny sack, as though attempting to read through their greasy backs. Then his coldly speculative gaze returned to me. Finally he grunted, rolled himself a limp cigarette, lit it, and deliberately led his next card. The hand ended in silence. In silence we pivoted, bringing me next to the stove. I was in need of its warmth.

I was already in a mood for my sleeping bag but Ed, once committed to combat, was insatiable. His peremptory "Now, just one more round" became routine until he looked up at the end of a deal and found me asleep. Once he accepted the inevitable and the cards were packed away he returned to normal and sent us home full of hot tea and renewed friendship.

I was too tired to remove any of my clothes when we reached our tent. As it turned out, it was a good night for sleeping fully clad. But the wind fell with the thermometer and daybreak, clear and biting, saw us again on the way to Echo Bay.

We jog-trotted most of the way across the portage and were able to follow our earlier trail up to the heights with comparative ease. Where the path was protected by the timber there was scant drifting and, even on the bench, its indentation could be readily distinguished. We were soon at our first corner posts. No sign of other human activity was written in the snow. Relieved, we began blocking in the unblazed sides of our three claims.

We worked together. Had we separated, with each cutting line as he went, more ground could have been covered, but I was still too green to be trusted to gauge distance and direction on my own. I tagged along behind Beck, learning how to pace off the 1500 feet and to hold a true course despite obstructions in the path. Always there was the trail behind with which to check on the straightness of the course ahead. This was the advantage of putting in snowshoe claims, one I often recalled wistfully when later we were staking in the open season, for in summer the forest closed over one's wake with quiet finality.

Eric, in the lead, charted the course while I marked the necessary trees. Where the timber was scarce and there were longer than usual breaks in the line of blazes, I barked larger areas of trunk so they could be distinguished at a greater distance. In my enthusiasm over my first claim I marked practically every stick within range.

The ground kept rising gradually but I had become more accomplished on snowshoes. Occasional snags still outwitted me, but I was developing an instinct for avoiding them, and found myself thrashing about in the snow less often.

Beck led the way east from our original corner posts. Fifteen hundred feet later there was no sign of other staking. Here we put in four markers.

"Now comes the tricky part," Beck said, drawing an oblong in the snow to help explain. "We've done two sides of a three-claim block. Rather than take time to complete them one by one, we're going to chance running the outer line of all three. Forty-five hundred feet south of here there's a spot where the southeast corner of our present property needs to be marked. Fifteen hundred feet west of there we should hit the last stakes we put in the other day. It will neatly close in our ground."

"What if we miss the place where we should join up?"

"It will mean I haven't accurately plotted the spot for putting in the stake at the southeast corner," said Beck in a matter-of-fact tone. "Let's go."

It was a severe test of his navigational ability. A surveyor, working with the proper instruments and a trained crew, would have had no difficulty coming out at the right place on our original line but Eric had only a hand compass and was working at speed over rough terrain. Not only did he need an excellent sense of direction; he needed luck.

He had both. The luck included the fact that the stack of four corner posts we were seeking was located on a natural rock monument which jutted above the surrounding area. We were able to spot the stakes at a much greater distance than would normally have been the case. They were slightly to the left of the course Eric had been striking and an angle was created in our line when we shifted back towards them.

"One day," he said, "we can come back and straighten out the jog in that line but, even as it is, it's pretty good staking."

As he spoke it began to snow. Overcast had been developing almost unnoticed in our intense preoccupation, and the first heavy flakes caught us by surprise. Had the snow come five minutes earlier it would have prevented our sighting of the posts. As it was, Watt 1, 2 and 3 had been neatly blocked in. There were still the two internal lines to cut, but they could safely await our next visit.

We had decided that morning that we would lose no more time making lunch on the trail. We had stuffed raisins and chocolate into our parka pockets, eating them on the move when hunger demanded. With neither food nor utensils to pack, and no firemaking and cooking to concern us, we had been able to concentrate on covering the ground. The resulting extra mileage had enabled us to complete our mission before the snowfall destroyed visibility.

We made no attempt to backtrack after calling it a day, but followed the still-discernable, two-day-old trail we had left in our retreat to the ice of Echo Bay. The snow became steadily more blinding but I felt as though we were in familiar territory – even though the familiarity was based on one previous trip, mostly in the dark. Our trail was a thin ridge of security against a very large Unknown.

Once on the ice, we moved quickly. At the portage we had Beck's flashlight to depend on, but we used it sparingly even after darkness had fallen with the smothering snow. We were beginning to develop some of the instincts of the four-footed animals who threaded the draw by night. It grew milder, and we were perspiring freely as we came home.

The next day – February 27 – we were away to a late start, not leaving camp until 9:45, but we made up for it with feverish work, raising our total number of claims staked to 11.

That day was highlighted by our discovery of open ground

on the actual shoreline of Echo Bay. Waterfront property had a high morale value: the fact that LaBine's strike ran into the lake invested other coastal ground with glamor. The shoreline also made for accessibility. Above all, our discovery showed the magnitude of a mistake that had found its way onto the staking map. When Beck got out the blueprint after our line had reached the ice, it declared that the shoreline to both the north and south of us was officially non-existent. How far this unknown ground extended remained to be seen, but what was there was ours for the taking!

A claim's length to the north a single witness post stood just above the waterline, marking the beginning of occupied ground in that direction. When our own stake had joined it we struck south along the lake. Where the shoreline turned in a southwesterly direction we found another witness post marking the limit of the staking from that direction. All the waterfront that stretched between it and our own witness post was open to us, and it was probable that the ground running inland was unstaked as far back as our own inner limit.

An explanation of this major error on the staking map suggested itself as we trudged the ice just out from the coastline. A short distance from where we had hit the lake the land reared abruptly in a series of cliffs, each banded with streaks of tenacious, ledge-hugging spruce. If the earlier stakers had approached by water, the prospect of running line up this near-perpendicular wall would have been uninviting, particularly if they had been in a hurry. To the north and south were several more attractive points at which to start putting in posts. If, like ourselves, the parties had been staking first and prospecting later, they undoubtedly would have left the jumble of conglomerate until they had blocked in more accessible formations.

Our predecessors, one party to the north and one to the south, had probably filled their licenses without having to tackle the cliffs; or the descent of winter might have driven them off before they had completed what they had set out to do. In any event, when each had turned in a staking map, the officials who had correlated them had obviously assumed that one property joined the other – and had made the shoreline conform.

We walked a quarter mile out from the land in order to survey what we would be up against in running line over this formidable prospect.

"We're going to have to sneak up on this one," said Beck. "We can put in some witness posts by rough calculation while we're down here – just to discourage anyone who might come along and spot some unstaked shoreline. When we've done that, we can hightail back the way we've come and start running line up the shoulder of that mountain until we reach the lip of the upper cliffs. When we're there we can decide how to handle the cliffs themselves and where to accurately site the witness posts."

There was at least a mile of open coastline when we paced it off – roughly the length of four claims. Our witness posts cut, we now had a picture of the likely boundaries of the open ground. Everything south of our own northern line, everything on the broad back of the upper slopes until they dropped headlong into the lake, was within our grasp!

Approaching nightfall forced us to retreat before we could match the view we had had from the base of the cliffs with one from their crest. That would come later. Meanwhile, we were practically sure of 11 claims – with the possibility of several more when our survey was complete.

6

The next day was Sunday. Though neither of us was a church-goer, we decided on a day of rest. It gave us time to upgrade the comfort of our camp. The most important improvement was a drying rack, which Beck erected along the side wall, back of the stove. Even with the temperature well below zero, we had been returning from the claims with sweat-dampened clothing – our footgear, especially. It had been difficult to eliminate the moisture before re-donning our gear the next day, but the drying rack would correct that.

The Sabbath brought visitors – two prospectors who were camped near the mouth of Lindsley Bay. They appeared in mid-morning and remained most of the day, as dissimilar a pair as the bush was likely to produce.

Stokely, the older man, bulked large in his caribou parka. His apprehensive pink face, with its heavy stubble of white whiskers, told of a Bear Lake winter that had bullied him un-mercifully. His conversation invariably turned to the imminent arrival of the Spence-McDonough plane which would fly him Outside. He expressed himself in nervous bursts of verbosity, punctuated by long, melancholy silences.

Turcotte, on the other hand, was a scrawny little man in a tat-tered canvas parka who bubbled with gentle Gallic humor, his eyes twinkling as he spoke with first-hand knowledge of all the better-known Canadian mining fields. Turcotte had accepted the lake in all its excitement, danger, and challenge.

The strangeness of the Stokely-Turcotte partnership was underlined when I learned that, for all his gregariousness when he came visiting, the French Canadian was basically a loner, and he immediately returned to his natural state after Stokely had been picked up. Each, apparently, had come to Great Bear independently. I could only assume that their joining of forces had been an act of compassion on Turcotte's part. He had apparently been unwilling to let the older man suffer his fears alone.

Later in the day a third visitor appeared: none other than Heb Jackson, the man whose silver sample had allegedly melted all over the stove top. He disappeared immediately into De Melt's tent and when, after half an hour or so, Ed appeared in the door and invited us over, we had visions of being introduced to new and spectacular mineral samples. Certainly the tone of Ed's voice suggested that something of great moment was at hand. When we came close enough to catch the glint in his eye, however, we grasped the real importance of the summons. Jackson was a bridge player. We had a fourth!

It was late when we escaped to our own tent – long after Turcotte and Stokely had headed down the bay for their camp. The night was clear, cold and reassuring. There would be good traveling conditions in the morning.

We were up at 6:30 on February 29, and on our way in good time. It was cold and we could travel fast (we now trotted a good deal when we could move without snowshoes). At one point a white fox danced along the trail ahead, looking over his shoulder from time to time to see if we were still following.

This was to be my first day of independent action. At our now-established trail leading to the heights from Cameron Bay, Beck turned uphill but I carried on towards Echo Bay. Eric's plan was to complete the lines that would carry him to the lip of the eastern cliffs. While he was doing this, I would remain on the ice, rounding the headland and arriving at the waterfront edge of our claims. When Beck appeared on the cliff edge, he would be able to indicate where I should finally place our witness posts.

We parted, and I struck out alone on the ice. Before I was

clear of Cameron Bay, I saw a black dot moving towards me out of the immensity of lake and mountain beyond the entrance. I couldn't make out the shape; I thought it must be an animal. I squinted, half in apprehension. Then I realized that I was being approached by another human being. I felt a strange emotion: this was the first time I encountered anyone on Great Bear, other than at the little crossroads of the cove.

The sensation of sharing the lifeless panorama with this small dot of intelligent flesh was like nothing I had ever known. Though the other man and I were traveling towards each other, the closing of the gap seemed to take forever.

Finally, we stood face to face.

"Hello," said the man, coming to a halt.

"Hello," I answered.

The features framed in the parka hood were marked by frostbite, old and new, and the encrusted beard gave the impression of something that had recently been hauled from the depths of the lake and dropped on the naked ice. It was an ageless face, a coarse weave of whisker and scar tissue with two bright eyes the only indication that there was life back of it.

"You come from De Melt's?" the man asked. He was slouched with weariness.

"Yes. You headed there?"

"For a while. I need some sleep. Siwashed it last night."

You "siwash it" when you are caught in the open without camping equipment.

"It was a cold night for it," I said.

"Cold enough," he agreed. "I didn't do too bad. Got a fire going against a rock face and it was all right as long as I could stay awake to stoke it. Dozed off, though. Froze my hands some."

He had a small axe, snowshoes, a light pack and the clothes he stood in.

I told him that my partner and I were camped at the cove and he volunteered that he had come in from the Mackenzie side and had been around the field for a while. We said so long and went our separate ways.

As I reached the turning point at the mouth of Cameron Bay I had a final glimpse of him. He was at the head of the portage, a black dot vanishing into the scraggly wall of spruce.

Next day, talking to Ed, I discovered that the encounter had not been between strangers, though our bearded, frostbitten faces had prevented recognition. The man's name was Whittington and we had known one another at Fort Simpson. He was a prospector from a long way back – a veteran of the Yukon rush – and during our brief acquaintance on the Mackenzie I had plumbed him vigorously for reminiscences. What he had been doing walking the face of Echo Bay alone, and where he went after he left De Melt's, I never knew.

Thanks to our early start, Beck and I fixed all our witness posts that day. The number of claims staked rose to 15.

We had heard the sound of plane engines on three different occasions during the day and anticipation speeded us to camp. No aircraft had landed on Lindsley Bay, however. De Melt reported they had all been heading north, probably for Hunter Bay.

Life in the cove had quickened, nevertheless. Whittington had borrowed Ed's sleeping bag long enough to get some rest before taking off in mid-afternoon for parts unknown. A man named Lainey, whom I had also met on the Mackenzie, had arrived to take his place. And several Indians were also visiting the acting mining recorder – with a severe problem. They were out of tobacco.

De Melt, whose own supply was low, tried to negotiate for a tin of ours, but it was already obvious we were going to be hard put before the open season eased the situation. Since the Indians said they would shortly be returning to Fort Franklin, where they would have access to all the tobacco they could smoke, we were not in a self-sacrificing mood.

There were certain courtesies involved, however, of which we had yet to learn. Later that evening our tent door opened silently and a well-built, middle-aged Indian entered. He acknowledged our greetings with a nod and squatted beside us, close to the stove.

Attempts to establish verbal communication failed completely. In response to our increasingly ludicrous use of English and sign-language, our visitor would solemnly nod his head, but he remained quietly impassive.

Finally I realized his eye was on the tobacco tin among the personal gear at the head of my sleeping bag. My obvious awareness of his interest appeared to be all he had been waiting for. Without change of expression or glance for permission, he reached over and drew the can to him. Extricating a pipe from his parka, he filled it, lit it with a twig touched to the stove, and drew in the smoke with a sigh of satisfaction that was like a spring wind through the impatient forest.

This had an air of ritual. Having failed to get anywhere with our own brand of communication, Beck and I went along with our guest on his own terms. We stoked our pipes and smoked while we waited to see what his next move would be.

For the next 15 or 20 minutes we hunkered in a silence broken only by the indrawing and exhaling of Virginia blend – one bronze face and two once-white ones expressionless in the candlelight, with the upcurling smoke the only movement in the tent. Finally the Indian's pipe sputtered. He knocked out the ashes, returned the briar to his parka, rose and, without sound or change of expression, stepped into the night.

"Whatever it's about I hope it isn't compulsory for each of them," said Beck. "There are still another five or six Indians in Ed's tent."

But our caller never returned nor, obviously, did he pass the word to his friends. We retired early, with a great wind howling about the tent. I couldn't get over the idea that there was laughter in that sound.

March 1 brought a cold morning and a drifted trail. We put in a hard day's staking and returned well after dark. The double line of cliffs on the eastern boundary of our claims was making life miserable. I lost my axe-head while working on my first bunch of stakes and had a devil of a time recovering it from a five-foot drift. It looked as though our block would finally size up at 16 claims. We were both out on our feet when we got home.

The second day of the month brought the coldest morning we had yet experienced. There was an inch of frost on our sleeping bags.

Shortly after the breaking of a bleakly beautiful dawn, seven drivers and 30 dogs pulled into camp with a great shouting, yapping and cracking of whips. All were heading for Fort Norman after having staked their full licenses in the country to the north.

Four were white men who had left Fort Smith the previous fall and who had more than a thousand miles ahead of them before they would again see home. A glance at their outfits raised some doubt as to their ability even to make Fort Norman, which was at least nine days of hard mushing distant. Broken harness, tattered parkas, badly worn gear and slim rations told their grim tale of hardship.

The remaining three men were Indians. They appeared to be in better shape. The group stopped for an hour-long mug-up and to investigate the possibility of adding to their supplies. The white prospectors told us frankly that on their January crossing from Fort Franklin, a desperate trip, they had found themselves heavily dependent on their Indian companions. Now the Indians were slowing the fast pace they were capable of in order to remain with the party for the return passage.

Ed, who expected supplies on the next plane, dug into what little he had in a quick deal with the travelers. To be on the safe side he also arranged for Edward Blondin, an Indian who had been working for him, to take off immediately for Conjuror Bay where the latter had a cache of moose meat and fishing bait. If the airborne supplies failed to arrive Edward's reserves could become lifesavers.

One of the members of that motley dogsled caravan pushing its way across the white desert towards Fort Norman was Peter Baker. His name was a loose adaptation of what he had been called in his native Lebanon. Of all the hard-bitten company, the Arab had been bitten hardest. He was almost completely snow-blind, his clothes were ragged, his face thin beneath its black, patchy beard. His dogs were so crippled that they were teamed with those of another train. Seven scrawny animals were pulling a single cariole, though its load of gear and supplies was pitifully light. Four could normally have drawn it with ease.

In the moments before the sled train moved off, the mist of freezing breath from so many humans and animals gave the scene a theatrical quality – as though fog-machines were puffing to create an atmosphere of cold menace. Peter Baker provided a final touch of the dramatic. His dark features, his pained, peering eyes, his animated conversation and his quick laughter suggested something almost too vivid – a little larger than life.

The dogs showed no eagerness to put their weight to the harness when the command *"Marche!"* was sounded. Whips cracked, voices were raised, men added their strength to the effort of getting the toboggans in motion. Finally the last train was under way and disappeared around the bend in the portage track. For a time the sound of whips and voices drifted back through the draw. Once I heard Baker's high laugh. Then the quiet of De Melt Cove returned, the more marked after the passing clamor.

The day was already too far advanced to allow us another trip to the claims. I was silently grateful for this. My ability to take innumerable falls without damage had deserted me the previous afternoon. I had come down heavily on the ice, but had not suspected any real damage at the time. But when we clambered out of our sleeping bags to greet the dog teams, I experienced acute pain. The longer I was on my feet, the sharper the evidence became that I had wrenched my hip.

The thought was deeply disturbing. We were just getting under way with what we had come to do and time was precious. What suddenly concerned me even more, however, was the possibility of having Beck think I was shirking if I pleaded inability to go back to the claims in the morning.

I convinced myself that the one way to prevent my leg from stiffening further was to keep it in action. I went to work on the woodpile. The chopping was torture, but I persisted.

De Melt called no bridge party that night and I attempted to turn to writing. It was a short-lived effort. The day had been consistently cold and the twilight told us we were in for the lowest temperature yet. Even with the stove constantly stoked, my fingers soon lost their feeling on the typewriter keys. I had discovered that working in severe frost could shorten the life of the typewriter ribbon alarmingly. The stiffening of the inked fabric made it brittle and it was soon punched full of holes. It would have to be conserved carefully. My typing was abandoned.

We put green wood into the stove to hold the heat as long as possible. Using live timber for fuel was a recent discovery we had made. With its sap deeply withdrawn against the harsh temperatures, living wood made excellent fire once a good bed of embers had been established.

Our innovation had lengthened the period between the snuffing of the candle and the time the dwindling heat made it necessary to pull our heads inside our sleeping bags. There was half an hour or so when it had become possible to comfortably converse in the dark. These had become the most communicative minutes of the day.

We talked about our plans and the work in hand. It was also a time and atmosphere for confidences. At first these had a stag-party quality – reminiscences of mighty benders and amatory adventures, boastings of past accomplishments and explanations of past failures – all on the grand scale. This phase passed quickly, though, brushed aside by an instinct to abandon the exaggerated superstructure of experience and to get down to the framework.

Undoubtedly it was affected by our physical firming-up and by the environment. There was something tremendously positive about the lake, about its mountains, its spaces and all the elements that set its moods. Great Bear demanded simplicity. You had to live with the lake on its own direct terms. There was no room for pretense.

The quality of our talk took on this directness, and I began to learn more about Eric Beck.

His memories of Penetanguishene, the Ontario town of his youth, were happy ones. His family had been well-to-do and a brother had become a successful lawyer. His own interest had long been in mining but he had never got around to taking an engineering degree. A government-sponsored prospector's course had been his quick ticket to field activity.

The stock market boom of the twenties had carried him into the brokerage business, and he had planned to marry. But things hadn't worked out, and he expressed no regrets. If anything he was grateful that the Depression had caught him without domestic responsibilities.

His absorbing passion was the possibility of making a

major strike. Money was not the attraction. For him, the discovery itself would be the end of the rainbow.

Such single-mindedness hadn't made him insensitive to me, however. He was a good listener and patient in the presence of my greenhorn ignorance and general verbosity. He had at no time been critical of me. But that evening, as I lay in the dark with my hip throbbing, I found it difficult to explain my predicament to him. My reticence made little sense, but I was suffering from excessive pride. I wanted desperately to carry my share of our enterprise.

In the end it became easier to be open with Beck.

"I'm not sure I'll be able to go to the claims tomorrow," I blurted.

His reply had more relief than criticism in it. "I thought you were wincing today. Why didn't you sound off?"

"I thought it would clear up," I said.

"Probably it will, with a night's rest. What's wrong?"

"My hip. Came down hard on the ice yesterday."

"How about a shot of rum? This is what we brought it for. It'll help you sleep."

"It isn't hurting that badly," I replied, quickly.

Beck was suddenly amused. "If John or any of the boys were here they wouldn't believe it." He chuckled.

"Believe what?" I asked, with an edge to my voice. I knew what he meant.

"That you turned down a drink when you really needed it."

It was my turn to laugh. "I'm not sure I believe it myself."

"Well, don't worry about the morning," said Beck. "If you aren't up to working, I can manage on my own."

I slept reasonably well while the trees cracked through a pitiless night and the Arctic temperature steadily established itself inside the tent.

Our bags were heavy with our frozen breath on the morning of March 3, but we were up in good time and off to the claims. I had doubts about whether I could stick it, but as I warmed up with the work, the pain became more bearable.

Had the staking not been so close to completion, we might not have accomplished a great deal that day. But, tying up the final lines, we became almost insensible to weariness, pain or caution. Beck, working the upper cliffs, carried the main burden. The lower slopes and faces, though rugged enough, were within my limited abilities.

Our greatest problem was to reach the narrow benches and ledges where there were trees capable of carrying our blazes. In the process we encountered the first exposed rock we had been able to investigate on our property. This held particular fascination for Beck. He did some wild scrambling on the rock face, trying to get a closer look.

As I stood on the lake ice, I saw Beck almost directly above me, trudging the lip of a 500-foot precipice. As he encountered a rounded cornice of hard snow, his snowshoes slipped abruptly from under him and he sprawled towards the edge of the drop, clawing at the icy surface to halt his descent. Two or three feet short of the rim he stopped, literally teetering on the brink.

I held my breath. At that distance, there was nothing I could do. As I stared, he methodically cut a grip into the treacherous surface with his axe, loosened his snowshoes and crawled to safety. Without pausing to look back at the spot, he resumed his normal posture and continued on his way, completely absorbed in his exploration.

Beck was surprised to learn when we again joined forces that I had witnessed the little drama from far below.

"I know I was a damn fool to go so close to the edge without taking off my snowshoes," he admitted sheepishly, "but I was in a hurry."

There was still some light when we had completed the blocking-in and on the way home, in spite of a headwind and damp snow that found its way inside my parka, I was able to bag half a dozen partridge to replenish our fresh meat supply. My leg, far from having suffered from the day's effort, continued to loosen up reassuringly.

We had finished staking the Watt, Beck and Sydie groups of claims.

A night even colder than the preceding one failed to subdue our high spirits. I guessed that it was at least 50 below (a later check at Eldorado gave a thermometer reading of $-62\,°F$), but when I went outside before rolling in I remained far longer than was necessary. The biting cold of the night was matched by its beauty.

The aurora borealis swept the heavens with sinuous fire. In the phosphorescent light the islands in the bay seemed twice their normal size and the cliffs above the cove humped close and menacing. The ragged detail of daylight was flattened by the night, leaving an impressionistic image of savage strength.

My awe at the sight was more powerful than the knife-edged air pressed against my flesh, until a stab of crackling pain told me I had a frozen ear. I was reminded that, even if my mind wished to soar among the stars, I was still a prospector's assistant on Great Bear.

That night we took off nothing but our parkas and mukluks but even then it was difficult to sleep. The frost reached into my sleeping bag with clawed fingers, no matter what protective position I huddled into. Towards daylight, however, a wind sighed down the draw, the temperature eased, and I slept.

March 4 was a day for celebration. There was no need to return to Echo Bay's cliffs. Besides, it was a double birthday. In Edmonton my son Erik had turned five and, on De Melt Cove, it was Eric Beck's birthday as well.

How better to celebrate than by taking a long walk? After all, we had done 60 miles or so over the past week. We decided to make a visit to Eldorado itself.

Immediately after breakfast we set out over the portage, down the length of Cameron Bay, then out into new territory. Instead of turning east on Echo Bay's wide sweep, we turned west. To the left rose the red-smeared mass of Gossan Island; to the right the high, rough walls of the mainland; and far ahead lay the gap between Mystery Island and the headland that ended in LaBine Point. Stretched across the opening was the hairline division between ice and sky.

It was a 10-mile tramp from De Melt Cove to Eldorado but that morning it seemed like a stroll around the block. Soon Glacier Bay opened to the north, with the ice-fall from which it took its name visible at its head. Now Mystery Island lay immediately on our left. The Gibraltar-like rock standing dead centre in the throat of Echo Bay was rumored to hold fabulous mineralization. The silent island held fast its secrets. It was a thing of stark, commanding beauty.

Entering the five-mile breadth of ice between Dowdell and LaBine Points, we sighted the V-shaped inlet to the north which would one day be known as Port Radium. Sheltered from the wind and surf by a spike of mainland and a strategically sited island, a small group of log buildings huddled at the foot of a rocky slope. Here Gilbert LaBine had chipped the first multi-colored samples that had drawn us to Great Bear.

Ed De Melt had warned us that visitors were not encouraged at Eldorado, and that the two members of the crew there had been retained over the winter months simply to keep people from snooping around the property. The only sign of life as we approached across the ice was the wisp of smoke rising from the chimney of the two-story living quarters. We had been sighted from afar, for the door opened well before we reached the shore and two men moved down the steep beach to meet us.

The leathery hardrock miners greeted us in a guarded way, but they became affable when we identified ourselves.

"Come on in," one of them invited. "We've been waiting for you to show up."

"Oh?" said Beck, surprised.

"Sure," said the other. "We've had a pile of newspapers for you here for two or three days. One of the pilots dropped them in – special delivery from Wop May's wife. Said you'd be along sooner or later. Come on; you can read them over lunch."

We had our meal on a real table with a real bench to sit on. And there was real coffee – as much as I could drink. I had done without since we had come north, since tea went further and was the proven stimulant in the bush. My reunion with the beverage, enjoyed while sitting upright at a table, was practically a return to the fleshpots. Topping off an oven-cooked roast of beef, it produced a sense of well-being which was entirely appropriate to our mood of celebration.

Observing etiquette, we didn't press for information about the mine. Our hosts offered none. But I realized they were as happy to have us there as we were to be under their roof. I decided that the tales of their hostility to visitors had undoubtedly begun with callers who tried to pry into matters which the guardians had been instructed to keep to themselves.

We allowed ourselves just three-quarters of an hour at Eldorado. We enjoyed the full experience of striding about the room and reveling in the novelty of standing upright under a roof again, and peering out through real window glass at the inhospitable landscape which had become our habitat. Then, with our newspapers under our arms like businessmen returning home from the city in the evening, we started the 10 miles back to De Melt Cove.

That night we burned an entire candle. Cigars were broken out, and tea brewed. Until the early hours of the morning, the magic carpet of wrinkled newsprint carried us back to the world we had departed. It was a fascinating journey but I came back to my new reality without regret.

7

There were decisions to make on the morning of March 5. The foremost of these was which direction we should take in staking the balance of our 1931 licenses. Beck's sixth sense had told him the chances of picking up more open ground close to the center of the field were poor. The upper reaches of Lindsley Bay were more promising. There was already too much activity there for our liking, but there was no question that room for staking could still be found if we struck out far enough. Before breakfast was over the choice was made: we would go north.

This next stage would not be as simple as the Echo Bay operation. We would have to travel much farther, and there could be no heading out each day from our base camp. The camp would have to go with us.

If we'd been employed by a well-heeled company or syndicate, this would have presented no problem. We would simply have negotiated an agreement with one of the Indian dog drivers to transport us to the area we chose to explore. Beck Syndicate, however, was geared to operating under its own steam. Backpacking at this time of the year was out of the question. We would have to have a toboggan – something not likely to be easily acquired at De Melt Cove.

It was too nice a day to brood over it, though. The sun was brilliant, the temperature the mildest since we had arrived. While there might be certain things we couldn't do at the moment, there were others within our capabilities. For one thing, we could wash.

Up to this point, neither of us would have won a prize for personal hygiene. Discouraged by the difficulties of getting water – and comforted by the deduction that germs would find it difficult to operate in the temperatures we had been experiencing – we had depended on a brisk rub with snow for the cleansing of greasy hands or tablewear. Our faces had steadily darkened but with thickening beards and windburn to blame, we had paid this fact little attention.

We melted a full bucket. Soaping and rinsing our hands and faces in our shallow gold-pan was a forgotten delight; no snake shedding his skin could have felt better.

And there was still enough water left for our tablewear. Plates, cups and cutlery were shining when we were through, free of the evidences of meals long past.

Acting in faith that we would eventually come up with some means of transportation, we made the necessary preparations for moving camp. During our stay, the inner half of the tent had developed most of the characteristics of an igloo. Steam from the cooking had condensed and built up layer on layer of ice on the canvas farthest removed from the direct heat of the stove.

Occasionally, when the sheet metal had glowed red for a long period, the roof above the sleeping area would thaw. When that happened a rainstorm would develop. Since the heavy drops froze solid on everything on which they fell, we had learned the art of controlled stoking. While keeping the temperature livable in the immediate region of the stove, we had allowed the ice to continue forming where it already was established. It was now a thick, solid shell enclosing the inner half of the tent's interior.

This was acceptable as long as we were on the present site, but it was now obvious we were going to have enough weight to drag north without including chunks of solidified De Melt Cove atmosphere. An attack was launched against the igloo by beating its containing canvas with clubs. The shell collapsed in fragments and, when we were through, the interior of our home looked like a china shop after a visit from the bull. When it had been cleaned out, however, living conditions were improved and the tent could be folded for transportation.

Meanwhile the answer to our basic need was tinkling towards us down the bay. Specks in the distance resolved themselves into Edward Blondin and his merry-belled dog team and, bringing up the rear, the unfortunate Stokely. The Indian's cariole was loaded with the moose meat he had picked up at his cache on Conjuror Bay, and also most of Stokely's outfit. He was pulling the prospector's almost empty toboggan behind his own.

"I've had my bellyful," Stokely announced. "No plane is going to fly in here and take off without me. The Indian drove by just when I'd decided I was coming in whether I could drag my outfit with me or not."

He glanced behind him, as though the lake were a malevolent force at his heels.

Later, after Stokely had raised his tent, Beck dropped over to visit him. When he returned Eric looked pleased.

"We're in business," he announced. "The old man is ready to sell anything in his outfit at fire sale prices. He isn't just through with Bear Lake; he's through with the bush – period. The toboggan's ours. Got a fine heavy axe from him, too. Ought to make things easier for you on the woodpile."

Several planes passed overhead during the day and the moment an engine was heard Stokely popped from his tent, jack-in-the-box style, ran out on the ice and gazed appealingly at the sky. As the drone of each engine died in the distance, the grizzled prospector would shamble back to his tent as though the last chance for life had passed him by. Our attempts to draw him clear of his tension were fruitless. There was just one man he was prepared to talk to – the pilot of the aircraft which would fly him Outside.

Ed De Melt entertained at dinner that evening and the aroma of moose steaks was only slightly less entrancing than the act of eating them. Even more refreshing was the company of Edward Blondin, who had moved in with De Melt. The Indian possessed a serene dignity which seemed unruffled by his encounters with whites. Honesty was a guarantee of his friendship. Any attempt to exploit that friendship brought down a curtain of unforced reserve and a quiet withdrawal.

Blondin had intrigued me from the first evening he had driven into the cove after a long day on the trail. It was at least —30 °F and dinner was waiting for him in Ed's tent. Nevertheless his first act had been to see that his dogs were properly cared for. He had selected a sheltered spot to stake them out, ascertained that each was beyond fighting distance of the next in line, and that its length of chain brought each animal within reach of a favorable spot for curling in the snow. As he did so, each beast lifted its head as a pet might to a thoughtful master. This was something new in my experience of the half-wolf sled dogs, particularly in relationship to Indian drivers. I wasn't surprised to learn later that no one had ever seen Edward lay whip to dog except to break up a fight.

With the team waiting patiently – and confidently – Blondin then picked two fair-sized lake trout from the cariole and, laying each on the ground, cut it in three with his axe. An equal share was tossed to each of the five dogs. Then Edward offered me the final portion. It was so natural a gesture that I had no difficulty in expressing an equally natural gratitude – though it was a completely new experience to find myself an afterthought to the feeding of a pack of huskies. This incident was the firm basis for a lasting friendship with Edward. It had also provided Beck and me with a delicious fish chowder.

The night of the moose-meat feast had an inevitable conclusion – a bridge game. Blondin had played cards before, but never auction bridge. Before the contest was over he found himself with three teachers, each highly opinionated in the matter of his own system whenever he drew the Indian as partner.

With the spirited debates that broke out between the various teachers, the pupil could have been excused discouragement – even resentment. However, he remained the one calm member of the foursome. Though he developed little finesse, he had a forthright way of leading with his aces. This disorganized the opposition as often as it did his partner and by evening's end Edward's philosophical acceptance of the game had given way to a fine zest for it. It made the most painfully butchered hand enjoyable and even De Melt suspended his terror tactics – for this one session.

When Stokely ran out onto the ice the next day at the sound of another motor, he was not totally disappointed. This time the aircraft wheeled over Lindsley Bay and glided into the cove – the first plane to land there since McMullen had dropped Beck and me. The old prospector's assumption that this was a Spence-McDonough machine come to retrieve him was unsubstantiated, however. It was the Fokker "SL", a Canadian Airways craft flown by Ronnie George. The pilot was new to the lake, but was quickly accepted when he produced some mail and the opportunity for getting letters out. My packet of newspaper dispatches date-lined "By Air Mail" was no longer a fraud.

News from home made it clear the arrival of my copy would be most timely. The magazine market was still sick, and my newspaper stories from points farther south had been given a very modest play. Heart-warming though it was to have *any* word from home, the letters gave urgency to our preparations for the move north.

Next morning we started solving the puzzle of fitting a folded tent, the stove, our sleeping bags, food and other gear onto the seven-foot toboggan. Work was interrupted by the arrival of Walter Gilbert, who whooped into the cove in "SK", the Fokker workhorse already famous throughout the North. He had just hopped over from Eldorado and reported that Spud Arsenault was in camp, preparing to leave for some of LaBine's more distant property. Knowing that Spud was in the field was, in itself, a morale-raiser.

Gilbert was 32 and looked younger. He had a good wartime flying record and had been made a Fellow of the Royal Geographical Society for work he had done in peacetime. When Major Lockie Burwash made his expedition to the North Magnetic Pole in 1930 and discovered a number of relics of the long-lost Franklin expedition, Gilbert had been his pilot. Even in his brief stopover for lunch with us, he was stimulating company.

Our chief problem in stowing the toboggan's cargo was to avoid a load so high that it would topple over at the slightest list. By the time we finally succeeded, Gilbert's plane had departed – without Stokely. The old man, still preoccupied with the non-appearance of his airlift, seemed scarcely aware of us when we finally struck out across the bay.

I had heard bushmen declare that toboggan-hauling was the most grueling form of winter travel but, on our first hour out, there was reason to suspect that this had been just another yarn designed to intimidate greenhorns. While Beck and I shared the dragrope at the beginning, the load slid so effortlessly over the trail we were following that we soon realized it was possible to spell each other, leaving one man free to walk unburdened half the time.

It was perfect, windless weather, bright with sunshine. Within 15 minutes we had doffed our parkas and put on snowglasses against the glare. When De Melt Cove faded in the distance, we were fresher than we had been before takeoff.

Rounding an island on the far side of inner Lindsley Bay, we were confronted by two high-walled narrows – one straight ahead, to the north, the other at right angles, to the east. The sled trail held to the north.

Remembering the inaccuracies we had discovered in the map of Echo Bay, we decided to take the eastern gap. There was no trail and the toboggan now required both of us on the dragrope, but men had been here before. Witness posts were dotted along the shore.

The lofty walls of the passage drew steadily closer together, some of them offering displays of mineral stain, but we had no time for curiosity about other men's ground. Our full effort was sparked by anxiety to discover what lay at the end of the narrows.

We discovered, finally, that nothing opened out of the narrows. We had been traversing a blind alley, a handsome fiord whose end was blocked by even more spectacular cliffs than those that formed its flanks. Re-examining the map we realized we had made a serious error in judgment. At a time when we would have been thinking about calling it a day and pitching camp, we were faced with retracing miles we should never have covered.

After that the toboggan turned heavy as lead. There was lost distance to make up and, beyond that, more distance which we had no choice but to cover before sunset.

There are two sizable islands in the southern pocket of Lindsley Bay. One, which bears the name Mackenzie, is massive enough in its three-mile length to seem like mainland to the stranger. The other, unnamed and a mile or so long, is sufficiently precipitous to be mistaken for Mackenzie itself. This we realized as we emerged from our blind alley and continued on the course we should originally have followed. Our failure to identify the larger island had been our undoing.

Eventually, in the late afternoon, we emerged from the shadow of Mackenzie and faced two miles of open ice stretching to the northwest. On the far shore, obviously, was the channel to the north which we had been seeking. Spikes of spruce rose on low ground close to the opening and promised a campsite.

We were tired when we set a direct course for the grove, a course which carried us clear of the windbreak the island had been providing. We had not been aware of any breeze up to this time but now, as the light failed and the warmth of the sun gave way to the chill of the shadows, we felt it. It was not a strong wind. It barely stirred the loose, dry snow on the crust. But its whisper was merciless.

While we were moving it brought only slight discomfort. Straining at the dragrope worked us into a sweat, particularly after it became necessary to put our parkas on again. It was when we stopped that we suffered. Our sweat-soaked clothing stiffened almost immediately and the frost, encouraged by the wind, gnawed at us.

The answer was to keep moving. But we were no longer physically capable of sustained stretches: the strength simply was not in us. We made fair progress for a mile or so – about half the distance across the open bay – but from then on our ability to move was limited to ever-shortening spurts. For long moments, it was impossible to lift one foot in front of the other.

If we had reached this stage within range of Mackenzie Island, we would undoubtedly have retreated to it and taken a chance on camping on its hostile face. By the time we realized the extent of our exhaustion, however, the grove ahead was as close as the island astern. Now that the problem had been simplified to getting off the ice at any cost, the sensible decision was to hold to our course.

The toboggan had become a ball-and-chain. We had only to drop the dragrope to be rid of it – to move forward free of its torment. If there had been human habitation on the shore, we unquestionably would have done just that. But as far as we knew, no shelter existed except the tent which burdened us. We had to drag it with us to the grove, or risk death. In milder weather, it might have been possible to remain on the ice and take to our sleeping bags but, as the temperature fell to iron depths, it became obvious that we must continue our struggle to reach shore.

By the time the last light had gone, we were close enough that the spruce spires, rising with open sky behind them on their low spit of land, were visible in spite of the gloom. The last, desperate lunges that carried us to shore were never longer than a hundred yards. At the end of each we would stand shivering violently, our sweat-soaked clothes stiffening to suits of icy armor, until we could summon the will and the strength for another try. Perhaps it was the violence of our trembling that beat some life back into us.

The snow in the grove was four feet deep and powdery. This meant working on snowshoes as we set up camp, a difficult operation in thick bush, made worse by doing it in the dark. But we had made it off the pitiless face of the bay, and our relief somehow brought renewed physical strength. We set vigorously to work. The four-foot excavation in the snow went down, the tent went up, the stove came to life and, at midnight, we ate supper. It had been 12 grueling hours since we had last eaten, and we badly needed the food. The meal seemed like a thanksgiving feast. It had been one hell of a day.

Dawn revealed two things we had missed in the dark. One was the fact that our camp was not, as the map indicated, on the edge of a narrows leading into the next arm of Lindsley Bay. Instead, it was on a low neck of land that separated the two bodies of water. There was a short, comparatively level portage, but the absence of the water passage shown by the map justified our distrust of it the day before.

The second discovery was a camp a mile or so across the ice

to the east. We could see a large clearing, a cabin in the course of construction, and a cache of gas drums at the lake edge. We guessed it to be the new Spence-McDonough base. The thought that we had been so close to help made us feel foolish until we found the camp to be uncompleted and unoccupied.

We crossed the portage and moved up the bay to the north. The area was heavily staked for three miles. The ground beyond looked good, though, and Beck chipped off rock samples, his prospector's eye glorying in the first mineralization of the trip. We picked a site for our new base just beyond the last of the staking and close to the ground we wished to explore. It blew hard all night but our camp was well sheltered.

A windy, murky morning greeted us when we rose at 6:30 A.M. on March 9. We waited, hoping that conditions would improve, but by 9:00 A.M. the trees still bent under great gusts. Finally, we decided to chance it, as we would have the wind at our backs. We broke camp and made remarkably good time, despite a track so badly drifted it was barely discernable. We camped well beyond the last staking. A purple finch greeted us here with a song like a tame canary. We took pains with the camp and made it the finest we'd had yet.

On March 10, we traveled hard all day, but the formation we spotted was disappointing. We kept hitting granite wherever we turned. Returning towards camp we saw four men heading for the one part of the bay we had overlooked. We met a young man driving a dog team who informed us the newcomers were tying on to some 1930 staking. He also told us that two men were camped on a small island we had considered staking two days before. Panicked by the rush which had overtaken us, we threw in a claim in record time on the point where we were camped.

The warnings we had heard in Edmonton a month before were being confirmed. A staking rush aimed at beating the in-between was underway, and we were glad of our early start.

The knowledge that the Echo Bay claims were safely sewn up was a comfort as Lindsley Bay began to crawl with life, but we still had a number of licenses to fill before they expired at the end of the month.

On March 11, we crossed the bay in a chill, brisk dawn and

started throwing stakes in to the east. We were obviously hitting only solid granite, and were forced to resume exploring. We found nothing but granite, until at noon we packed up and cut back to camp at Contact Point (optimistically christened by Beck), blocking in three claims and partially staking two more. Some newcomers were staking the large island I had investigated the day before.

Next morning our island jumpers hailed us as we hit the ice. They proved to be units of a large force Colonel McAlpine had rushed into the field. They were staking indiscriminately, taking in nothing but granite as far as we could see. We lunched with them and learned that Great Bear was booming Outside. Encouraged, we put in four more claims on Contact Point, but discovered that both islands we had our eyes on were gone. Our formation was looking better all the time.

The next day was the 13th of the month and we had 13 claims yet to stake. We worked steadily – 11 consecutive hours on snowshoes – and staked seven claims.

Among these were two small islands on which we located our first real mineralization. There was a good quartz vein, well sprinkled with bornite, chalcopyrite and iron. We had hopes for something better (gold!) but were almost afraid to consider it. Eric named the islands after my wife, Ernestine, in the wild hope that they would go down in mining history.

On March 14, after our second wash in warm water since hitting the lake, we headed for another group of islands which I felt lucky about and, wonder of wonders, they weren't staked. What was more, they showed good formation, with all the minerals of the Ernestine group, though iron predominated. We squeezed them into two claims and spent the raw, misty afternoon prospecting them. We came home heavy with samples.

The next day would have to be our last in this territory, unless we happened to strike something startling. Grub was running low. We were all set to do some intensive prospecting on the island claims and possibly look over the adjacent mainland. But a mean wind blew out of a clear sky and brought snow squalls. We were flailed and battered on the open lake, the blast biting to the bone. We were forced to retreat to the tent.

This was the first time we had been driven to shelter after having committed ourselves to a day's work. The fact that we had just found two new veins of quartz and calcite on one of the Ernestine Islands made it even harder to give up. We would have to return to De Melt Cove the following day and this was probably our last look at the new staking before the breakup.

But the combination of wind and cold was unbearable for more than a few minutes at a time. Even with a toque under my parka hood I froze an ear badly. It remained extremely susceptible to further frostbite for the remainder of the winter. I made another discovery: it is the ear on the leeward side that freezes first in a crosswind.

Our campsite was well chosen, with excellent shelter even under the punishing wind. We had not been the first to appreciate it. In a foray for firewood, I had come on the skeletons of two large Indian lodges, the poles bleached paperwhite in the many years since canvas or hide had covered them. Their symmetrical strength rose against the sky, a memorial to the hunting or fishing parties they had once housed.

Here was firewood if I wanted it, tinder-dry and already cut. But the ghost lodges still stood when I returned to our own camp. They were a mystic link with the ancient Bear Lake People.

We left the wooded point on the morning of March 16. The wind had continued to howl through the night but our need for provisions left no alternative but to return to our supply dump. There was a steady soughing in the upper branches of the spruces, with fine snow eddying down, as we loaded the toboggan. It sounded ominous, but we were still hoping it wouldn't be bad when we emerged from the trees.

The trail was drifted by snow as dry as ashes and the toboggan lurched and pulled. When we crossed the portage into lower Lindsley Bay the wind rose higher and lashed us without mercy. The crossing to Mackenzie Island, an ordeal on our outward journey, was equally hostile to our return. We were stronger and fresher than we had been eight days earlier, but so was the wind. Our one break was the discovery, in the narrows between the island and the mainland, of a new camp on Mackenzie's lee side. Here we found warmth and a good fill of

tea when we were hailed by Colin Bowen, a young Northman I
had known from the previous year. He and his partner had
been prospecting some property on the island.

Colin, wisely, was denned up for the day. However, just
after he had put the tea on, sleigh bells sounded out on the ice.
We were not the only ones on the move. Through the tent door
we spotted two dog trains approaching over our back trail. We
were joined by the drivers, who were working for McAlpine.
They remained just long enough to drink a mug of tea and
thaw thumbs frozen while crossing the stretch of open bay.
Our hearts rose when they told us they were heading for De
Melt Cove. It meant they would break trail for us.

We gave the dog teams a quarter of an hour's start, then
resumed our journey. For a perfect mile we traveled in the lee
of the island beneath a sun grown suddenly friendly. The trail
was a greased skidway and the toboggan became so magically
light we broke into a jog trot out of sheer relief.

With only three miles to go a weird light settled over the
lake. The sun vanished and the clearly printed trail the dog
trains had left only 15 minutes before danced crazily, then
disappeared altogether. We slowed down and moved warily,
feeling for the packed surface with our moosehide-clad feet.
When we missed, we sank to our thighs in soft snow off the
track.

Then the trail lost itself even to this haphazard method of
navigation. We trudged in circles and felt for it, but our efforts
were hopeless. A long, hard drift, abutting the track, had obviously led us astray and dropped us off into the deep snow
again. Through the ominous light, we could dimly see the
gaunt head of the mountain that rose above our base camp.
Wearily we slipped our feet into snowshoe harness again and
set a direct course across the bay. The wind rose viciously and
flurries of snow began to lash the lake.

Polar explorers have written of the strange optical illusion
that occurs at the frozen ends of the earth. The whiteout is a
light that at mid-day may prevent a man from seeing chasms
that yawn right at his feet. The phenomenon made our last
three miles shakingly unreal. The dragrope sagged and
strained, the toboggan bucked wildly, and our snowshoes

sometimes rose so sharply that their curved tips struck our knees. We were fighting our way across humpback drifts – but to the eye the bay's surface was as flat as a paved street. We were incapable of avoiding the punishing hummocks, which came with irregular jolts, much like atmospheric disturbances in a clear sky. At one time I had the impression the bay had frozen to the bottom of the toboggan and that we were pulling the entire landscape after us. Groggy and numb with cold, I could not swear to anything that happened in those last three miles. We reached camp at dusk and stood over a red-hot stove for two hours while our ice-shelled, sweat-saturated clothing dried on our backs. We could not go more than three feet from the fire without beginning to tremble again.

The thawing-out was done in Ed De Melt's tent. When we mumbled something about pitching our own camp he brusquely told us not to be damn fools. We didn't argue with him and unrolled our bags beside his stove. We must have been in bad shape. He didn't even raise the possibility of a bridge game.

8

In the rapidly shortening period before the in-between sealed off Great Bear for several weeks, the rush was developing steadily. De Melt Cove was bustling and, at the Echo Bay end of the portage, another little community was springing up. Also, De Melt reported one day that Spence-McDonough's base, already bearing the unlovely name of Smat (Spence-McDonough Air Transport), was functioning and that several prospecting parties were establishing their headquarters there.

Rivalry between the three camps was keen, with two major prizes to be competed for. It had been announced that a wireless station would be set up by the government on either Echo or Lindsley Bay before the open season. It had also been made known that a permanent mining recorder would be assigned to the field by Ottawa while it was still possible to fly him in. Whichever settlement managed to claim either of these would take a long lead over its rivals, and if it could attract them both, it would become the metropolis of Great Bear.

For the moment, De Melt Cove, lying athwart the sled-track between Smat and Cameron Bay, was enjoying the best of both worlds. It was the crossroads for practically all the traffic moving between Echo and Lindsley and was also developing its own identity. When Beck and I had gone north it had been left with three residents – one a transient. Within a week of our return, it was headquarters for more than 20 men and 50 vociferous dogs.

We discovered that not only were there additional tents adjacent to De Melt's but that the community had jumped the creek. On the far bank was a complex of superior-looking canvas dwellings. Whoever had put them there obviously had not been under the financial restrictions imposed on Beck Syndicate. Planes had been working overtime for this outfit, and had supplied them with a lavishness we had previously encountered only at Eldorado.

"They're called the Great Bear Lake Development Company," announced De Melt, enunciating each word portentously, "and they own the best property on Spark Plug Lake. It was some of the first staking. Rich – mighty rich."

Setting up our own camp again was simple. Our frame was still standing and, better yet, the ground was still clear. We had simply to rig our dwelling and bank it with snow. It was a pleasant contrast to our first ghastly session of De Melt Cove homemaking.

Comfortable though we were after digging in, a visit to the new camp across the creek filled us with envy. The Great Bear Development men were also under canvas, but their tents were floored and walled with expensive flown-in lumber. Not only could the occupants stand upright, but there was enough space for them to turn handsprings if they were so inclined. The mess tent had a proper iron stove – plus tables and benches for the diners. In the office was a broad worktable covered with maps, blueprints and other papers. I visualized what it would be like to sit down in such magnificent accommodation while writing my stories. I had never really learned to enjoy cradling my typewriter in my lap.

As we were becoming acquainted with our neighbors, a plane dropped into the cove and delivered the development company's chief engineer, J. A. Reid, and another load of supplies. At the controls of the machine was the senior half of the Spence-McDonough corporation. Bill Spence was a compact, relaxed and apparently tireless airman. He left his motor running while the cargo was unloaded and was away again almost as quickly as the last package was out of the cabin. This was his routine every time he flew into the cove. I had barely time to ascertain that old Stokely had finally made his escape.

"Oh, sure," said Spence. "Flew the old boy out myself. I've seen plenty of men eager to get in here but never one as eager to get out. He was the Bear Lake rush in reverse."

The day also brought our first emissaries from the settlement on Cameron Bay. Dark-complexioned Jack Wiley belonged to a family that had been prominent at Fort Chipewyan for generations, a family steeped in the fur trade. His companion, Jack Carey, was a stringy Northman from the hardrock mining country. They were as ready to talk about what they were up to as most men in the area were reticent. Over a cup of cocoa they announced they were the advance party of a company whose plans could be trumpeted to the entire field.

Murphy Services, they said, would shortly be opening on Cameron Bay, prepared to supply anyone with practically anything – grub, boats, dynamite, overnight accommodation, transportation, the works! Its partners were naturals, covering every aspect of such an undertaking. Gerry Murphy, the administrative head, had recently left the government service at Fort Smith, where he had landed in 1920 after failing to make a fortune in the Fort Norman oil rush. Vic Ingraham, married to Jack Wiley's daughter, had done everything from driving a team on the Fort Smith portage to operating a Northern butcher shop. Tim Ramsey, though a tenderfoot to the Territories, was not new to business. His father had been the merchant prince of Edmonton.

This was exciting news. It was one thing for the big mining companies to make their exploratory thrusts, for prospectors to invade the lake and leave their corner posts as indications of their possible return, but when seasoned businessmen announced their intention of becoming permanent residents a new phase was at hand. I envisioned the shadows of skyscrapers, cast across the snows of Echo Bay.

The volatile Carey provided most of the information. Murphy and Ramsey, he informed us, would arrive before the in-between suspended flying, setting up shop with what it would be possible to bring by air. Ingraham would follow by water after the break-up, transporting the first of the company's bulk supplies in the schooner, *Speed.* Meanwhile the advance party was establishing itself on Cameron Bay which, they were certain, was the most strategic location in the field.

That night our neighbor across the creek entertained. J. A. Reid was a model of the respected Canadian mining engineer – mature, erudite, practical, unobtrusively tough. Many of the same qualities were evident in his crew. All had obviously been carefully selected. There was a professional camaraderie among them, but Reid received the deference rated by an established leader.

Spark Plug Lake, where he was ultimately headed, was in the jumble of high ridges three miles to the west. Until the ground cleared, he intended to remain based at the accessible cove.

The evening had two highlights – coffee (a Bear Lake status symbol), and a brief conversation that came just as we were leaving.

"I've been reading your stories in the papers Outside," Reid told me. "There must be a shortage of office space in your present quarters. Feel free to use ours if we aren't in it ourselves. We'll be away frequently."

"What are you doing tomorrow?" I asked eagerly.

"Help yourself," laughed the engineer. "We'll still be settling in."

Next day my typewriter ran wild in its new and encouraging surroundings. Before I paused there were 3000 words. I had barely edited the output when McDonough – the other half of Spence-McDonough – dropped in with a new load of supplies for my host. He was, he said, flying directly back to McMurray. Next day my copy was on the telegraph wire.

My sense of well-being was tempered on the morning of March 19th when a breezy young man in a blue toque stuck his head in the door and introduced himself as Fred Failes of the *Northern Miner*. The presence of a reporter from the weekly bible of the Canadian mining industry was proof of Outside interest in Great Bear, but it also meant I no longer enjoyed a monopoly. Moreover, the newcomer was on a full time journalistic mission, while my primary responsibilities were to Beck Syndicate.

Failes had just come from Eldorado and brought us

another batch of newspapers Vi May had sent there. He also said he thought there was some mail for us, but had felt it was safer to leave it for our own pickup. This was enough to launch us towards Eldorado the following morning.

On March 20, we repeated the 20-mile trip to LaBine's and back, in perfect walking weather. It was worth the trip. The mail brought exciting news.

A hot deal was in the works for the Echo Bay claims; and Ernestine wrote that the North American Newspaper Alliance was going to take my articles at $25 a column.

John Sydie's letter to Beck urged him to get out the recording forms for our claims at all speed. We had so far put off the tedious task of filling these out properly for forwarding to Fort Smith and final registration, but now we set about it. The job took the best part of two days, with the heaviest work falling on Beck, who had to draw two maps of each claim. I attacked the forms themselves, making so neat a job with my typewriter that I quickly won the admiration of the Acting Mining Recorder.

"Never saw anything like it," De Melt exclaimed. "You don't know how good that looks after all the hen-scratching I've had to put up with from the other prospectors. How about typing out a few of the worst of these other forms when you've got the time?"

"Anything to help," I said, recalling Ed's thoughtfulness in our hours of need.

I had reason to question my big-heartedness before a day had passed, however. The cove had become loud with the jingle of sleigh-bells as six dog trains and seven Indians trotted in to swell the population. Their teamwork as they set up camp was pretty to watch: some raised the single tent that served the entire party, while others staked out the 35 dogs and cut firewood. Less attractive was the early revelation that they were accompanied by the documentary evidence of their staking activities. The number of illegible forms that showed up soon had Ed appealing to me for massive aid with my typewriter.

Most of the new arrivals were young men but among them was a patriarch of striking mien. While others of the party ran behind their toboggans, jumping on the little platforms at the rear from time to time for breathers, Susie Bouton sat comfortably within the moosehide walls of his cariole. Above a blanket pulled halfway up his chest – like a passenger in a steamer-chair – his high-cheeked features were completely impassive. A pipe with a curved stem seemed to grow on his chin and, apart from the odd occasion when he flicked his long whip to remind a dog that it wasn't pulling its weight, his arms remained folded on his chest.

He called on us that evening. His pipe undoubtedly required filling. However, he made no move towards my tobacco tin until he was invited. When his pipe was drawing satisfactorily, he revealed himself to be a fascinating conversationalist.

His English required careful following, not because of any shortage of vocabulary, but on account of its marked accent. Compensating for the latter was an artistry of intonation and a dramatic use of sign language.

He was, he said, very old – "maybe 30 years". The yardstick he used was unfamiliar to us, for by Gregorian calendar he had undoubtedly seen at least 70 summers. As he proudly carried us back to the great days of the Bear Lake People, it was impossible to determine where his own life began and where it merged in the tales his father and grandfather had told around unnumbered campfires.

One thing was certain about Bouton's forebears – they had been mighty hunters and the tales of their exploits were tribal lore. One of them (he believed it was his grandfather) was the man who had killed the fabulous 200-pound beaver. Not only had it been a monster; it had been great with magic and all the arrows and shots that had rained on it across the years had bounced from its impregnable hide like hail from a teepee roof.

Susie's father – or grandfather – or perhaps it was his great grandfather – had consulted a famous medicine man and had been given the secret of how to outmatch the magic beaver. Nothing, he was assured, would break the animal's pelt except a silver bullet. So Bouton's ancestor had saved the necessary precious metal, had cast it in a ball, tamped it firmly in his "muzzle-load" – and brought to a triumphant conclusion the

200-pound beaver legend. The narrator launched on a further tale of how the magnificent pelt had been used, but we were never quite able to overtake him in that chapter.

On March 26, the stubborn hope there might still be a few fractions to pick up in the Echo Bay region took us back there, but 15 miles of tramping revealed how forlorn a hope it was. A web of snowshoe tracks covered the hills. Others with the same idea had preceded us.

Cameron Bay itself was much changed. Its surface was heavily scored with the ski tracks of several planes that had droned in from the south. At the clump of tents which now marked the end of the portage we found Jack Carey with a happy collection of mail for us – letters, newspapers, even a parcel to mark my birthday.

There was a relayed wire, too, from the Edmonton Journal, urging me to step up the coverage of the rush. If this was any indication of the level of interest in Great Bear in the outer world, it was obviously an evening for breaking out a couple more of our precious cigars. We obeyed the impulse as soon as we were back in camp.

I was wakened the following morning by Beck's hand on my shoulder.

"Do you hear what I hear?" he was asking anxiously.

"Hear what?" I mumbled.

"That!" pronounced Eric.

Music – rich, fervent, melodious – filled the air.

Bewildered, I stared around me at the familiar walls of the tent and the comfortless face of the still-unlighted stove. Then I realized that what we were hearing was actually welling from De Melt Cove.

"Someone must have flown in a gramophone," I suggested.

"That's it," exclaimed Beck with relief. "I'm glad you hear it, too, though."

"Fine time to turn it on," I grunted, noting that daylight was barely at hand. "Wonder who the joker is?"

I climbed from my bag, poked my head through the tent fly and scanned the surrounding dwellings. It was not difficult to locate the source of the sound. There was a light glowing in the tent the Indians had pitched on the slope above. The music was that of a male chorus.

I crawled back into my bag and we listened. Slowly the nature of the singing became clear. We were hearing a hymn, rendered as I had never heard one before.

The high, metallic voices of the Indians filled it with bell-like harmonies and it might have been specially written for the natural amphitheatre against whose walls it echoed.

"I've got it!" I said suddenly. "It's Easter – Easter morning!"

I remembered that there were two days in the year for which the Indians and Eskimos crowded in to the missions if they were within traveling range: Christmas and Easter. Northern clergymen had invented a special calendar for native converts who seldom came in to the settlements. Holy days were prominently marked on it. Though I had failed to note Easter Sunday in my diary, Susie Bouton and his friends had kept accurate check of it in theirs.

The chained huskies, usually transformed to a yelping chorus at a strange presence or sound, uttered not a yap throughout the entire two hours of the service. Even the early morning axes of the prospectors, intent on replenishing low supplies of firewood, fell silent as the woodcutters stopped to listen.

The gaunt cliffs, hemming in the camp, became the towering walls of a primeval cathedral. No whip cracked, no sleigh dog strained at the harness all day. The sight of the Indians, usually as active as a colony of beavers, remaining quietly in their camp, had its effect on the rest of us to whom Sunday had become only one more period of daylight in which to keep up with the rush. It was an Easter morning to remember.

We took the day off to mend torn parkas and mukluks worn thin by friction with snowshoe harness.

A blizzard, wiping out the trails that night, kept us confined to camp the following day. I was glad of this when I discovered that during the evening Chief Jimmy Soldat had joined his tribesmen. Pinned down by the weather, we had plenty of time to entertain the chief and to yarn.

Still apparently in vigorous middle age, Jimmy was by long odds the best known of the Bear Lake People. As early as 1908

Melvill and Hornby had written their appreciation of his vigor and knowledge of the country. Stefansson and Douglas had depended on him. Where Indians generally had stopped short their caribou hunting in the Barrens when they reached the Dismal Lakes – the instinctive dividing line between themselves and the Eskimos – Jimmy had pressed on to establish friendship with the traditional enemies of his people. By any measure, he was a formidable man.

Despite his long association with whites, his command of English was still limited. It was vastly superior to my knowledge of Hareskin but it made for maddeningly slow going as he stitched bright colors into my patchwork knowledge of Great Bear history. It was particularly frustrating when he was recalling his times with Father Rouvière, the missionary he had introduced to the Eskimos and who later was to die at the hands of some of his Coppermine converts. I would have treasured an adequate translator!

De Melt told us the chief was traveling with a Mounted Policeman who was making his winter patrol from Fort Norman, and that the officer had paused at Cameron Bay. When the storm blew itself out and the first dog team had broken trail across the portage, we trotted over and located the law, temporarily established in Jack Carey's tent.

Corporal Makinson was typical of the force; clean-shaven, smart even in his trail gear, filled with Northern wisdom, quiet humor and unforced decisiveness. He was accompanied by an Indian special constable, a large, grinning fellow by the name of Isadore, whom I had met at Fort Norman in 1929.

Makinson and I saw a good deal of each other during the next few days. In one way our interests were identical. We were both reporters, interested in the same developments in the same field. The difference lay in our attitudes towards what we encountered – in my tendency to tell all and do little about it and in Makinson's relaxed capacity for keeping his own counsel and causing things to happen.

There was a bridge game at De Melt's that night that was remarkable for its restraint. Makinson played his cards as he did everything else, efficiently and unobtrusively close to his chest. Ed was less intimidating than we had ever found him, even when he went down two on a small slam bid.

Beck and I continued on to Smat next day with the policeman. The place had become unrecognizable since we had last seen it. Well-built log cabins started at the water's edge and climbed the cleared slope above. Several planes came in and out during our visit. The ubiquitous Freddy Failes of the *Northern Miner*, having set up shop here himself, flaunted a civic roll he had prepared, on which there were more than 30 names. Moreover, he produced the bodies to go with the names. As far as he was concerned, Smat had already become the capital of Great Bear.

His trump card was a pleasant young fellow who turned out to be Sergeant Rainey of the Canadian Corps of Signals. The latter confirmed that he would shortly be setting up his wireless station and that anyone who wanted to be in constant communication with the Outside would be able to do so at Smat.

Foremost among the new residents was Major Lockie Burwash, explorer, former Commissioner at Fort Smith, and now head of a sharp-looking crew of prospectors. Dr. Kidd, of the federal geological survey, was also making his headquarters here. He was already acquainted with the field from the previous season and oldtimers spoke with admiration of his ability to traverse the crags on his metal-shod skis. Here, too, was Prince Galitzine, a tall and handsome young Russian who carried his title with unassuming simplicity and who had flown in his own plane from Edmonton.

Though thoroughly partisan in our loyalty to De Melt Cove, it was impossible for us to maintain any sense of rancor towards the northern settlement, particularly after Charles Chellew, now cooking for Spence-McDonough, had prepared us a civilized meal. It was too fine a day for jealousy, in any event. As we were driving back across Lindsley Bay the sky was spotless and the trail a glazed joy. Makinson's dogs jingled along effortlessly, putting a necessary touch of pressure to the harness only from time to time, and our party alternated in forerunning and riding luxuriously in the cariole. It seemed incredible that it had been over this same surface that Beck and I had staggered, numb and desperate, on our previous crossing of the bay.

The festive atmosphere reached its peak when we got back to the cove and were immediately invited to the Great Bear Lake Development camp for a celebration. Beck had leaked the fact it was my birthday and Reid and his crew had set the stage properly for De Melt Cove's first major social event. The dining tent was warm, the cook had produced a magnificent cake, and the company was in brilliant form.

I was 31 years old, and I found myself alternating between feeling half and twice my age.

Before Great Bear I had begun to feel at least twice my age. I thought about it that night, encouraged by the night itself. The stars were out when we crossed the draw to our own tent. The shadows of the surrounding heights were more tranquil than menacing and, even with the stove dead, it was mild enough to lie with my head outside the shelter of the sleeping bag – and to let my mind feel its way over new ground.

At first there were interruptions. The night was so still that every sound of every camper settling down in his bag, every growl of every dog burrowing himself deeper in his private hole in the snow, was sharpened and magnified. After a time, though, there was only silence and the sense of my own thoughts moving, unfettered, across it.

I recalled what had happened earlier that week when one of the men from an outer camp had descended on us with the results of his favorite diversion – the making of moonshine hooch. He had a gifted touch with dried fruit and the other ingredients necessary for the creation of forked lightning. The party in Ed's tent had set the tethered sled dogs into baying competition. I had been present but had emerged cold sober. This was revolution.

I thought about the six quarts of rum still stowed under our tarpaulin, untouched since our arrival. True, they were labeled "Emergency Supplies" – but there had been more than one occasion on which the lowered state of our bodies and spirits had been close enough to an emergency state to justify emergency treatment.

My abstinence could be explained, of course, in practical terms. Discipline was needed to meet the demands of Great Bear. The flabby muscles I had brought in with me had hardened. Perhaps this physical well-being had become so precious that fear of losing it, even if only for a morning-after hangover, had become strong enough to keep me on the wagon.

There was more to it than that, though. There had been the influence of the remarkable relationship I had developed with Beck – the man I had been warned was the last fellow with whom I should attempt to live in the testing intimacy of the bush. I thought of the regard that had developed between us within a week of our starting to live as one another's shadow. The key had been honest communication. We had said what we felt when we felt it; he without reticence, I without frills. It was more than common sense – I knew I was developing a growing mental resiliency along with toughening muscles.

I remembered something that had happened on the hardest of our marches which defied rationalization. During those back-breaking experiences on the drag-rope, when my leaden feet had threatened to outweigh my determination and failing strength, when my mind had cried, "This is the outer limit" – somehow I had quietly walked out of myself. I had stepped clear of the exhausted, frightened, hurting man chained to the toboggan and its burden, which could not be abandoned without abandoning life itself. Another me had walked alongside the figure swaying on the end of the drag-rope. I had been two people and when one had been completely spent, the other had moved over and taken the strain.

The experience of this was strange – disturbing, and yet heartening. I could clearly recall what I had seen exposed in my burdened self as I had tramped in freedom alongside him. It was no more than any perceptive friend would have seen – the limited sense of responsibility, the self-pity, the belief no bigger than the man himself. The significance lay in the fact that I was of course, more than a detached observer.

Might it not follow that the man moving in freedom was the *essential* man – that there was a foul-up to be straightened out somewhere which would enable the prisoner of the drag-rope to find unity with his other self? I decided that it was a man with at least some degree of freedom who said "Thanks, I think I'll pass," when the moonshine went around the tent that night.

The world as I lay there thinking was very still.

"Take it easy," I said to the darkness. "For all I know, this is the way a man becomes bushed."

9

The Indian population continued to swell as new dog teams appeared from both north and south. You were never sure when they left camp each morning whether they were in search of more claims or more food. It was becoming clear that the native people were coming close to familiar territory – the rim of starvation.

There was a glint of pride in the old eyes of Susie Bouton when he reported he was the one hunter who had recently brought in anything bigger than a ptarmigan, but it was a wry triumph. The moose he had shot was a small one and when the band went short the hunger pangs were communal. A number of fish-holes had been chiseled and the catch occasionally included a 25-pound trout, but with half a hundred dogs to be kept in working shape there was never enough left over for their masters.

There were consultations with a worried Ed De Melt. His various middleman services were not working out as well as they had done when he had been dealing in a less crowded market. His operation was not up to the pressure of numbers.

Word had drifted across the portage, too, that the official Mining Recorder, McKay Meikle, had been flown in to Cameron Bay and had set up his office there. That would mean bureaucratic inflexibility and further complications for Ed's free-wheeling approach to enterprise.

On April 4 Corporal Makinson, looking sterner since the plight of the Indians had become more obvious, reappeared with Chief Jimmie Soldat. There were more consultations. The next morning the original Indian contingent broke camp and started across the lake for more familiar and friendly shores at Fort Franklin and Bear Mountain. We sent them on their way with a good feed of Beck Syndicate bacon. It was the first fat they had had for several days and they needed it. There were more than 200 miles of hard driving in which to burn it up.

Makinson, Chief Soldat, Nere Robert, and some of the later arrivals remained a day longer and again there were meetings in De Melt's tent. The principals kept their counsel but we had the feeling there was a straightening out of some complicated agreements made with the now-departed Indian stakers.

The following morning the cove was almost as quiet as when we originally arrived. The corporal had resumed his patrol, Jimmie Soldat had again moved off into the vastness of his domain, not a single dog was left to set the cliffs echoing to its howls, and even the crew across the creek had temporarily left home to stake some fractions Ed had suggested to them. The silence was intense.

We had little time to savor it. John Sydie had been urging us in every mail to get our claims properly recorded and now the opportunity to do so existed at no greater distance than the other end of the portage.

McKay Meikle, the Recorder, was proof that the regulated mind of a civil servant could be successfully married to the flexible soul of a bushman. Short and wiry, with a finely carved nose supporting rimless glasses, he had shrewd, direct eyes. He knew the mining regulations to the last line of fine type and made sure that those who did business with him shared the knowledge before claim forms became acceptable. The surprise came after business was done and his mind had been released from the last questioned staking map. Then he revealed a broadly refined intellect.

Even among the mining engineers, of whom there now were several in Cameron Bay, Meikle retained the aloofness of official authority. His standards and beliefs were definite. This was in sharp contrast to my often confused and questioning state.

Our initial visit was not one to recall with pleasure. Meikle brought bad news. There was a technical error in our forms for the Echo Bay claims, which had already been flown out to Fort Smith. De Melt had been absent from the cove on the day we completed the papers, and had not been able to witness them. There was a legal way to handle this – up to a point. We had elected Beck an Acting Recorder for the occasion. Unfortunately, in his brief term of office, Beck had inadvertently witnessed his own signature. Meikle had brought back the forms from Fort Smith to be validated.

This small slip created real difficulties. There was now a definite danger they might not get out to John Sydie before breakup isolated us for at least six weeks. Even after Meikle had put them in order, they would have to be returned to Fort Smith before being forwarded to Ottawa. It might well be June before John had the necessary documents with which to take advantage of the hot offers he had reported. By that time the market would be flooded with snowshoe claims, imperiling our plan for the further financing of Beck Syndicate.

The setback made it seem necessary to remain close to both the recorder at Cameron Bay and the wireless station at Smat until the question of our 1931-32 staking was cleared up.

It couldn't have happened at a worse time. Our 1932-33 licenses had become valid on March 31 and we were poised to strike out on the longest expedition yet planned.

Had our prospecting plans been confined to either Echo or Lindsley bays, there would have been no great difficulty. In either area we would have been close enough to duck in to Cameron Bay on short notice. But another name had been ringing in our ears: Conjuror Bay.

Bill Mills, second in command at Great Bear Lake Development, had already made a scouting trip with one of his companions to the mountainous pocket that forms the southeast corner of the lake. Conjuror was the bay from which Gilbert LaBine had started his tramp up the eastern coast two years before. Bill, while giving away no specific information, had said quietly, "I like it. We were too early to see much but when it gets warmer and the cliffs clear I wouldn't be surprised if someone finds a mine there.''

I was partial to Bill's judgment. He had brought a copy of Joseph Conrad's *Almayer's Folly* to Bear Lake. After many bookless weeks, my already-established respect for the tall, middle-aged Mills became complete. Beck shared my regard: Bill had impressed him as a mining man who knew his business. Our decision to explore Conjuror Bay as quickly as possible was a unanimous one.

There was a certain compensation for the delay we now faced. Waiting for mid-April would mean improved weather conditions. The days were lengthening swiftly and, though the temperature occasionally dipped to $-20\,°F$, the sun was making itself felt. It would speed the disappearance of the planes but it would also hasten the melting of the snow from the rock formation.

The pause also left us free for the long-overdue building of a cache. Three well-located trees close to the tent had been marked for this ever since our arrival. We now sawed them off, 10 feet above the ground, as the legs of the triangular platform on which our supplies would henceforth rest in greater safety. Empty bacon tins had been saved as sheathing for the upper lengths of each support, denying a grip to the claws of climbing marauders. Trees close enough to be springboards for a leap to the platform were felled.

While animal life in the area was limited, we had seen white fox and mink, and Edward Blondin had reported the presence of the arch-villain among campwreckers – the wolverine. It was good to have the risk behind us.

It was an impressive structure, big and strong enough to hold two or three tons without crowding. When the supplies back of the tent had been carried up the ladder they made a ridiculously small stack in the center of the cache. There would be less than 500 pounds there when we hit the trail again. We invited De Melt to share the new facility.

Final contacts with the Outside brought hurried meetings and partings. Pilot after pilot dropped in to say, ''So long until open water.'' Walter Gilbert, one of the last, brought a tall, erect and grizzled man who looked strangely familiar. It took a couple of minutes to be certain. Then there was no doubt. It was George Douglas, en route to Hornby Bay. For the few minutes he was with us we were transported to the Great Bear which had once welcomed only those hardy souls willing to face the violent 90 miles between Forts Norman and Franklin.

As though offering extreme contrast, the next day saw a dainty little Puss-Moth buzzing into the cove. From it stepped, of all things, a woman! Her pilot introduced her as Princess Galitzine and himself as Bill Holland. They had thought they were dropping down on Smat and a reunion with the prince, but had failed to accurately identify their destination from the air.

We persuaded them to remain at the cove long enough for us to do our best by the first member of the opposite sex we had seen since leaving civilization. Tea was served with all the finesse at our command and the visitor seemed to enjoy herself. Hope was expressed she might persuade the prince to transfer his operations from Smat to De Melt Cove. Finally we instructed Holland on the location of the Spence-McDonough base and the Puss-Moth purred on its way.

The anxious debate as to what might happen to our wo-manless Eden ended 48 hours later. A visitor from Smat reported that neither the charm of De Melt Cove nor the better living conditions of the settlement across the bay had been sufficient to hold the princess. She had returned South the day after her first experience of Great Bear.

The prince, however, remained at the lake. His own plane had recently suffered a broken strut but while this was patched with drill steel and the aircraft flown Outside for proper repairs during the breakup, Galitzine remained in the field, traversing it on foot like the rest of us.

Not all the planes joined the final rush Outside. For the first time there were operational flights on the lake while the disintegrating airstrips on the ice of the Athabaska and Slave rivers ended flights to the south. Frank Barager of Canadian Airways remained at Cameron Bay and continued trips as far as Fort Resolution. Cal Mews of Spence-McDonough maintained short charter flights out of Smat. All had made the necessary preparations for shifting to floats when the ice gave way to open water.

1929 air mail flight: The Red Armada at Fort Resolution.

*Great Bear: first
view of Lindsley Bay.*

The stone cliffs at the entrance to Echo Bay.

Pete Baker, waterborne.

Edward Blondin hitches his team for the trail: 1932.

Eldorado Mine, circa 1933.

Eldorado: Cyril Knight, Charles LaBine, Stanley Graham, John Rogers, Punch Dickins, Gilbert LaBine.

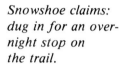

The first claim posts: Eric Beck at Echo Bay.

Snowshoe claims: dug in for an overnight stop on the trail.

Gerry Murphy: unofficial mayor of Cameron Bay, 1932.

Andy Cruikshank and Harry King, Echo Bay 1932.

Bill Jewitt, pilot and mining engineer, 1932.

Ted Watt: Marooned at Conjuror Bay.

Conjuror: Beck tries to regain use of his legs.

Breaking the in-between, June, 1932. Hours ahead of a human deluge.

Cameron Bay, 1933. Log cabins and a float base, one year later.

Meanwhile the tempo at Cameron Bay had quickened dramatically with the arrival of Gerry Murphy of Murphy Services. Gerry was both a visionary and an activist. His civil service career, which had followed a private setback in the Fort Norman oil rush of 1920, had been one in which he had frequently strained against the bars of his gilded cage at Fort Smith. Now he had managed to spring the door and his wings were spread in exuberant flight.

In the large tent which the two Jacks, Wiley and Carey, had erected as his temporary headquarters, Murphy entertained on the very evening of his arrival. It was no backwoods catch-as-catch-can affair. Fifteen of us sat down by invitation to a feast centered on a monumental turkey which had arrived with our host. With it went all the trimmings. The whip-sawn table and benches cut by the advance party could not have been more impressive had they been polished mahogany.

Murphy, at the head of the board, was a completely happy man. Sandy, stocky, and of soldierly bearing, he had brought a lively army record North with him. The mark of it was still evident in the rake of his beret, the well-shaved cut of his jaw and the well-laundered clothing. His speech was as clipped as his moustache.

Once a wild man with the bottle, he was on the wagon now. It wasn't difficult, though, to visualize him as he had been. Crackling laughter frequently accompanied his words, and his eyes danced with a warm-hearted deviltry. Before the evening ended he had taught everyone the proper rendition of *When The Ice Worms Nest Again*, a tune that was to become the Murphy Services theme song.

We returned to the cove that night bathed in Gerry's aura of optimism. Crossing the portage we decided to strike out for Conjuror Bay as quickly as we could pack, taking a chance that John could straighten out the fouled-up claim forms without us.

At five o'clock next morning, however, the weather took over. We were pinned down by two weeks of the wildest fluctuations of atmosphere that had yet come boiling across the vast lake.

It began with a blizzard: 24 hours of unbroken storm, with

the wind raging straight from the north, the snow driving in horizontal, blinding sheets and the temperature dipping lower and lower. I ventured only as far as the camp across the creek and floundered up to my thighs, the path being completely obliterated. The gale wrestled noisily with the tent and the fine, dry snow sifted constantly through the fly and the spark-holes.

There was no letup the next day. Temperatures were colder still and although the snow stopped falling at intervals, the gale kept the air filled with it. Snow hissed incessantly against the canvas, and the tent strained lop-sidedly like a drawing sail. Barager came bumping into the cove in the teeth of it and we had to give him a hand to get the plane out of the deep snow he ended up in. He bolted for Cameron Bay and called it a day. He showed iron nerve to be out at all. He was looking for Bill Storr.

Storr was an Arctic coast trapper who had come down from Coronation Gulf with Purcell, his partner, the previous year and had done some staking. They were again due, the only party to cross the Barrens on foot in the present season, and Barager had been assigned to a pre-arranged meeting after which he would air-lift them Outside.

By April 20, the storm still howled. It wasn't difficult to imagine men going mad after a long period of being storm-bound in cramped quarters.

Some men, nevertheless, maintained their sanity by refusing to stay stormbound. Gerry Murphy and Colin Bowen appeared out of the smother, having plowed across the portage with a wireless message they had discovered awaiting me at the Consolidated camp.

"I had a hunch it's good news and shouldn't wait," Gerry grinned.

His instinct had been sound. The Journal had word of an important discovery of new ore at Eldorado and I was being urged to provide something straight from the mine's mouth. The paper sounded properly excited about it.

"What do they think I am - a polar bear?" I demanded, showing Gerry the wire.

"If you're a patriot you'll become one," said Murphy. "Do it in easy stages. Come back to Cameron Bay with me tonight and lay over as the guest of Murphy Services. Then, tomorrow, you can take your time getting to Eldorado.''

In the end Beck and I shouldered our sleeping bags and followed him back across the portage. There was no sign of the trail on the three lakes and the wind got a good swipe while we labored across. Murphy Services' hospitality was appreciated when we reached it.

The next day, we went to LaBine's and returned safely to Cameron Bay only by the grace of God. The first of several disasters occurred when Beck fell through some thin ice, saving himself from a complete ducking only by presence of mind. He lay quietly on his face when his legs went through, suppressing the instinct to thrash about and complete the breakthrough. Then, gently, he eased himself back towards my helping hand and firm surface.

Later, crossing a low neck of rock which juts out into Echo Bay, we both went over a sheer ten foot drop which was blotted from sight by ground drift. Fortunately we landed in soft snow.

On the return journey we were punished severely by a head wind, the ground drift being so vicious that flying ice particles cut the skin on my nose and set it bleeding.

But the trip was worth all these troubles. Charles LaBine's reputation as a tough, gruff customer had preceded him – and he lived up to it. A mountain of a man without surplus flesh, he was unsmiling as he fed us a hot lunch. Certainly he did not share the Journal's sense of urgency about publicizing Eldorado.

"The stuff's there," he growled, "so we don't need any build-up. It's when you haven't got anything that you need your company's name in the papers. We're miners, not promoters."

I agreed reluctantly and let the subject ride until there was time to consider a new approach. Then I remembered a recent article by a well-known Canadian writer. He had complained that the country's established industry was suffering because of capital wasted on remote mining gambles. The piece had had the provocative title of "The North Can Wait." LaBine admitted he had read it.

"What do you think of it?" I asked.

Charles regarded me across the lunch table with a hostility I prayed was intended for the writer of the article. After several uncomfortable seconds he spoke.

"Eat up," LaBine said abruptly. "We'll look around when you're finished."

There were two pits, one at the water's edge and one at the top of the draw leading upward from the camp. A natural pathway offered access to the latter. As we mounted it there was an explosion at the crest of the hill. Smoke and flying debris stained the skyline. When we reached the 15-foot deep trench at the base of Gilbert LaBine's legendary hanging wall, the dynamite fumes were still curling among the heaps of rock which had just been fragmented. Already, a number of parka-clad workers were selecting chunks of ore that required no concentration to proclaim their richness. The miners were heaving these to the lip of the hole, where other men stacked them in rough piles.

We looked at a chunk of dirty-looking stuff that had just come out of the pit. It weighed about 100 pounds.

"Silver?" I asked Beck.

"Not all," he said dryly, scratching the chunk with a piece of rock and drawing a long, metallic line wherever he touched. "Only about 50 percent. Maybe not that much."

A worker in the pit called, "Do you want to see something pretty?"

I clambered into the hole. Projecting from the face of the rock, was what could have been a slightly crumpled piece of business-size notepaper – except that it was leaf silver.

The entire wall might have been taken from a crazy miner's dream. Silver, in leaf and wire forms, jutted everywhere. Even to the inexpert eye, pitchblende was present in startling quantities. Copper cropped out like gold bricks thrown in for good measure. These were only some of the minerals present. Every primary color showed in the various oxide stains.

Work was being concentrated on a shoot of highgrade ore measuring 40 inches in width. Where the ordinary silver mine reckoned vein widths in inches, Eldorado figured them in feet. Elsewhere assays of tens or hundreds of ounces per ton were the rule. At LaBine Point they ran into four figures.

The highgrade ore was being hand-cobbed and sacked in

preparation for being shipped Outside with the open season. To meet the high cost of transportation, Charlie told us, no silver ore was being shipped which ran under 2000 ounces to the ton.

The same policy held for the pitchblende. The growing shipment which awaited the breakup was worth between five and six dollars a pound. Ore of lesser values, though it would have been considered rich in a more accessible location, was being cast aside to await the coming of mining machinery to the camp. I asked LaBine when that would be.

"We've got our program," he said, "and there's no reason to hurry. We're looking a good many years ahead and a lot will depend on what we can do to improve transportation. How soon we get our concentrator going depends on the oil fuel from Norman Wells and coal from the deposits on Bear Lake. Both the oil and coal operators are working on it now. I'd say our mill will be running next year. For the time being we've got 20 men here who will go on looking over the property. The highgrade ore we take out by hand will help with operating expenses as we go along.

"After all, it's only two years since Gilbert made the discovery. We've just scratched the surface and we're not going to hurry it just to make a show. Eldorado doesn't need any ballyhoo."

We walked down the hill to No. 1 pit. It was at lake level and would undoubtedly flood when the ice ceased to seal it off. Now, though, it held its crew of workers, blasting and prying off the black chunks of pitchblende. Its knobbed and bubbled protuberances were streaked with bright yellow, violet and pink.

We stood on the rim of the hole while the great wind, sweeping from the lake, hurled fine snow and small rock fragments on the hooded men below. The latter worked without letup, enthusiastically identified with their undertaking. I turned to LaBine, as massive as the rock his men were attacking.

"Picture of the North waiting," I suggested.

For the first time since we had met, Charlie smiled.

I had my story: the next job would be getting it onto the wireless.

We stayed at Cameron Bay that night, and hiked across the portage in the morning. It was rotten going. The trail had been completely wiped out by the previous day's blow. I banged out my story, then immediately headed for Smat. I had to break trail all the way and the eight miles, normally an easy two hours, took more than three. Sergeant Rainey, the Signals man, volunteered some cautious good news. It had begun to look, he said, as though the bulk of the wireless traffic was going to center on Cameron Bay; perhaps he would be justified in moving his station there. I told him I would remember him in my prayers. It was his opinion that the Almighty paid scant attention to the supplications of the blatantly self-interested. I said I would keep remembering him anyway.

On April 23, Cal Mews attempted to get away with some of MacAlpine's men he was to fly to Contact Lake but it turned mild by morning and he couldn't get the plane to lift clear of the soggy surface. I started home from Smat at 10:30 A.M. and had another heartbreaking trip. Navigating the soft ice was like walking through glue and my mukluks were soaked through in the first half mile. By the time I made camp I was exhausted and I lay like a log for the rest of the day. Towards evening the wind rose again in its full fury and bombarded the tent with drift.

The next day, it rained! It didn't start until I was almost across the portage with some wireless messages I had offered to deliver to Murphy and Meikle. I got across, then had to wait at Cameron Bay until 9:30 in the evening, hoping the rain would stop and the weather tighten so the path would freeze. I struck out, but another downpour began when I was halfway home. It was cruel going, with the darkness and the rotting trail: I sank to my thighs in slush several times. It continued to rain hard all night.

Several days of consistently warm weather began.

On the 26th, the first flare of sunshine broke through the overcast. Travel was nearly out of the question, even for short distances, on the deep, slushy surface. It was possible to go for wood on snowshoes but the harness became quickly sodden. However, without them, we were virtually wading.

We were eager to be on our way to Conjuror Bay and

fervently hoped for a hard freeze to make it possible. But spring had come to De Melt Cove, and we were enjoying its first outbursts. One night at 4 A.M. an amorous ptarmigan perched on our ridge pole and wakened us with his raucous wooing of a nearby female. Beck routed him by yelling and shaking the tent but he was back at 6 A.M., again wrecking our dreams. This was too much and he stopped a .22 bullet. A sad affair, but he made a delicious stew.

After a day or two of glorious sunshine, the snow continued to sink but there was still a great deal to go before the lake ice would be fit for travel. We did a washing – our first real cleanup – and were visited by our first fly and our first mouse.

On the 29th, temperatures began to tighten. We took an exploratory trip to Cameron Bay; the portage surface, though rough, was fairly firm. At the settlement there was bad news about Bear Lake's domestic air service. Barager, on the point of taking off for Resolution, had blown a cylinder head and was grounded until repair parts could be brought in by open water. Doc Robertson had also had bad luck and his aircraft would be out of action until it was able to operate on floats.

Unlike other pilots who had acquired the medical title as a nickname, Robertson had the sheepskin that went with it. He had earned his M.D. after coming out of the Air Force at the end of World War I and had practised in a small Ontario town. In time, he decided he preferred flying operations to those performed in hospital. An excellent pilot, he was later to become Chief of Airway and Airport Division for the federal government. Nevertheless, when he came North he brought his doctor's bag along as a matter of course. The failure of his aircraft now meant that Cameron Bay could be sure of having its own medical officer during the in-betweeen season. With the nearest regular physician 400 miles distant, this was a comfort. Doc was also a no-nonsense bridge player and an articulate philosopher. He would contribute much to the establishment of Cameron Bay as the Athens of Great Bear.

Before returning to our own end of the portage we told Murphy we intended to head for Conjuror Bay that night if the freeze was sufficiently sharp. It was always a good idea to have someone aware of where you were likely to be found if your return should become long overdue. Besides, Conjuror Bay was well off the beaten track.

"What time do you figure you'll be passing through here?" asked Gerry.

"Midnight, probably," said Beck. "It should tighten up around 10:00 or 10:30 but the days of crossing the portage in three quarters of an hour are over. It will take twice that time to make it with a loaded toboggan."

"I'll stay up for you," offered Gerry. "Come in and have a mug-up. You'll probably need it."

We pulled out at 10:30 P.M. The trail was gouged with great potholes into which the toboggan pitched every few feet, dislodging the load as it came to a dead halt. At midnight we were between the first and second lakes.

We back-packed half the load the rest of the way over the portage. At 3:00 A.M. we passed Gerry Murphy's darkened tent. We never knew how late he waited. It had taken us four and a half hours to travel three horrible miles.

10

One thing might have been said for the villainous state of the portage: by contrast, it deepened our appreciation of the good surface offered by Echo Bay. Under the recent rain and sun, the snow had sunk and solidified. It was a vast skating rink, streaked in places by new, dry snow. The toboggan slid feather-light except where the glaze had been dulled by snowy bands. We quickly learned to anticipate these, breaking into a trot when we saw one ahead and riding through its ashy grip with the power of our worked-up momentum. It became a sort of game and, in our joy at being under way again, we played it like boys.

At 4 A.M. we paused on a finger of Gossan Island long enough to brew a mug of tea. The air was marvelously clear as the sun lifted above the rim of mountains and ran delicate feelers along the dark shoulders of the bay. Directly above, the new light touched the red of the gossans, rusty iron deposits which gave the island its name. They glowed brighter and brighter, as though the forbidding heights were being reheated and molded to gentler contours. With the warmth of the tea and the fire working on us, the illusion was complete.

Once we were under way, however, the cold breath from the lake chilled us once more. The breeze was barely perceptible – not strong enough to send the loose snow slithering across the glassy surface – but we could feel it readily on our bare faces.

Moving towards the long southern entrance to the bay, framed between the mainland and Mystery Island, we were once again heading into fresh territory. For the first time the satisfaction of encountering new ground was not tempered by uncertainty of its geography, for at long last we had an accurate map.

It had arrived shortly before we set out – a special, advance edition of the air map made by the Topographical Survey of Canada. Covering the entire coast from Hunter to Conjuror bays, it had been rushed into production the previous month, just in time for McKay Meikle to sell us a couple of copies when we needed it most. There were a few parts of it still indicated by dotted lines, areas where there had been cloud when the survey planes had photographed the coastline. But the part that concerned us was shown in clear and accurate detail. On this trip, there would be no danger of fruitless invasions of blind fiords.

When we had inched past the sombre fortress of Mystery Island we were, for the first time since our arrival at Great Bear, completely clear of the land. In the unlimited visibility of that crisp morning, the featureless sweep of ice to the west reminded me of the ocean. Yet it had something coldly and pitilessly its own.

When we finally rounded Dowdell Point, the large headland named after one of Gilbert LaBine's prospecting companions, we had been on the move 14 straight hours and sleepless for more than 30. For some time now, we had been casting hopeful eyes towards the shore, searching for an accessible beach with at least minimal shelter and fuel. There were spots where the otherwise craggy coast was glacially flattened and gravel-beached but these places were without a spear of timber. Then we spotted a miserable clump of brush surrounding a single spruce tree.

There was wood enough to cook lunch and shelter enough to rig our tarpaulin as a lean-to. It was unnecessary to unpack the tent, so the bulk of the toboggan's load remained stowed for a quick departure after we had slept. The brightness of day was no problem when we climbed into our sleeping bags. We could have slept under arc-lights.

A blizzard roared in from the lake in the early evening. The flailing of the tarpaulin didn't disturb our dead-sleep, but driven snow, sneaking into the bags and melting on our necks, finally woke us. We waited, hoping that the blow was only a passing squall. Finally there was no choice but to unpack the tent and raise it in the shelter of the lone spruce.

It was a difficult operation. We did a good deal of foraging before we had our tent poles. The wind was playful with the bellying canvas. It was two in the morning before we were able to return to our bags – and another 24 hours before the weather changed.

Then the wind sighed and disappeared. The sun blazed. Most of the new snow had been whirled from the lake and, to the south, a clear trail to Conjuror glistened.

We put in nine hours on the ice. It was a mean day's work – 16 miles of travel on the glassy surface.

It was an exhilarating time up to the last two miles. Then it got rough, with jagged pack-ice upsetting the toboggan time and again and necessitating the relashing of the load after every second or third spill. The farther down the coast we moved, the more fields of uptilted ice forced us out from the shore. These told of fall storms that had exploded against the land, and plummeting temperatures that had paralyzed the convulsed floes. By keeping just clear of the outer rim of the turbulence, though, we were able to find a fair traveling surface. The distance from the land remained uniform – about two miles – and we were able to maintain a straight course down the lake.

We were badly burned by the sun reflecting off the ice. Even behind snowglasses, our eyes suffered from the glare. Our noses, cheeks and lips were painfully swollen.

The shoreline, as it unfolded, became increasingly steep. But the sight of it kept our blood warm, particularly when, by our reckoning, we were in sight of Richardson Island. That 30-mile long mountain is Conjuror's protector against the full force of Great Bear's gales, the outer line of the island continuing that of the mainland. There is a narrow entrance to the inner waters at its northern tip. We were nearly abreast of this pass before we realized we had found it.

The sheer coastline, apparently without break, was sliced cleanly, as if by a sword-stroke, to reveal the quiet waters within. Conjuror Bay lay ahead, its throat less than a mile across, the black cliffs on either hand making it seem narrower. Before we reached it, we had to cross a two-mile band of icy chaos. In the next hours we traveled several times that distance, as we followed innumerable likely looking leads through the floes, our bodies and equipment taking heavy punishment.

Often the passes through the jagged ranges of ice angled off 45 degrees or more from our intended course. Many ended in traps. We moved in a series of rushes, collisions, capsizings and bone-jarring falls. The number of times the load had to be restowed and relashed was beyond counting.

We touched shore at the mainland tip of the entrance. A half-moon of cliffs, facing west, returned the inscrutable stare of the lake, and offered no shelter against an onshore wind. We remembered the pummeling we had taken on Dowdell Point. Within the arc of cliffs was a gradually rising sand beach, already blown clear of snow in places and spiked with a few stunted spruces. The trees stood well apart from each other, emphasizing the barren loneliness of the place.

The entrance was, at this point, still two miles wide and the formidable pack ice had forced its way up the narrowing channel. Beyond the inner hook of the cove, however, smooth surface was visible.

"Well?" panted Beck.

"I'm all in," I told him.

"So am I," Eric admitted. After a thoughtful silence he went on. "If this weather holds there would be nothing against camping here until morning."

"Even if the weather broke we could make it around the corner to a sheltered campsite in an hour," I added.

We took the chance. Tented and fed, we slept long and gratefully. The next day, even the scimitar of cliffs appeared half friendly in the fresh sunlight. We cooked breakfast in the open, enjoying the sensation of sprawling on the dry, warm sand and reveling in the blue distances of Richardson Island. Then Beck focused his interest closer at hand.

"Have you noticed that formation up there?" he asked,

pointing to the heights at the inner curve of the cove. "That dark section eating into the cliff just above the ice-slide."

"I hadn't," I confessed. "Couldn't you find something easier to get at, though?"

"It would be possible to climb the flank of the slide, then work along its top, keeping close to the bare rock," said Eric slowly. "I could cut steps in the ice."

His fascination with the lofty band of dark-colored formation was unusual. I was the one who normally became enthusiastic over any unexpected coloration of rock, my ignorance investing a valueless bornite stain with all the virtues of an Eldorado. Beck was forever having to bring me down to reality. His sudden determination to get a closer look at the pocket in the cliff was an indication of something really exciting.

"I'll take no more than three or four hours," he said. "If I can't make it a useful visit by then we'll have to leave it for later. Can't afford to push the luck we had last night. We'll need to move to shelter well inside the bay before the day's out." He paused, then added, "I think maybe I'd better tackle the cliff alone. There's not much room up there."

"Fine," I replied. "Four hours will give me time to jog over to Richardson Island and see if it's as good-looking close up as it appears to be from here."

We set out in our separate directions. I reached the island, to find snow still deep in the draws. Any exposed rock failed to reveal so much as a stringer of quartz. However, the afternoon sun shone high and the Conjuror's mood was still benevolent when I recrossed the channel.

I hoped I would find Beck glued to the cliff face, still caught up in the fascination that had drawn him there. I set a return course that would land me at the foot of the slide. My partner was nowhere in sight, however. I decided he had completed his investigation. Though the snow was still fairly deep on the floor of the cove, it was preferable to the rough ice of the channel, so I headed across the beach towards the tent.

Halfway there I encountered a track freshly broken in the crust. It was odd: there were no identifiable prints, human or animal. It looked more like a toboggan trail except for its inconsistency. In tortured swerves it wandered jaggedly in the direction of the tent.

Suddenly, with a jolt of alarm, my mind connected the impressions in the snow with the absence of any sign of Beck. Ahead of me the tent stood quietly in the sun. With Beck returned it should have been taken down by now, in preparation for the move into the bay. Its silence was ominous.

I broke into a run. I realized something of the truth – a man had been dragging himself here, or had been dragged. When the snow gave way to the bare beach the marks were still visible in the sand. They led to the door of the tent.

When I came closer, I heard the terrible sounds of a man in great pain.

Beck was lying belly down on his sleeping bag. His thin face looked like a death mask. The flesh stood out, unnaturally white where his snowglasses had protected it. His eyes were wide in a parchment-like skull which wind and glare had aged. His scraggy beard was stark and black. The quart of emergency rum was beside him, already a third gone.

He gasped the bare details of what had happened. A foothold he had cut at the top of the cliff had given way, and he had chuted down the ice slope and crashed into the windrows of rockfall protruding above the snow at the bottom. Knocked unconscious, he had no idea how long he had lain there.

He had no sense of time either, about the terrible journey he had made, crawling and dragging himself a quarter of a mile back to the tent. One hand was badly battered but the serious pain was at the base of his spine. His legs were useless. I could not tell whether this was because the pain was too great, or whether he was paralyzed.

I got the stove burning so that the tent became comfortable, then examined his back. There were no open wounds – only swelling and discoloration. There were no obviously broken bones. The words "internal injuries" kept turning over in my mind. I had written them often enough as a reporter to know they were bad news. My wife Ernie, from her nursing experience, had remarked once that people suffering such injuries frequently died on the third day if they weren't going to make it.

There were times before the night was out when I doubted if Beck, far from making the third day, would last the first. He moaned pitiably in his suffering.

As I did what little I could for him, the tent swayed in a sharp, cold wind off Great Bear. Gusts of blown sand sizzled against the canvas and whipped under its unanchored skirts, stinging the eyes. We breathed grit.

The half-gale blew out of pure spite and a clear evening sky. It was intent on hurling us into the foot of the cliffs. The lightly secured tent came close to ripping free from its poles with the first hard blast.

The loose surface of the beach offered no serious support for stakes, but I managed to rig a sort of sea-anchor before the blow worked up to its full force. The empty toboggan, weighted down with the heaviest rocks I could move, was put out to windward and all our spare rope secured between it and the peak of the rear tent poles. This was where the wind's pressure on the canvas was centered and, when the firm counter-strain of the anchor was established, immediate disaster was averted. Then I piled other rocks on the tent skirts. While they didn't prevent the sand blast from spurting along the floor, the walls ceased their wild whipping and it became possible to make dinner.

Beck showed no interest in the smell of frying bacon. Repeated shots of rum had taken some of the edge from his cries, but it was impossible to tell how much pain he was feeling through his delirium. Now and then he became articulate and called for the bottle. The rum unquestionably eased his suffering and lengthened the merciful spells of unconsciousness. He fell asleep, but cried out at any movement of his body. The sounds were shouts from a nightmare.

I was having my own sort of nightmare. Sleep was impossible. I worried that the screaming wind, blowing furiously all night, would carry the tent away. And I worried about the long-range implications of the disaster.

On the credit side, Beck was still alive. He had taken his fall close to home and in decent weather. Had he been at a distance I might have had difficulty finding him before the cold finished what the fall down the cliff had begun. We had plenty of grub, which wouldn't have been the case if the accident had occurred later in the trip.

On the debit side there was no saying how badly he had been hurt. The likelihood of internal injury made it impossible to move him, and the doctor was 25 miles away. We were completely trapped by the ice, in any case. Should he turn worse, I would have no choice but to leave him to get assistance, but that would mean at least two days – weather being favorable – during which he would be unattended. The shelter was miserable, yet, until Eric could move, the camp must stay where it was.

I felt an even deeper despair. This was May, the last month in which we could prospect before the breakup and the inundation of stakers. This was the last chance to justify the faith of those who made it possible for us to come here.

Beck was still alive – and still suffering – in the morning. Despite the large quantities of liquid he had taken, he had passed none of it, heightening my fear that something was seriously wrong internally. I prepared to take off for Echo Bay that evening. At the eleventh hour, however, Beck showed the first signs of a reoperative drainage system.

By the next day, the fear of serious internal injuries had been virtually dispelled. It was obvious, though, that Eric would be confined to his bag for some time and incapable of traveling for a longer time after that. I set about improving our camp in preparation for a lengthy stay.

By May 5, Eric was much improved. He refused to lie down, and insisted on trying his legs despite the pain of rising. Once up, he found he could navigate slowly with a pair of sticks. Methodically he began shuffling up and down in front of the tent to get the feeling back into his limbs. He was a gallant, pathetic and humorous sight. Such spirit would hasten his recovery, I hoped. I investigated the cliffs back of the camp and tramped the northern tip of Richardson Island. I returned with not a thing to show for it except a pair of aching feet, and a face cracked from wind and sunburn.

That night the snap and bang of the whipping tent woke me time and again. I could well imagine men going mad under such conditions.

But wind or no wind, I was determined on my plan for the day. I was going to take a look at the broad reaches of Conjuror Bay where the map showed it opening out at the end of the seven-mile inner channel. This was what we had come to do and Beck encouraged me to make the thrust. Even though I lacked geological know-how, I could at least identify mineralization if I found any. Somehow, a sight of the main bay would take some of the sting of failure from our expedition.

The trip took seven hours of steady walking. There was little need for snowshoes, the surface being firm and generally smooth once I was past the narrowest part of the entrance. Recurring snow squalls limited the visibility, however, and made for comfortless travel. For six of the seven hours I had to keep my head pulled deep in my parka hood.

The inner channel was from a half to three quarters of a mile wide and, from time to time, I edged close enough to one wall or the other to get some idea of the formation. The weathered pink of granite was unrelieved on the faces.

A break came when the channel finally opened out into the great bay. For 15 minutes the wind dropped, the snow ceased and my eyes swept the panorama of bold inlets and mountainous islands. Conjuror, for those few minutes, was free of malevolence, smiling with promise. If only there had been two of us, fit and eager, to share it!

Then a new squall spouted out of the channel and obliterated the bay, breaking the spell. With Conjuror again veiled, it was easier to start the return journey.

Shortly before reaching the basin I had noted two small islands, not much more than reefs, near the west wall of the channel and had marked them for closer examination on the trip back. I approached them now, with the driven snow in my face. If I had been less hurried, I would have advanced on the narrowed passage with caution, knowing that the closely confined waters on Great Bear were subject to currents that chewed at the under-surface of the ice. Lost in thought and with my head deep in my parka, however, I was unaware that I was striding into trouble until it was upon me.

There was an undulation of the ice, then a growling sigh beneath it. Before I could spring back my right leg had broken through. I yanked it out, soaked to the knee, and found myself staring down through the hole it had punched.

Bear Lake's waters are as clear as they are cold. Through the port I had created, the stones at the bottom of the channel seemed only inches away. But I knew it was much deeper: there was plenty of water in which to drown.

I stared at the crystal depths and felt the ice shift and sough beneath my mukluks. I was aware that if ever I had had reason for fear it was now. But something weird was happening to me. Perilous seconds were moving by while I was caught in utter timelessness. I realized my situation fully: I knew the odds were strong that I would break through completely. I knew if that happened I would never make it to camp even if I managed to pull myself back on the ice. The cold would finish me. Still, I didn't panic. I was motionless and unhurried as I considered these facts. Then I knew something else. I knew I wasn't afraid.

I inched off the groaning ice that quaked beneath my feet. It was as if someone had pushed out a plank to bridge the way to solid surface.

Once more heading up-channel, I was conscious of having experienced the most profound moment of my life. A religious man might have said he'd encountered the intervening presence of the Almighty. Long after the immediate danger had been left behind, I had the feeling of being in trustworthy company. I was scarcely aware of the physical effort of bucking the blizzard until the cliff-encircled tent took shape in the swirl ahead.

Until then I had been anticipating the sharing of my adventure with Eric. I had felt certain the strange experience was communicable. Yet the sight of the tent made me weary in body, and suddenly cautious. A night's sleep would leave me refreshed and better able to recount the unexplainable, I decided.

That night I told Beck of the glimpse of the bay, of the formation I had seen along my trail, of the breakthrough on the ice, of my luck in escaping a ducking. The spiritual experience would have to keep until morning.

A heavy fall of snow smothered the wind sometime during the night and, in the calm that followed, I slept. After 12 solid hours, I woke just long enough to determine that the weather would be unfit for another foray. The dismal snow continued to fall, although the temperature was barely at the freezing point.

The day was one of enforced inactivity, and it brought a new and dangerous psychological problem.

Up until now, neither Beck nor I had expressed any serious moodiness or bad temper, despite our close companionship and shared hardships on the icy face of Great Bear. When either had briefly arisen, the cause had invariably been some uncontrollable caprice of the lake. Since our personal feelings had had no power to change Great Bear's ways, our anger and frustration soon dissipated themselves, without causing undue strain in the confines of the tent.

The difference now was that we suddenly began reacting to one another with deadly, unspoken abrasiveness.

It began with my inability to say what I had intended about my experience on the ice. The overnight delay had not helped me to become articulate. Instead, I decided that if I tried to tell Beck, I would be inviting amusement, even scorn. I lapsed into a self-protective silence that spread to the simplest domestic issues and Eric was left to interpret it as he chose.

There was no rational excuse for this. Ever since the night, months before, when I had experienced such difficulty admitting I might not be able to carry on next day, I had been conscious of how important it was to maintain the lifeline of honest speech between us. I had, I thought, anticipated every threat to it that might arise and how I would head it off if it appeared. The possibility of my own irrationality, however, hadn't been taken into account.

If Beck had been his normal self, he might well have eased us past the trap, but the odds were too heavily against him. For days he had been the pain-wracked, frustrated prisoner of the cove that had crippled him. Faced by a silence that could have suggested criticism of his part in our common misfortune, his early expression of bafflement turned to one of smoldering resentment.

The strange and terrible conflict which grew between Eric Beck and me, and which shattered our partnership on Great

Bear, had its background in many things I can view now through the dispassionate perspective of time and my later experience in life. The narrative of our half-year on the lake records its growth and the feelings I had at the time, almost exactly as I set them down in the diary I was keeping. I was then incapable of sorting it out for myself, and in the weave of the telling, it is better to leave it that way.

I have thought since, however, that factors contributing to my behaviour must have included the huge anxiety I felt over the need to have a successful staking trip. The economic stress of the Depression cannot be overemphasized. I was the father of a small son, with another child due at any time. I knew my wife to be in desperate circumstances. I must have seen Beck's injury as, at least in part, self-invited. I was trying to stifle anger at him for taking chances on the cliffs – chances that put both of us in peril. Instead of finding a way to say this, I let it fester inside me, and the anger came out in inappropriate ways. I can apologize for this, but I cannot change it. I lost faith in him as an enlisted man might in an officer, lost it at the precise moment when the two of us were most interdependent. And something in me was ashamed. The shame grew, too. In my immaturity, I let the blame crystallize on Beck himself. But he knew me, knew how I had behaved under stress. To one trying to find his manhood, that knowledge was dangerous, and made me hate him.

Even during the time on Great Bear, I was well aware of the "bushed" phenomenon. I'd heard all the famous stories about this bizarre psychological upheaval, which is said most often to arise between two individuals who have been isolated together for extended periods. There are tales of prospectors shooting one another over trivia. In one famous case, a trapper was acquitted by a jury of his peers after having killed his partner, who whistled the same tune over and over again. It was widely speculated that Albert Johnson, the Mad Trapper, was bushed when he went berserk in 1932. Before committing myself to the Great Bear trip, I had given these stories hard consideration, in light of the fact that I barely knew Eric Beck and would be isolated with him for days or weeks at a time. But I had brushed aside such negative thoughts. Getting away from the city and its pressures had become more important to me.

When the conflict arose, I didn't connect it with being bushed. But perhaps we were. It was fortunate, in a way, that I had my diary in which to monitor the seismic events. I recorded the rumblings as they occurred, and released my anger in some limited way, as well. I have deleted the uglier parts of that confessional, less in self-protection than out of a sense of perspective. Still, the conflict can be traced through the events which follow.

Determined to keep active that day, I did some housekeeping and made a batch of bannock with the last of our flour. Knowing how rapidly our supplies were dwindling put further strain on our taut nerves. The accumulating miseries of the whole ill-fated trip had closed in on us. When Eric rose late in the afternoon, sitting up for a smoke, the anger in the eyes he turned on me matched my own.

Wordless, we were like two men in an imperiled mine, conscious of the air swiftly exhausting itself, yet helpless to restore it. The tent was no longer our security against the elements. It was a prison whose walls compressed a poisoned atmosphere.

An explosion was inevitable and it came at dinner time. A few grains of coarse sand, rasping against Beck's teeth as he bit into the fresh bannock, was all it took to detonate it. The sound was as jarring as the clang of an alarm bell. Along with the accusing eyes that were turned on me, it broke the last of my self control.

I had barely time to grab my parka and plunge from the tent before my pent-up rage escaped in a torrent of obscenity.

The enclosing cliffs seemed to allow little more freedom than the walls of the tent had done but I lurched blindly through the snow-blurred twilight. The moisture of the early part of the day had become frost-hardened and the treacherous glaze underfoot broke sharply under my furious strides. I pounded on, physically exhausting myself.

Eventually, having circled the cove, I came to a halt a short distance from the tent. One hard truth had finally managed to work its way to the surface of my mind: if there was hope of saving anything whatever from the wreckage of our partnership, I would have to stop behaving like a hysterical moron.

At any cost, I must guard my temper in future and make the best of the appalling situation. As my self-control returned, I rehearsed the careful speech I would make when I returned to the tent. Beck made it easier for me, though. By the time I came through the fly, nothing was to be seen of him except the back of his head projecting from his sleeping bag.

Asleep or not, he continued to lie still while I finished my cold supper, washed up and rolled in. Lying in wakeful turmoil as the hours passed, I suspected he was waiting out the silence, hoping I would break it and give him something to shoot at. There were times, however, when he undoubtedly slept. His pain was still constant, but it was only in slumber, when he shifted position, that a moan escaped him.

He had obviously reached a decision similar to my own by stove-lighting time in the morning. There was some desultory domestic conversation but no mention was made of the previous night's blow-up. We each moved warily around anything that had potential for touching off another explosion.

That tense time set the pattern for our remaining days at Great Bear. On only one brief occasion would my temper again break loose. There would be times, even, when the lake and our business with it would draw us toward something resembling our original relationship. But the wounds never healed. The touchstone was gone. Hardships that had once inspired trust and respect became ready sources of suspicion and resentment. The unending effort of keeping our feelings under control was more exhausting than any grueling winter march.

On May 8, passable weather gave me the excuse to explore a long bay to the east which we had noted on the map. In the course of 20 vigorous miles, my mind became refreshed and my instinct for frankness came close to a comeback. But just short of the camp I had a bad fall on the ice and the pain, which lasted for a couple of days, dragged me in on myself again. There I stayed.

Beck kept making his forays out of the tent, trying to walk, but he was far from fit for travel. Our food supply was going down alarmingly. I hunted ptarmigan at night, without any luck. I told myself again that the trip was a dead loss.

The next day, it was blowing and raining, and the ice was

covered with water, putting an end to my hopes of prospecting. Beck's efforts were only putting him in worse shape, physically and mentally. He took to his bag, cursing everything from the weather to the first butterfly it produced.

I had to scale the cliffs to find any firewood worth burning. It blew hard at night. My greatest worry now was getting Eric back to Echo Bay before the grub ran out.

On May 10, a heavy rainfall was mixed with wind and hail. Eric seemed as low as ever but crawled out of his bag when I managed to stalk a lone ptarmigan in the rain. The fresh meat was a badly needed lift.

For the next three days it rained. The heights shed their snow at an amazing rate. Half a dozen cascades came to life on the surrounding cliffs, crashing noisily to the floor of the cove and running across the beach in brawling streams. As they flooded out into the bay, the surface of the ice sank deeper and deeper under water. In some places the overflow found drainage in the deep ice cracks that existed even in midwinter, and the gurgle of these catch-basins was added to the sound of the waterfalls and streams.

The runoff imprisoned us even more securely than the pack-ice had done. There could be no traveling across the surface water that now hemmed us in.

My hunting trips were seriously limited. It was necessary to cling to the base of the cliffs, whichever direction I chose to go. This was exhausting and fruitless. The ptarmigan became scarce when we needed them most. Where we normally had picked off an adequate supply on our regular travels, hours of determined hunting now failed to produce a feather. In the ptarmigan's place the Arctic raven turned up with increasing frequency.

The boreal raven was already established in northern lore as a bird of ill omen. Vulture-like, the black bird is said to show up invariably when misfortune is close. He is big and funereal, with a voice like a cracked bell.

The ravens always stayed just out of gunshot range, lumbering profanely from tree to tree or hopping among the rocks. Even though it was difficult to imagine eating them, their skill at making a man feel like prospective carrion encouraged my killer instinct.

On May 13, our supplies were approaching the vanishing point. But at 4:00 A.M. – now well lighted as the sun arched higher from dawn to dawn – the sound of ptarmigan conversing on the beach awakened us.

The conversation of the ptarmigan in mating season is distinctive. The jay chatters a good deal, displaying his feelings like a child not yet able to articulate. The Arctic raven mutters maledictions and sounds of contempt. But the ptarmigan is not only a voluble conversationalist. He forms his words precisely and with little repetition. Anyone who has been with him in the wilderness for a month can, if he wishes, readily follow his line of thought.

I knew instantly that we were hearing a male and female who were agreed on the subject but not on the manner of approaching it. Gently parting the tent fly, I confirmed this. They were only a short distance away, the male attired in the black head and scarlet comb of the mating season. The female had not yet shifted to the protective brown she would wear when nesting time came, and was still dressed in the pure white of winter. They were pacing the beach, keeping their distance but arguing without pause.

I fired from the comfort of the tent, with only the rifle's muzzle protruding. The cock died instantly, in the middle of a sentence. The hen, regarding him questioningly, remained long enough for me to reload the single-shot weapon and to fire again.

She took off with a rush of wings but I felt certain she was hit. Bullet-straight, she flew into the deepest pocket of the cove, an area thick with scrub and still floored with snow. I took after her. There was no sound when I reached the snow field, nothing to guide me, but unerringly I ran into the bushes to the spot where the bird lay dead, the white of its plumage barely distinguishable against the white of the background.

Retrieving it, I had a moment of mixed amusement and awe. A snapshot of a man standing in his long johns, his bare feet deep in snow, displaying a lone ptarmigan as an African hunter might pose with his first elephant, would have been good for a laugh in any album. But I was amazed at the accuracy with which I had been drawn 300 yards to where it was barely possible to see the black of the bird's eye against the snowy bush.

The birds were processed as both stew and soup, with little discarded except the feathers. Feeling better after our meal, I raised the possibility of making a move. The weather had stiffened at last. It was plain we could delay no longer. If we failed to take advantage of the present moderate freeze, we might not be granted another. Starvation was at our elbow and, disagreeable as the thought of traveling with Beck in his present condition might be, the alternative was worse. We could move with the chill of evening. Eric agreed, though without enthusiasm.

We committed ourselves to the gamble at nine o'clock on the night of May 14. During the afternoon, in preparation, Beck took the sticks with which he had learned to walk and rigged them as gee-poles on the rear of the toboggan. Gee-poles are usually reserved for dog-drawn carioles, to enable the driver to steer the sled from behind when it is being hauled along a rough or winding course. In our case they would be needed as we negotiated the pack ice. The anticipation of that ice wracked us increasingly as the hour of departure neared. The memory of our arrival rose to haunt us. The poles would give Eric something to lean on for support, taking part of the weight from his still-weak and hurting legs, while I supplied forward power on the dragrope.

We negotiated the pack-ice in an hour.

It was something of a miracle. The dreaded tank traps which had so punished us on the way in to Conjuror had been blunted by the warm weather of the past week. The razor-edged ridges of ice were now bulbous mounds over which the toboggan slid easily. There was, however, a new hazard. The depressions between the mounds were filled with snowmelt. In some instances the day's drop in temperature had been sufficient to form an ice covering that bore our weight as we crossed the pools. In others, the ice-sheet would collapse and plunge us to our knees in freezing water.

This was hard enough on me but it was sheer hell for Eric. The sudden swing of the gee-poles as the toboggan slewed wildly down the flank of some glassy mound twisted his back. The sudden drops as the ice broke jarred him from head to foot. At first he was able to confine himself to the relief of swearing, but as the wrenching became worse, he cried out in agony.

"Hold up, hold up!" he finally yelled.

I ignored him. Perhaps it was intelligence, perhaps desperation, but I threw myself even more frantically against the dragrope. I felt certain that if we stopped now Beck would never get started again. As we drew farther from the shore and my breathing became more labored, I knew this was also true for me.

Either we won this long, long sprint or we lost the race.

The swaying toboggan and the collapsing ice had been the earlier targets of Eric's curses. Now he directed them at me. But he held his grip on the gee-poles. To the almost uninterrupted sounds of his pain and rage, we continued to plunge forward – stumbling, slipping, falling, but instantly picking ourselves up and never losing our way. Panting and trembling, we finally came to the smooth desert of the outer ice.

We lay down and let the breath build up in us again. A scrap or two we had saved from our last meal revived us when we had the energy to eat it. A flock of ptarmigan whizzed out of the pre-midnight dusk, startling in their sudden appearance so far out from shore, and instantly were lost again in the half-light. The Conjuror was giving us a farewell fly-past.

Beck said, "Forget what I was shouting back there. Let's go."

The ice was nearly perfect – as it needed to be under the circumstances. We reached our earlier campsite on Dowdell Point at 3:00 A.M. Half a dozen slices of bacon we had hoarded as the grub-pile finally vanished were now broken out and laid reverently in the frying pan. The aroma was almost as satisfying as the taste.

Eleven hours after we had challenged Conjuror's pack-ice we rounded the point at Cameron Bay. There were still narrow bands of snow dusting Echo Bay and we had no steam left with which to break into a run before we charged them. The toboggan had to be dragged through them. Towards the finish it felt as though my arms and legs were being torn loose at the joints.

Eric's endurance and fortitude had been unbelievable. He

was still lurching doggedly along until we came through the neck of Cameron Bay and the settlement, its chimneys busy with the smoke of breakfast-making, greeted us from less than a mile away. The sight of it finished Beck. His legs buckled.

There was a pleasant piece of shoreline close at hand, sheltered, clear of snow and warmed by the sun. I unshipped Eric's bag and stretched it under a big tree where the ground was even and soft with fallen spruce needles. The day was beautiful and there was no immediate need to pitch the tent. However much he might be hurting, Eric was asleep the moment he was in his bag.

It was incredible how fresh I felt as I walked down to the end of the bay to do business with Murphy Services.

11

Under winter conditions I could have crossed the portage that day and replenished our supplies from the cache. Murphy, however, warned that it was now an extremely hard passage, with the trail obliterated by slush and the ice of the lakes deep in run-off. He advanced me enough grub to keep us going for a day or so and promised to send Doc Robertson over to see Beck when the flying physician returned from a visit he was making to another camp.

The spot where Beck lay appeared even more attractive as I cooked our first unrationed meal. Sheltered by a large spruce, it commanded a lovely prospect of Cameron Bay in one direction and the Southwest Arm in the other. There was little underbrush in the immediate park-like area and the well-treed slope that rose behind showed dry timber, white against the black of the conifers, that guaranteed fuel. I drew these details to Eric's attention when he awoke and he agreed we might as well put up the tent on the spot rather than moving on to the settlement. In fact, he said, maybe we should make this our permanent base.

Fortune continued to smile. Twice as I was erecting the tent I laid down my axe long enough to shoot ptarmigan that wandered into camp. Then, in the evening, when Gerry and Malcolm Campbell visited, we learned we had become the first citizens of Cameron Bay's permanent site. The thaw had revealed that the present settlement stood on muskeg, and plans were already under way to move it to the location we had just chosen for ourselves.

It was a tribute to our visitors that only after their departure did I realize I was entering my third successive day without sleep. I turned in and slept for 13 unbroken hours. When I woke it was to the music of water running through the tent. Disintegrating snow fields higher up the slope had released three busy rivulets, the confluence of which was just above our dwelling. The hurried digging of a gutter through the center of the floor confined the invading waters to a reasonable area of our living space.

By midnight the frost turned off this particular torrent but turned on another beyond the tent walls. The freeze, improving traveling conditions on the bay, brought the first waves of dog teams moving the settlement to its new site. The shouting of the drivers, the barking of the animals, and the general commotion of logs, supplies and other cargo being hauled up the bank made me grateful I had already accumulated a reserve of sleep. But there was no real hardship in listening to the beginnings of the new Cameron Bay. It was like hearing the tramp of a triumphant army.

On May 16, I made a trip to the cache. Swirling streams wiped out the trail time and again and I waded a great part of the way, up to my knees in ice-water.

De Melt Cove was a dying community. Ed, the founding father, had departed for Hay River and home. J. A. Reid and his men, the last remnants of population, were packing for the move to their property on Spark Plug Lake. They hadn't yet struck their living quarters and I was able to share a meal and, before the cook's oven, to bake some life back into my benumbed feet.

Joe Dillon, guardian of the staking parties that had crossed the lake in winter, was currently employed by Reid in the move to Spark Plug. Of all the Indians, Joe was the most fluent in English. He could speak it colloquially, was conscious of it, and overdid it. He had picked up other accomplishments in his close association with whites – some worth possessing and others which he would have done better to discard. His ability

with the dogwhip was typical of his mixed gifts. It was an of-
fence to animal lovers, but there were those who said they owed
their lives to his being able to lash a team into motion long after
the beasts should have been dead in their traces.

Having loaded my packsack with as much food as I could
hump over the portage, I reached an agreement with Joe to
move the rest of the outfit to Cameron Bay when he had fulfilled his contract with Reid. It would mean a long trip around
the coast – 25 miles at least, now that the portage was im-
passable to heavy loads – but Joe said he would be driving to
Cameron Bay in any event and he seemed eager for the
business. Visualizing what it would be like to back-pack the
500 pounds, I was equally eager for him to have the job.

Doc Robertson, appearing from the north as I was about to
take off, was a welcome companion on the trip back to camp
in the evening chill. The portage wasn't much better than it
had been in the heat of the day and I was 50 pounds heavier,
but Robertson's dry humor was an antidote to the wet
journey.

His report after checking Beck's condition was also reassuring.

"He's had a rotten jolt, obviously," he said, "but without
an X-ray examination I can't prescribe anything more than
he's already doing – keeping active within reason. The body's a
tough mechanism and it's got excellent built-in repair
facilities."

Spring arrived properly in Cameron Bay next morning. I
woke to two liquid notes – one the now-familiar singing of the
stream running through the tent, the other the full voice of a
robin. When I tumbled out to try to spot the latter, I was confronted by another sign of the season. Where our harbor
joined Echo Bay there was a broad, black patch of open water
on which serenely floated a pair of mallards and three glistening gulls.

The other musician, the stream, competed with rising vig-
or. It became necessary to build a log floor above it to keep the
tent habitable. Once started, this urge towards local improvement would not be halted. There was a knoll nearby, now
completely clear of snow, and here the tent was re-erected.

This was no ordinary roof-raising, though. It was preceded by the building of three-foot log walls. When the tent was mounted on them we were able, for the first time, to stand up straight in our own home. Even after the floor had been fitted in, we could walk upright indoors. It took getting used to.

Coming back from Murphy's and the inevitable bridge game that evening, we found a big, lustrous mink posted on our path leading up from the ice. There was no real darkness at any time of day now and the lovely beast couldn't possibly have been taken by surprise. He stood his ground as we approached, and glared at us as we halted 20 feet away. It seemed almost as if the animal were protesting the human invasion of his wild domain. Then the sinuous body silently vanished in the forest.

On May 18, Joe Dillon arrived without the contents of our cache and with a plausible story about his dogs being out on their feet after moving Reid. The prospect of moving our stuff across the portage by hand, with the portage in such shape, was not pleasant. It had to be done right away: our supplies were very low.

There was no question that Dillon's dogs were tired but, the way Joe traveled, this was normal. Our guess was that he had heard there was shortly to be an exodus of the teams now moving Cameron Bay to its new site and had decided this offered a better business prospect than hauling our outfit on the long trail around the coast. So he had come high-tailing, light, across the portage.

Any other teams we might have hoped to employ were leaving that same evening for Fort Franklin. They belonged to Bill Boland, the trader at Franklin, and several men from the Fort Norman region who had combined a staking expedition with giving a hand in the moving of the new settlement. They had waited until the last moment before making tracks for home. It was a long drive and the open water at the head of the bay was reminding them that the ice would not hold indefinitely.

Watching Bill Boland take off that night was unforgettable. He had a team that matched his own personality. Spirit and experience were beautifully integrated in the five powerful brutes, a bitch and four of her sons from a single litter. There was more German police dog than Husky in the strain, and they were well fed, and well cared-for. When the trader came to harness them, the young ones leaped on him like house pets, strikingly different from most sled-dogs, who snarled resentfully or accepted their working posts with bitter resignation.

The mother, who ran as wheel-dog immediately ahead of the cariole, barked sharply from time to time at her energetic offspring, but perhaps they realized they were headed on the 200-mile run home, for there was no suppressing their eagerness. Boland, working as though it was a familiar experience, lashed the rear of the cariole to a tree before he laid out the harness, then fitted his team, a dog at a time, into the traces. The moment an animal's gear was adjusted he began to pull, held back only by the strength of the restraining rope and the deep roots of the tree.

The expression of the bitch was a study in mild irritation, parental pride and worldly wisdom. When her own turn came for the harness she stood, slack in the traces, for a final minute of relaxation. Her example did nothing to improve the behavior of her sons. They continued to put passionate, unrelenting strain on the leather. They were like arrows tensed for the release of the bowstring.

When Boland finally slipped the rope they shot down the bay. The driver took no chances on attempting to run with them, but leaped on board the cariole the moment it moved. The dogs were still going full gallop when they vanished around the point, the bitch apparently joining in the fun now that it made sense. We couldn't know how long they would continue this way before settling down to the regular jog-trot of the trail, but if ever flesh approached the secret of perpetual motion, Boland's animals did.

On the night of May 20, there was a good deal of frost and a second trip to the cache became imperative. Beck, who had been extending his walks in the camp area daily, declared himself fit to accompany me. He stood up to the trip and 90 pounds of supplies returned with us, but the grueling experience made any thought of repeating the journey out of the question. When we reached Cameron Bay again at 5 A.M. Eric was nearly as bad as he had been when we arrived from Conjuror.

We were still asleep in the middle of the afternoon when a loud voice roused us. Poked in the doorway was a battered fedora topping a prominent nose and a pair of laughing eyes. It took time to identify them. When we had seen Peter Baker three months before he had been a snow-blind, scarecrow figure in the company of the stakers retreating to Fort Franklin. The face inside the parka hood at that time little resembled the healthy-looking Arab who now greeted us.

"I'll be damned!" exclaimed Beck. "You're supposed to be back at Fort Smith, settling down for the rest of your life."

"Oh, no," said Pete. "I like this country."

Over dinner he admitted that the crossing to Franklin with starved dogs, tattered gear and frostbitten men had been hard, but not unusually so. No one had died. It hadn't shaken his belief that Great Bear was to be the brightest star in the Northern heavens. Lying over at Fort Franklin until he could restore his outfit, his one objective had been to get back to the east shore as quickly as possible.

"And now," he grinned, childlike in his triumph, "I am here."

He still had one of the dogs with which he had originally arrived, a mighty animal named Stunt, and he had managed to pick up others at Fort Franklin to round out a team. He had also acquired a broad-beamed, 20-foot canoe and had brought it along on his toboggan. Half its length extended beyond the tail of the sled, but by loading his cargo in the nose of the boat, he managed a state of balance. His outfit, like the team, was lacking in uniformity, but it was sufficient for his needs. Food seemed to be his most marked shortage. There were, however, a couple of large lake trout in the bottom of the canoe, one of which went to the dogs as we inspected them.

"You don't seem to have arrived any too soon," I observed. "Were you able to get game as you came along the shore?"

"I didn't touch the shore after I left Franklin," Pete replied casually.

"You mean you came straight across the lake?"

"Sure. Why not?"

"What did you do for shelter? What would you have done if you had run out of food?"

"Oh, the weather was good – a little snow, maybe – a little wind. When we stopped the canoe made a good windbreak. If it snowed we got under the canoe – and I would pull the tent over my sleeping bag if it was too cold. We always stopped by one of those big cracks in the ice – the kind that go right down to the water. When I put in my lines there were always fish."

"But how did you keep your direction so far out of sight of land?"

Pete shrugged and a flash of teeth showed against the dark, deeply burned face. "The sun came out nearly every day and, even if it hadn't, Billy, my lead dog, would have known where to go. He is very clever."

Then Baker became Ahmed Bedaui Ferran again and quoted some of the poems he had written in his native Arabic. The music of them was not dependent on the translation which followed. Pete was a fascinating companion – worldly wise, childlike, philosophical – in swiftly changing moods. For him the world was divided sharply into good men and bad men, with the good men predominating. He had a particular feeling for the Indians and spoke readily in two of their dialects.

An instinctive trader, he had started his Northern career in the early twenties, selling soft drinks on the portage between Fitzgerald and Smith. Branching into the fur business, he was the subject of a bewildering divergence of opinion among the old timers. If his generosity to us was any yardstick of his merchant skills, it was a miracle he had remained solvent. It is pleasant to record, however, that in his eighties he became a well-to-do councillor of the Northwest Territories.

One thing was certain. He was a master fisherman. The secret of his existence on next to nothing during the long crossing of the lake was plain enough when he began to pull trout from Echo Bay. He was an artist in the setting of a line, his sensitive fingers twisting a loose loop which allowed a fish to get up speed as it made off with the bait. When the hook jerked into its jaw it stayed there. We never lacked for trout steaks after he came.

I told him of our difficulties in reaching the cache.

"Don't worry about that," he said. "When my dogs are rested I must go over and call on my friends in Smat. We can go by way of your cache and bring your outfit back here.''

Nearly a week passed before the trip could be made. Rain, sometimes torrential, made life miserable for us. Beck and I were confined for long, comfortless hours in the little tent, and the abrasive relationship we had brought from Conjuror Bay steadily worsened.

Things might have gotten out of control if it had not been for Pete Baker's frequent visits. Quick to detect the strain between us and wise in the ways of the bush, he played us with all the skill that he applied to the lake trout. There were no opportunities for brooding when he was present. An inveterate teller of tales, he could abandon facts for poetic license with an almost imperceptible changing of gears.

Had there been something tangible at the heart of the strain between Eric and myself, Pete would probably have rooted it out on the occasions when he had us laughing with him in spite of ourselves. As it was, I couldn't have offered him a clue had I wanted to.

The days were miserable and wet. We often lay in until noon to save what little dry wood we had and to pass away useless hours. I braved the storm to get in new supplies of wood and to gather cold moss for chinking up some of the worst holes in the log wall. Beck, going for water, went through the ice and was soaked to the waist. The noise of the gale, tearing at the tent, robbed us of sleep. The month was rushing by at an alarming rate and we still had nothing to show for it.

Between Beck and me, open communication had become restricted to the barest of working essentials. I decided to make a run to Lindsley Bay with Pete Baker.

The day started atrociously late. By 2 P.M. when I had finished putting the camp in shape and was prepared to pull out with Baker, Eric had shown no signs of undertaking the all-important prospecting on our Echo Bay claims which he had promised to do. I addressed a few unvarnished words. They were received in silence but he pulled out for the claims. It was our one outbreak of open hostility.

Opposite Glacier Bay, just inside LaBine Point, Pete and I encountered Bill Jewitt, Consolidated Mining and Smelting

Company's man in the field. A brilliant engineer who was obviously headed for the top of his giant mining corporation, Bill piloted his own plane and was an accomplished bushman who eventually covered on foot anything that looked good from the air. He was a deceptively quiet and companionable fellow for a big-time operator. We had been friends at university and the reunion on the ice led to dinner at the Consolidated camp.

The food was good but the news was better. Bill told me in confidence that he had instructions from Outside to check over the Echo Bay properties of Beck Syndicate. A possible buyer!

It was only five miles back to Cameron Bay and, for a moment, I found myself thinking, "Eric must hear this before the evening is out. It's the biggest lift we've had since we came here." Then I recalled our acrid parting. But it could not entirely dispel my joy. When Pete and I arrived at Eldorado later that evening I was still airborne, planning what I would accomplish back home in my imminent solvency. I would retire all my debts, and buy a new home for Ernestine – or should we build...?

There was another reunion at Eldorado. Spud Arsenault was there, his head swathed in bandages. Rumor had reached Cameron Bay that he had been hurt while prospecting beyond Dowdell Point – that he in fact had tangled with a bear – but it sounded like one of those tales improved by repetition.

"Well, it's true enough," the battered Arsenault insisted. "And don't get any idea I went looking for it. Gunnar Berg and I were sleeping in the open when this Barren Lands grizzly comes sniffing around. Maybe I tried to brush him off in my sleep – like he was a mosquito. Anyway, first thing I remember was the roof falling in. He only took one swipe at me but he sure parted my hair.

"I had a revolver under my sleeping bag. You're in bad with the Mounties if you have one in here but it's easier than packing a rifle. So I came up shooting. Don't think I hit anything – too much blood in my eyes to see – but the bear took off. Gunnar made me come back with him here to get patched up. I guess he was right, but it sure hasn't done our prospecting program any good."

I was sympathetic but couldn't pass up the opportunity to

remind him of the evening in Edmonton when he had under-
taken to bring my firstborn a Barren Lands grizzly next time he
came Outside.

"You're not likely to get such a chance again," I reproved,
"and Erik is going to be heartbroken when he hears how you
muffed it. The least I can do is give him the impression you
really tried."

"You don't have to tell him," Spud protested.

"I'll have to tell the world," I answered. "Men don't wres-
tle with grizzlies every day, you know."

My son forgave Spud readily when the facts had been explained, but whether Spud would forgive me after the story
had been published Outside was something that remained
longer in doubt. The yarn had a background that encouraged
embellishment, even though Doc Robertson, who had stitched
the gash in Spud's scalp, made clear it had been no laughing
matter.

The six-mile shoreline from LaBine Point to Lindsley Bay
was known as The Labrador. Anyone who had ever seen
Canada's north Atlantic coast readily grasped the parallel.
Throughout its length The Labrador presented an almost un-
breached wall of dark precipices, with small, offshore islands
jutting above the lake's surface like uneven teeth. Along this
grim strand, in the thin dusk preceding midnight, Pete and I
set out after a final mug of coffee at Eldorado.

I suggested the canoe might be left behind so the toboggan
could run light but Pete was firmly against it.

"It will be better to load your outfit into the boat than have
it stacked high on the toboggan," he said. "A canoe is a good
thing to have this time of year."

Driving up The Labrador, I became more convinced than
ever that I had been right. The weight of the 20-foot craft added to what was already hard going for the dogs. The lake surface was in a state of frigid upheaval adjacent to the little
islands, and the outer sweep of it had candled under the
warmth and rain of recent days. It thrust up in billions of
minute spikes, cutting the sled dogs' feet.

Billy, the lead dog, was the first to start leaving pink paw-
marks behind. When the ice showed no signs of improvement,

Pete halted the team and examined their feet. Even Stunt, the cast-iron wheel dog, had a bloody one. There was a delay while Baker tied 16 moccasins on as many paws. When we got under way again, the dogs ran more easily, but before we rounded the turn into Lindsley Bay, dabs of red seeping through the moosehide were again being stamped on the ice.

It was better going inside the bay and by 2 A.M. we were drawing into De Melt Cove. Fresh difficulties faced us as we closed the shore. The run-off from the steep slopes had already brought the creek to boiling life and it, in turn, had undermined the offshore ice. There was a 25-foot moat of open water along the entire front of the cove – except at one point where a bridge of small floes had drifted together.

Pete halted the dogs 50 feet from the gap and edged cautiously forward to examine the possible crossing. He reached a quick decision.

"That ice will hold," he said, "but you'd better hang onto the side of the canoe."

He yelled, "*Marche*, Billy!" and snapped the whip. As the dogs lunged forward, he continued to exhort them with cries. We charged straight for the ice-bridge, Pete on one side of the canoe and I on the other, each with a hand on a gunwale as we ran. The jumble of thin pack-ice rocked and grunted as we hit it. Once I felt my foot go through briefly, but our forward speed gave the floes little time to betray us and, before the shouting Pete needed to pause for breath, we were safely ashore.

The Arab walked along the line of dogs, patting each proudly and speaking words of praise. Stunt was the only one who showed appreciation. He stood happily on his strong legs, tail up and head raised. The others curled on the ground the moment they knew they wouldn't immediately be roused again by the whip. It had been a tough haul.

The cove was a melancholy sight. Only our cache suggested there had ever been people here. In the half-light, amid the shadows cast by the spruces, the naked poles that had once been the pillars of a community were one again with the trunks that had never known an axe. With much of the snow gone, the nature of the draw itself had changed. Trees and rocks that had become intimates in their white trappings were no longer recognizable. At its best this had been a hard camp – but it had been home. I realized this was probably the last time I would ever see it. And, seeing it, I found it already strange.

Baker was noisily gathering firewood. Like most things he did, he had his own expansive way of going about it. He neither cut down trees nor cut them up when they had fallen. Anything that was dry enough to burn and within his ability to pull bodily to earth was fuel for his fire. Once his kindling was alight, he fed it with limbs up to 15 feet in length. The resulting blaze would have been bright enough to signal a rising of the clans. It filled the draw with leaping light. The ghosts fell back into the shadowed depths where the portage track once had led.

Man and dog, we drew into the great circle of warmth and relaxed. Pete brewed tea, manipulating the pot with a long pole. The heat was too great to approach the coals directly. There was something ludicrous about watching the little kettle leap to a boil on a fire better suited to a blast furnace.

By the time the flames had subsided, forerunners of the early sun had slipped down the bay. It was full daylight when the contents of the cache had been loaded into the canoe and the embers of Pete's beacon carefully doused.

Recrossing the ice-bridge was more difficult than our original mad dash. The load on the toboggan was now substantial and, even worse, the rough shoreline made it impossible to work up any speed before challenging the moat. The dogs scrambled readily enough over the jumble of ice-pans but as the weight of their burden came behind them, there were ominous heavings and groanings beneath the toboggan.

"*Marche! Marche!*" screamed Pete, his whip exploding over the straining animals.

The dogs had gained footing on the solid ice and Pete and I were pushing the canoe like charging linemen by the time the bridge collapsed.

We could feel it going and had just time to leap into the craft before it found itself afloat. Propelled by forward momentum and the hauling of the dogs, it touched the rim of the firm ice almost immediately. Jumping from the bow to dependable footing, Baker and I had the canoe clear of the water in a matter of seconds. The curved prow of the toboggan, still projecting at the boat's bow, provided a perfect skid for the operation.

Pete gave the dogs a brief breather, then we were on our way to Smat.

It was a fast, light-hearted trip. There was enough early-morning chill for good surface. The previous night it had been necessary for me to run ahead of the dogs to keep them on a consistent course, their tendency being to veer away from the wind when there was no forerunner to follow, but today they were completely responsive to Pete's shouted, *"Hue!"* or *"Tcha!"* when a change of direction was required. Even with the contents of the cache as added load, it was possible for either of us to ride the toboggan when the mood was on us. Mostly, though, we trotted alongside, talking and singing in the spell of a spectacular dawn.

It was 6 A.M. and Smat was barely rousing itself when we arrived. There was an almost completed but still untenanted cabin on the beach and we spread our bags on its floor and slept for a couple of hours until its builders appeared to resume work on it.

The day developed into the warmest we had yet experienced, perfect for visiting but unfavorable for resuming the journey. Pete made the rounds of the friends he had come to see – they included practically the entire population – while I provided Sergeant Rainey with enough copy to keep his wireless key as warm as the day.

We hung around until evening, hoping the temperature would drop and improve traveling conditions. We pulled out shortly after eight o'clock but ran into a driving rainstorm on the open lake. We were soaked through immediately but continued to plug ahead, The Labrador offering not the slightest shelter. It was still pouring at midnight.

It was all I could do to set the pace for the dogs. At least the myriad pinpoints of candled ice had been blunted by the heat wave, but we had to don rubbers over our moccasins in an attempt to keep our feet dry while traversing the never-ending pools of water. This was quite as difficult and uncomfortable as the spiked footing had been. The rubbers drew on our feet like suction pumps, particularly after water had slopped into them while crossing the deeper pools. They were crippling me so badly I abandoned them and let the ice have its way with the soles of my moccasins – and my feet. By journey's end the footgear was practically soleless.

The rain let up a couple of hours after midnight, shortly before we turned into the narrow channel between LaBine Point and the chunk of rock at its tip. The little island, though rugged, offered our first chance to rest.

Soon we had a fire going, and the kettle boiling. We stretched our weary limbs before the flames. Drowned rats though we were, the sogginess had not penetrated to the core of Pete's amazing spirit.

"What a country!" he exclaimed, raising his arms to the clearing skies and the dawn already tipping the mountains. "Why would a man with any sense ever want to be anywhere else?"

There was something deeply stirring in the new day as it touched the rain-drenched ramparts of Echo Bay. Pale light ran like quicksilver over the island where we paused, bringing a theatrical outline to the scattered scrub and softening the deep scars in the rock.

"Put another log on the fire," suggested Pete. "We're in no hurry."

I moved to the most promising clump of timber and was about to put my axe to a dry stick when a stack of four posts, only a few feet away, caught my attention. With the curiosity that burned at every encounter with claim stakes, I gave them a quick examination.

"Come here, Pete," I called, quietly. It might have been a holy place.

Baker padded over and read the metal tag on the Number One post that held my eye. Its information was still legible where it had originally been inscribed in heavy pencil on the white face of the stake. It was the first post Gilbert LaBine had raised when he claimed Eldorado – the length of tough, warped spruce that had touched off everything happening at that moment, and everything yet to happen, on Echo Bay.

12

At Cameron Bay on May 29, Beck busied himself packing and unpacking and giving indications of another move. I hadn't been consulted about our plans but any action was OK by me.

My return with the supplies had done nothing to improve the atmosphere in our tent, but I immediately joined in putting the camp in good shape for a quick takeoff into the field. A new cache was built within 24 hours and food and equipment selected for our first open-season prospecting trip.

This, Beck finally informed me, was to be a strictly overland expedition, with Eagle Nest Lake – well inland from Echo Bay – as our goal. It would mean that everything we brought along would have to ride on our shoulders. Beck had every reason to pack and unpack many times, for the loading of the sacks called for extreme selectivity. Food and gear had to be worked out to the most economical load that would allow the longest range.

Beck's choice of Eagle Nest Lake as our destination was one detail with which I had no quarrel. It was one of the two inland bodies of water which the new map acknowledged by name. Contact Lake, nearer and already well-known, was the other. Although a number of them were quite large, the myriad of other lakes remained nameless.

Not only was Eagle Nest well beyond the existing staking, it had been partly under cloud when the survey plane had photographed the area and some of its outline was indicated by dotted line, suggesting a certain amount of guesswork. It was a phantom lake, and yet worthy of a name. For me, these were omens that the new lake would be cradled in richly veined formation.

This should have been a time of glorious anticipation. The bared slopes now invited thorough prospecting and it was near enough to the time of sustained midnight sun to permit a 24-hour working day for those who wished it. As things stood between Beck and me, though, the unlimited light, destroying the ordered framework of night and day, intensified the strain.

Our raw nerves reached their most acute state when Beck suddenly decided to walk to Glacier Bay for a talk with Jewitt – this on the evening of the day he had said we would leave for Eagle Nest. He started off at 10 at night and returned at seven in the morning – just as I rose charged with a tremendous urge to get into the field. At three in the afternoon he was still dead in his sleeping bag and I was seething with impatience.

A target for my pent-up nerves presented itself in the form of a bear that lumbered out of the bush to the water's edge on the other side of Cameron Bay. Grabbing the 30-30, I took off in pursuit and succeeded in exhausting myself in a fruitless attempt to hunt it down.

Pete was with Eric when I returned.

"You'd better get some sleep," the Arab greeted me. "You'll be getting up early tomorrow."

"Pete's driving Meikle to the end of Bay 66 in the morning," Beck offered. "He doesn't see why we shouldn't go along."

"The Government will be paying the fare," grinned Baker, "and Mr. Meikle won't mind if you rest your packs on the sled now and then."

The Mining Recorder was making a short inspection of the staking around Bay 66 – so named because parallel 66 North passed neatly through its tip – and his outfit was not so heavy that Stunt and his fellow sled dogs had any difficulty pulling the two extra packsacks we added to the load.

Though we were well acquainted with the outer reaches of Echo Bay, the long thrust of Bay 66, its eastern extremity, was new territory. It was an encouraging introduction, with a cloudless sky, the ice still firm underfoot, our packs riding on the toboggan and Pete and Meikle providing good company. Above all, it was a relief to trot along in the knowledge that, after the galling delay, we were about to resume our undertaking to the shareholders of Beck Syndicate.

At the end of the bay Meikle and Pete started over the mile-long portage to Contact Lake. We could hear at its other end the dull boom of George Moody's men dynamiting their way towards another good investment for John Michaels. With bed, board and shelter for the next 10 days on our backs, Beck and I turned toward the low hills, endless lakes and alder-filled swamps to the east.

It was hot going and we drifted southward from our intended course, losing our bearings on several occasions but always managing to extricate ourselves. By evening we were on the outer fringe of the staking. Although we had toiled many miles we had only accomplished four in a direct line. We made camp on the shore of a boggy lake.

This was my first serious experience of backpacking. The emergency trips across the portage to Lindsley Bay had given me a taste of it, but to have a 50-pound load of food, bedding, and cooking utensils suddenly become a permanent part of my body was a strain. It was not unlike my first experience of snowshoeing except that my shoulders, rather than my legs, took the brunt of it. The pain was sharper, this time.

Slipping the pack at the end of the day brought a wondrous sense of lightness. I felt almost as if I were in danger of floating away on the next breeze. One advantage the packsack had over snowshoes was that it actually became lighter, the farther we trekked. Mineral samples were added from time to time, but the food's weight decreased as we used it, steadily reducing the load.

On June 1, we headed into little-known territory. We traveled through granite all day. Encountering a racing torrent, we bridged it with a tree.

Here, I had another close call. A partly trimmed branch of our makeshift bridge tripped me halfway across. I ran desperately forward as I lost my balance and toppled into the rapid. Fortunately, I was close enough to shore to grab an out-jutting spur of rock. Otherwise I undoubtedly would have been swept away. Beck made a side trip alone while I lit a fire and dried out.

It was hard, hot going during the remainder of the day, with more delays caused by steering a poor course. We located ourselves on a pretty lake by suppertime, however.

Of all the overnight campsites we ever made this was the loveliest. Traveling light, we had only a small tarpaulin for shelter and shared a single sleeping bag and flybar. As long as the weather was fine we simply used the tarp as a groundsheet, then opened out the bag and pulled it over us. As yet we had been untroubled by insects, so the flybar went unused. We lay in the open, with nothing above us except the sky.

I thought unwillingly of the grizzly which had attacked Spud Arsenault in these regions. Nothing was said, but our axes were invariably positioned within ready reach before we pulled the sleeping bag over us.

The setting in which we spent that first night of June was such, however, that the thought of any Barren Lands grizzly invading it seemed preposterous. There was a delicate beauty to the lake, in contrast to the harsher surroundings to which we had become accustomed. The rock faces along the opposite shore were touched with pastel shades, the birch trunks above them so white they glowed against the backdrop of blue green conifers. Ice still covered the lake from shore to shore but it was deeply candled and glinted like silver filigree.

The sun sank tentatively behind the hills to the northwest and the light softened. The birds became silent, but the stillness and the lustrous, indirect light brought new beauty. I knew I needed rest but I found it difficult to close my eyes on the untouched world that surrounded us.

Finally I drifted into sleep. Sometime during the midnight hours I wakened briefly when I felt a light breeze on my cheek. The sky was still clear, however, and the air warm, and I gratefully drowsed off again. In a dream I thought I heard the whisper of spring moving across the winter-weary land, or perhaps the tinkle of a million small, silver bells. When I awoke and looked at the lake in the full light of morning, I knew that the sound hadn't been a dream after all. Where ice had sealed the lake from rim to rim, there was now nothing but the sparkle of deep, blue water. The tinkling in the night had come from the disintegration of uncounted glassy shards, ringing against each other as they finally separated under the encouragement of the passing breeze.

A range of mountains, tall and black across the intervening lowland, beckoned us eastward. Breaking camp early, we moved toward them, hoping the mountains would reveal a more promising type of formation than had so far greeted us. The consistent pink granite which thrust above the swamps was colorful enough, but it was completely barren of mineralization.

We spent a strenuous day, working through tangled alder swamps and over beetling cliffs. We were determined to pierce the granite barrier by evening and kept on long after we were tired. We finally camped on a small lake within hailing distance of our main objective, Eagle Nest Lake. The rock there was not startling but we were out of the granite and our real work could begin. All the small lakes we passed were rapidly breaking up and the spring leaves were coming out. We had stumbled on a cow moose and her calf at one point. Without weapons we were no danger to her, though we would not have shot her even had we been armed. There would be no chance to stockpile the fresh meat.

We decided to work out from this camp the next day and left our packs behind. We hit an array of cliffs to the south and unearthed a copper and hematite showing in a small vein. It was not impressive enough to stake, however. We plugged on. After some hard going, we cut over to a long lake to the east and worked back along its shore. We were staggering when we reached camp late in the evening. The mosquitoes were out and hungry (for the first time) and we found it necessary to rig the flybar. It rained hard for some time after we turned in but we were dry under the tarp.

We made another foray from the same camp, this time across Eagle Nest Creek and up a nameless river to the east. It was a beautiful stream, with splendid rapids every quarter mile or so. The country on the far side looked very promising but the river was much too formidable to be rafted. We found some big quartz veins. They were barren except for a bit of hematite. We were cutting down on our meals, to conserve supplies.

Summer was by now positively exploding. Flowers sprang up underfoot almost as you watched and the leafing birches dotted the hillsides with shrapnel puffs of light green. Once, in a heavily sheltered spot, we saw the last of an unusually deep snowdrift releasing the blueberry bushes it had smothered the previous autumn. The first snow must have come early, for the bushes had been laden with ripe fruit when they were buried and fresh-frozen. Now the berries emerged perfectly preserved, making delicious eating for the few hours before they began to ferment in the heat.

On June 5 we broke camp and pushed southeast into the same region we had covered two days before. We found some fairly decent formation and came on another copper showing. Again it was too insignificant to stake. We made camp early on another gem of a lake.

Supper was bacon and bannock – again. The constantly greasy diet was playing havoc with our stomachs.

I was deeply alarmed by the first signs of this. The stabs of pain were severe enough to wake me from the heavy sleep of near-exhaustion. They seemed to have most of the indications of acute appendicitis. Any symptoms that might have been actually lacking were quickly supplied by my imagination, then further stimulated when I remembered how isolated we were.

I found myself desperately figuring how long it would take Beck to return to Cameron Bay if my condition worsened and I was unable to move under my own steam; how long it would take Doc Robertson to reach me; how much he would be able to do if I required emergency surgery. The agony increased in proportion to the time I spent trying to figure out its cause.

At its height I remembered Conjuror Bay and the fearlessness I had felt when I should have been scared white. I admitted to myself that I was damned scared now. The confession helped me to stop fighting the pain and to lie quietly rallying my stampeding forces. Slowly I relaxed. My throbbing gut became less violent, and the fever – real or imagined – subsided. Within the hour I was asleep again.

This was not the last time our grease-rich diet caused us discomfort, but on later occasions I found myself able to escape the tension that came with the pain. Once I was conscious that fear was most of the problem, I seemed capable of meeting it with relative calm.

On June 6, we pushed a couple of miles north through swampy country, but when it became obvious that we would see no rock in that direction we wearily swung about and headed east along the shore of the long lake – a beautiful body of water at least eight miles from end to end. Like the river that fed it, it was nameless. We came on quite a good showing of mineralized quartz veinlets in a most unexpected spot: on the wooded lakeshore, where most of the rock was concealed by overburden. Later we found some splendid formation. I was all for going to work with the axes and putting in stakes but Eric ruled against it. He collected a number of samples, though, to pan for gold when we got back to Cameron Bay. I was disappointed over his decision. The time was dangerously close when the summer rush would be on us. I wanted to fill my licenses without delay.

The next day, we broke camp on the long lake, crossed Eagle Nest Creek and put in a hard day plugging north along the east shore of Eagle Nest itself. The formation there was disappointing. Thanks to our improved condition, the day's progress was very satisfying and we were at the north tip of the lake when we camped. It had turned clear and chilly, dispersing the mosquitoes so that we didn't need the flybar at night.

On June 8, we were working towards home and back into the granite again. The country on this leg of the trip was low and marshy; our feet, usually wet, were saturated. Grub was down to fighting rations and I limited myself to a pipe and a half of tobacco a day in an attempt to make it last.

This march produced a welcome break in our diet. In midafternoon, plowing through some of the most wearying swamp and brush barriers yet, I began to feel the shortage of fresh food with unusual anguish. "What I'd give to sit down to half a dozen fresh eggs done sunny side up!" I exclaimed.

The words were barely out when a partridge exploded from a clump of brush just off our course. The sound was so close, so thunderous, that it stopped us in our tracks. The bird was still in flight when Beck hurled himself at the spot from which it had risen. A moment later he was shouting triumphantly, "Well, what do you know!"

There were six eggs in the nest. We candled them against the sun and could see they were fresh-laid. Silently we shed our packs and while Beck got out the frying pan, the bacon grease, the salt and pepper and the dinner service, I kindled a fire. Once the six eggs were in the pan, I felt a twinge of guilt.

"I wish we'd found them without seeing their mother," I said. "She's going to feel badly when she comes back to that empty nest."

"Happens to them all the time," countered Beck, salting the sizzling morsels. "She'll just lay another clutch when she comes back – probably better ones than these."

It was a convincing argument, clinched by the aroma rising from the frying pan. They were not large eggs but we ate them slowly and sat for five or 10 minutes enjoying the memory of them before we started again towards Echo Bay.

Next day, we were off to an earlier start than usual and we found ourselves just short of Surprise Lake (prospector-named) by two o'clock. Here Eric decided to check over the lines and posts of a set of claims we had heard had lapsed. While he did so I made camp. I was keen to get back to Cameron Bay. Not only did I want food in my belly, clean socks on my sore feet and the sight of a few faces again, but it was essential that we refill our packs and get out on the next trip as soon as possible. I had given myself two weeks to get my staking done. After that I had agreed to become a full-time reporter, and would have little opportunity for prospecting.

The supposedly lapsed claims proved to be still in force. We pushed straight through to Bay 66 next morning. Any hope of finding a quick road to Cameron Bay evaporated as we reached the shore. An expanse of steely water, stretching as far as the eye could see, had replaced the glazed surface down which we had driven with Pete 11 days before. There was one homeward path now: the deeply indented shoreline which not only curved miles away from the direct route but which fell steeply into the lake along much of its length.

Luckily we had reached top physical condition. Even with the briefest noonday pause to wolf our last crumbs of food, it was evening before we struggled onto familiar ground – our own Echo Bay claims. Snags had ripped our clothes, sharp rocks had bruised our feet, and an aching hunger had weakened us when we finally climbed the heights beyond which lay Cameron Bay. Far below, thin pillars of smoke rose pink in the midnight sun.

As we picked our way down the slope, lurching with fatigue, it became evident that the big move at Cameron Bay had been completed. There was no sign of life at the head of the portage, but at the entrance to the bay we had difficulty identifying our own tent among the new log structures and tents which now surrounded it. The place was transformed.

We worked our way down through the trees to the water's edge and finally stood directly across the bay's narrow entrance from the new community. Here we paused. It had not been long, really, since we had last seen other human beings, but it was fascinating to simply watch them move about in the little town they had created.

When we finally shouted, the windless evening encouraged echoes to bounce from wall to wall of the bay. *Hello ...hello...hello...* they mimicked. From the door of Murphy Services' now-completed log headquarters, Gerry emerged and shouted back. Again the echoes took charge, creating such confusion that we eventually had to space our conversation carefully in order to make it intelligible. Once identified, we got quick action. The president of Murphy Services made a personal project of it, rowing across in one of the skiffs and ferrying us to civilization. It was just four weeks since we had landed on the point from Conjuror Bay.

Gerry pressed supper on us: fresh trout, all we could eat. We indulged in the luxury of tailor-made cigarettes, a wash in warm water and plenty of chatter.

The weather provided a perfect epilogue to the trip. That night it began to rain, a 36-hour, steady downpour that worked itself up to a point where its thunder on the canvas made it necessary to shout to be heard. But the sound was not powerful enough to prevent sleep. In the brief times when I did wake, it was to gratefully realize where we were – and to have a flash of what it would have been like had the storm caught us traveling. It was worth being wakened if only to sigh in dry contentment, then drift back to sleep again.

Indoor confinement also gave Beck time to bake our mineral samples, both those collected on the trip we had just concluded, and the ones brought back from the northern islands. After submitting the chunks of ore to a protracted heating on the red-hot stove top, he laboriously ground them to a coarse sand for panning when the sun returned. The light was required if the precious "colors" were to be detected.

The deluge ended on the afternoon of June 12. With the sun blazing almost straight overhead, we found a quiet spot on the narrow beach which had been revealed below the tent by the final thaw. Here Beck hunkered over the gold pan, for the first time assuming its rightful role after months of serving as a wash-basin. Eric deposited some of the granulated ore in it, covered the contents with water, and began the rhythmic, circular motion which would wash away the slag and allow the heavier, metallic element to settle to the bottom of the pan.

There was *something* there. That much was plain even to me. Peering over Beck's shoulder, I could identify a glinting substance that became more and more consistent in the dwindling sludge of dark sand. After awhile I was more aware of what was happening to Eric than of what was happening in the gold pan. His face was beginning to shine brighter than the stuff showing through the film of gently swirling water.

"By God," he said finally, "there *is* something!" Before he put the magnifying glass on the showing, Beck was confident there was both gold and silver. We almost burst with excitement. But the gleaming dust proved to be only copper and magnetite.

It was a nerve-wracking business, this testing. The next day more samples were washed, with the same negative results.

Beck decided we shouldn't head out again until Pete Baker could transport us to the end of the bay by canoe. Pete was in Smat, but got back on June 15 with word that we could expect the first plane in the next day. There was instant excitement, and I had no doubt it would rise to fever pitch when the engine was heard. The prospect of mail was a thrilling one. I spiced my day's work with a visit to the Echo Bay claims and opened up a hematite vein for nearly 20 feet. The mosquitoes were bad, and drove me in earlier than I had intended.

Anticipation of the plane's arrival suffered a setback next morning. Low clouds marched in from the north in sullen procession and their speed made it clear no aircraft would be challenging such headwinds. The same was true for the day that followed. Edginess supplanted our glad expectation.

By next week, the scene of the newly reported strike at Contact Lake would be 10 minutes' plane run from Cameron Bay, but today it was as distant as Edmonton, a thousand miles away. For the past few maddening days of our more than two months' isolation we had been practically cut off from ourselves as well as from the outside world. Everyone was taut with the slivers of news that had worked their way across the hills.

The ice of Echo Bay no longer offered safe travel. A few days before, Pete Baker's dog train had plunged through the treacherous surface ahead of him. Fortunately he not only had his canoe aboard the sled, but he was sitting in the craft when the ice gave way. He picked the dogs out of the water, paddled to solid ice and drove home – riding the canoe all the way. There was a hundred feet of water where he went through.

The planes had become the only link with the Outside and we waited anxiously. With drifting ice still making other harbors hazardous for landings, there was no question that the first herald of the open season would touch down on the completely clear waters of Cameron Bay.

From the north Major Burwash and his men glided in by canoe. Gerry Woods found his way over the hills from Spark Plug Lake. Cal Mews and Fred Rainey appeared at the end of the portage, bearing wireless word from Smat that Walter Gilbert was at Resolution – waiting out the bad weather.

The tent was seldom short of dinner guests, candidates for sleeping-bag room on the floor, and fresh sources of news. Most welcome was Jack St. Paul, the rotund, dark-jowled, and vigorously cheerful brother of Charlie St. Paul, Gilbert LaBine's co-discoverer of Eldorado. Jack and his partner,

Colin Campbell, owned the ground directly north of our Echo Bay claims. They had built a cabin there and had been doing some extensive prospecting since the snow had gone. What they had found, they admitted, pleased them.

"Incidentally," said Jack, "what we like the best is mighty close to where you tie on to us. You knew what you were doing when you staked that stuff."

When at last the great day came, the birds were its heralds. I never understood their system for regulating singing and non-singing hours in a land where there was no nightfall or dawn. I took them for granted, along with the unplanned change in our own habits which, while we were in camp, found us following the sleeping routine of night club habitués. It was usually three in the morning when we put our heads down, and we got up again when we were slept out.

When we took to our bags on the morning of the 18th, the birds were probing the new day with tentative pipings. It was apparent that they were obtaining a clear echo, for the pulse of their singing took on a power and cadence it had not possessed since their return to the North. The wind, which had been twanging off-key bass notes on the spruces for the past days, reacted with lilting runs in a higher register. Swords of sunlight pierced the dull cloud cover with increasing frequency, whetting themselves on our canvas roof. It was difficult to sleep. The ear was too wakeful.

Most of us were up for the conventional breakfast hour, though work beyond the limits of the settlement had been abandoned and that which was done within it was mostly the fidgeting of hands trying to conceal their tension. We sat around and told stories, but even that seemed unimportant. Sentences ended half-spoken in the listening silence.

Noonday arrived. The sky was now completely clear and the birds moved unnoticed about the domestic business they must complete in the short and urgent season allowed them. The sounds and silences of the morning were broken by the rattle of stoves being stoked and the sizzle of frying pans. The odors of cooking, heavenly in their effect a few days earlier, now had a little more impact on the senses than the evergreen perfume of the hillside. Lunch was made to kill time – to do something because there was nothing else to do.

Then it was there, a buzz at first so faint that it was an indistinguishable note in the low-key insect chorus that had developed with the falling of the wind. It might have been a bad-tempered bulldog fly displaying a mounting determination to storm the screen on Murphy Services' front door. But it continued with a greater persistence than any insect sound – rising and falling, departing and returning – until it touched off a sudden barrage of yells from cabin and tent.

"It's here!"

Eager men spurted from every door, ran downhill through the haphazard alleys and converged on the point, where there was an unlimited view to the south. The sight of the speck above the Southwest Arm's handsome mountains was, in a way, anti-climactic. Emotion had struck initially through the ear and we were still concentrating on sound, even when the dot in the sky enlarged and a blue and gold Fokker took shape – even when it soared above us in an exploratory pass, identifying itself with the big "G-CASL" painted on its wings and flank. The roar of its single engine, filling the bay with thunder, was the real climax of the arrival.

When the pontoons had kissed the water and the machine taxied close to shore, we recognized Andy Cruickshank at the controls. He pointed the plane towards the arc of sand that offered natural shelter on the northern edge of the settlement. As we stood waiting to greet him, I realized that this was the very spot where the mink had confronted us when Beck and I had been the only residents of the townsite. That had been just a month ago! It seemed like half a lifetime.

Some of the sparkle went out of the occasion when Andy, urged to land the mail almost as soon as the floats nosed onto the sand, announced, "Sorry, boys. No delivery today."

Postal Inspector Hale, he explained, was at Resolution, on his way in to establish an official post office at Cameron Bay. The accumulated letters of the in-between season would be coming in with him, to make the opening really memorable. The reaction was savage. Everyone roared disapproval.

It was something, though, to have a word-of-mouth account of the Outside. Andy and Harry King, his engineer, did their best to oblige when they were paraded to Murphy Services' restaurant and cut in on the half-finished lunch. Their intention, they said, was to return to Fort Rae as soon as their express cargo was unloaded and to be back before the day was out with the first of their passengers. We tried to remember they were men in a hurry and to give them a chance to down their lunch, but there were so many questions that clamored for at least brief answers that it wasn't easy. That they managed to eat at all was something of an accomplishment.

Cruickshank, fortunately, had been a Mounted Policeman in the Yukon for a few years after the war and had retained a clipped, matter-of-fact ability to report essentials. The Outside, he said, was still very much in the grip of the Depression. It was worse, if anything, than it had been before the in-between season. Great Bear had been taking a merciless battering from the gloom-and-doom financial experts in the Eastern newspapers.

"About the only other thing worth mentioning," grinned Andy between passes at his caribou steak, "is that there is a crowd of people waiting air passage from McMurray or boating down the Mackenzie who don't seem to have read the experts."

He personally delivered the first of the men of faith before the day was out, winging back to Rae and landing three passengers at Cameron Bay that evening. Two of them were of my own age, prospectors named Charlie White and Carl McKee. The third, also a prospector, was an erect, white-haired man whose eyes snapped humorously through steel-rimmed spectacles. When he jumped ashore from the pontoon it was with a sure and agile foot, though I happened to know he had reached his full Biblical time allowance, for I recognized him from my cub reporter days. He had been Assistant Superintendent J. D. Nicholson of the Alberta Provincial Police. I also remembered him from my boyhood, when he had been Sergeant Nicholson of the Northwest Mounted Police, the nemesis of some of the West's most dangerous criminals.

"J.D." had joined the Northwest Mounted Police in 1885, when the force had been enlarged to play its part against the

Riel Rebellion. It is on record that he rejoined in 1939 when the intelligence branch of the RCMP was reinforced for its role in the second world war. But he had much more than durability. This was plain within hours of his landing at Cameron Bay.

Gerry Murphy was his host on the first night but, in the morning, J.D. scouted the ground with a long-experienced eye and picked his campsite. It was a beautiful spot on the edge of the park-like plateau just above the cluster of downslope dwellings.

Halfway through the raising of his tent he glanced about him sharply. Something obviously was missing. He was thoughtful for a few moments, then headed into the bush with his axe and returned with a tall, straight timber. His labor over it in the next half-hour was mystifying but we kept our distance and our counsel. J.D.'s sense of humor was genuine, but if you pushed it too far you ran into the austerity of a top-flight policeman.

When the pole was skinned and white, the grizzled worker raised it before the framework of his tent, sinking its butt into a hole that ended quickly at the permafrost, then bracing it with rocks. He stood back and examined it carefully, making certain it rose at an exact angle of 90 degrees to the ground. Finally he went to his packsack, produced a small object and, returning to the pole busied himself at its base.

From the edge of the clearing we saw the object climb the pole as Nicholson manipulated a line and pulley. At the mast's peak there was a sudden burst of color as the breeze caught the released folds of a Union Jack. It was the first flag we had seen unfurled at Great Bear and its brilliance, against the deeper shades of the background, was startling.

J.D., ramrod straight, stood back and regarded the banner silently for a moment. Then he returned to work on the tent. Every evening while he remained at Cameron Bay, the bunting was lowered, and every morning it broke anew at the masthead.

13

A human deluge was not long in following Andy Cruikshank in, though there was a hiatus of 24 hours in which only Walter Gilbert showed up, flying his favorite Fokker "SK". I had reason to be grateful for the interlude. Not only had Walter been able to filch one of my home letters from the officially delayed mail, but he was under instruction to scout the landing conditions in other parts of the field and invited me to go along.

An offshore wind at LaBine Point had cleared the bay of ice and we were able to have a quick look at Eldorado and to enjoy supper with Charlie LaBine. Next we looked in at Contact Lake. George Moody, exhibiting the typical mining engineer's restraint, showed us the silver samples he had been blowing out of the hillside. Compared to what we'd seen at Eldorado they were modest, but to a man who had been unsuccessfully peering through a magnifying glass for the slightest trace of precious metal in his own samples, the fernlike patterns of native silver stood out like bullion.

Around midnight we dropped in on another inland lake, a lonely place large enough for landings and takeoffs but meaningless within my knowledge of the field. Walter was happily mysterious about it until he had beached "SK" briefly, landed for a short walk along the shore, then taken off again for Cameron Bay. By that time I had worked things out for myself.

"That didn't give you much chance to prospect those claims," I said.

The aviator chuckled. "No," he agreed, "but I've got someone who'll do it this summer. Same boys who staked them for me last year."

Later I asked, "If it's any of my business, what did you accomplish by that visit?"

Walter, seldom at a loss for an answer, looked more boyish than usual. "I guess it does something for you to be on your own ground," he said finally, "even if only for a few minutes." He regarded me suspiciously. "OK, have your laugh."

I assured him it was no laughing matter. I told him how I had felt when, returning from our trip east, I had encountered the corner posts of our Echo Bay claims.

"It's not as though the ground really belonged to you," I said. "You know it will lapse someday unless it brings in a mine. But somehow it gets a tighter hold than land you own outright. It's like being handed a chunk of Canada and told to see what you can do with it."

"You're a sentimentalist," Walter told me. "I'm practical."

"Write me a letter," I returned, "when you've worked out the practical value of the visit we just made to your claims."

June 20 was a day of constant turmoil and excitement. Punch Dickins arrived with Walter Hale and a deluge of mail. With the general hullabaloo and the writing of letters to go out with Andy in the morning, I was at my typewriter until after midnight.

Among the arrivals was one of the team responsible for most of us being at Great Bear. Charlie St. Paul was slender, middle-aged and quiet. He showed no instinct to trade on his fame as Gilbert LaBine's partner, seeking anonymity among his fellow prospectors. It told something of his character that a good deal of the small fortune Eldorado brought him eventually went into a game preserve near Kazabazua, his native village north of Ottawa. Here he granted protection to a number of moose, elk and deer behind miles of high wire fence.

Gilbert LaBine, I knew, was the antithesis of his partner. Powerfully built, with aggressive features, he was very much the man in command and made sure everyone knew it.

On June 21, the camp was again a boiler factory. We received some fresh meat and vegetables and celebrated by having Punch Dickins and Hod Torrie to dinner. Hod had come in to superintend the repair of Frank Barager's plane. In the evening a party got under way. For the first time since coming North I dipped into the booze. I didn't get tight, though, largely because Beck *did*. He started talking in a way that threatened all our future staking plans.

Like many a quiet man after he has hung on a good one, Beck made up for past silences. Little we had done or hoped to do escaped his loosened tongue around the campfire that night. As it happened, no direct harm was done to the Beck Syndicate. But I reacted strongly. It was as if Beck had deliberately sabotaged everything we had dreamed and labored for.

It was understandable that I should be on edge. The mail from home had triggered anxiety. The hardships in Edmonton were as great as ever, though Ernie's faith that they would soon be alleviated by good news from the North had been firm. I yearned to justify her trust and confidence.

Under these circumstances, Beck's indiscretion aroused the specter of disaster. My thoughts raced from anger and frustration to rebellion. If there was one last thing I did as a member of the Beck Syndicate, it would be to fill my 1932 licenses!

The next day I announced my decision. I tried to do it quietly but my voice was unsteady and melodramatic before I was through.

"I'm going to put in those 18 claims even if I have to do it on my own," I declared, "and I'm going to start on the stuff near Eagle Nest Lake. I know you don't think it's any good and I know I haven't got the experience to contradict you, but I've got a hunch about it and I'm damned if I'm going to let those licences go to waste."

Beck's head might still have been aching. He seemed more pained than angry. When he spoke, he was surprisingly dispassionate. "If that's the way you want it, I guess that's the way it will be. There's no need to go alone, though. I'd like another look at that country. We can pull out tomorrow."

So we struck out. Once again we were fortunate in making a quick passage to the end of Bay 66. White and McKee, the two young prospectors who had flown in with Cruickshank, brought us a letter of introduction and we had done what we could to acquaint them with the field as we knew it. They had a canoe coming in by water but it would be well into July before it arrived, and in the meantime they had every intention of making the most of being early on the ground. They had rented one of Murphy Services' whipsawed skiffs and were taking off for Contact Lake. We were invited to go along as far as Bay 66.

The advantages of water travel over backpacking were strongly impressed on us as we rowed on a straight course past the shoreline across which we had so recently struggled to Cameron Bay. By the time we grounded at the end of Bay 66, Beck had made a deal with our companions. We would join forces for the next few days, they supplying the boat and we the experience of the country out east. Eric explained that we already had our eye on ground we intended to stake but, apart from that, each party would have first claim on anything it turned up.

The mile-long portage to Contact Lake was well defined, with not too severe a slope. For all its heavy hand-hewn timbers, the skiff was a manageable burden. The problem was not its weight, but the fact that it occupied both hands of the carriers beneath it, leaving no way to deal with the mosquitoes.

In the early days of their appearance, the insects had been fat, languid and generally good-natured. Now they had turned tireless and vicious. When they swarmed beneath the upturned skiff they took full advantage of a man's inability to retaliate. The screened comfort of George Moody's headquarters at the end of the portage was an unusually welcome haven.

But there was more than shelter from the flies. Visiting was our old friend Turcotte, late of Lindsley Bay. Even bundled in his winter gear, the French Canadian offered little wind resistance, but in his summer outfit he seemed almost entirely lacking in physical substance. What there was of him, though, was catgut on a steel frame and the warmth and liveliness of his personality was enough for six men.

He traveled with us the greater part of the next day, heading for one of the smaller lakes on the way to Eagle Nest.

A larger man would have made our total load more than the skiff could handle. As it was we were left with less than an inch and a half of freeboard. The water was glassy, though, and Turcotte, apart from being a powerful oarsman, was, as usual, traveling light. From the insignificant bulge of his packsack one might have suspected that he depended on a miniature magician's kit for his food and shelter.

Three short portages and two small lakes beyond the inner end of Contact we parted from our nimble-tongued friend. When we reached the outer limit of the terrain in which portages were practicable, we cached the skiff and began a hard tramp across the hills. There was no stopping until we had reached one of our earlier campsites near Eagle Nest. It had taken us three days to reach there originally. Thanks to the skiff and our better knowledge of the country we were just 24 hours out of Cameron Bay.

Like ourselves, White and McKee were the field party for a syndicate. They had been largely grubstaked by railwaymen from the Edson CNR divisional point west of Edmonton, and miners from the adjoining Coal Branch. Carl McKee had been a locomotive fireman far enough down the seniority list that the Depression had squeezed him out of a job. He was a tall, modest man who appeared to be more naive than he actually was. Charlie White was stocky, somewhat older, and had been around. He talked readily, confidently, and had had a good deal to do with the organizing of the syndicate.

They had an excellent outfit. It was built around a light, easily rigged tent, with a sewn-in floor and a sensible netting arrangement at the entrance. Within a few minutes of slipping our packs this canvas shelter was available. The insects that had infiltrated it were eliminated by a few shots of repellant, after which perfect peace reigned inside. Though the whining torment had not, even yet, reached its peak, Beck and I had already had enough experience of doubling up under a single flybar to deeply appreciate the sanctuary provided by our traveling companions.

On June 25 it rained heavily as we broke camp and moved over to the location of our prospective claims. We did some prospecting despite attacks by the mosquitoes. Eric grew positively glum over the worthlessness of the stuff. To my inexpert eye the vein looked better all the time. Again we had a wonderful respite from the insects at night, though they roared like a breaking surf outside the tent.

Next day, the Doris block of six claims (named for John Sydie's wife) went in after a hard burst of work and I was in a much better humor despite my bitten and burning hands and face. We started early and it was 8 P.M. when I finally dragged into camp after running the last line. The mosquitoes were absolutely blinding as I put in the final posts at the lakeside. We probably would have staked more but White and McKee were eager to get back and, as we were dependent on their boat, their word was law. The relief of crawling into the clear air of the tent after the mosquito-filled swamps was enormous. There was an outcrop of sharp rock under me but I slept like a top.

McKee and I had taken to each other readily, particularly after we had talked for a couple of evenings and found how much we had in common. Carl had felt completely secure in his job firing the big locomotives that worked the steep grades into the mountains out of Edson. The loss of his work and income hit him hard.

When the Edson Coal Branch syndicate was organized, he had friends among the railwaymen who still had money to gamble on such a venture. This, rather than any knowledge of prospecting, had earned Carl his place on the field staff. The syndicate had raised enough money to pay their prospectors modest salaries, and he was in a better position than I. His faith in Great Bear's future was almost as great as my own.

There was not the same empathy between White and Beck. Eric was normally as reticent as Charlie was breezy, and this became more marked when the fine points of prospecting were under discussion. Beck later remarked that if White ever made a strike, chance would have a very heavy hand in it.

Clambering back over the hills to retrieve the skiff on June 27, we became painfully aware that blackflies had joined the mosquitoes. Of the two, the mosquitoes were the kindlier. They at least signaled their attacks. The flies worked in silence, with delayed-action venom. Again we were thankful for George Moody's refuge when we reached Contact Lake.

George took me aside after dinner. "I don't know what your staking plans are," he said quietly, "but we've been making an interesting discovery around here. The idea that there's nothing worth looking at in the granite just isn't so. We've been prospecting the south side of the lake more thoroughly than we did last year. The granite's still there, right along the length of the shore, but it's not as solid as it looks. There's some interesting stuff intruding. We've thrown in a group of claims almost straight across the lake from here. You could do worse than tie on to us."

There I was with an urgent need to fill my 12 licenses and ground recommended by a bona fide mining engineer had been laid practically at our feet!

I managed to get Beck in a corner, and passed him the word. He, in turn, isolated George for professional discussion. When he rejoined me he was in the grip of one of his rare bursts of enthusiasm.

"It sounds good," he declared. "In the morning we'd better tie a dozen wildcats onto George's staking. Once the word gets out there is promising stuff in the granite, this place will be plastered."

"How about White and McKee?"

"It's their break, too. Our agreement with them still stands. We've decided to stake 12 claims tying on to the Contact Lake Mines group. The rest of the south shore is theirs."

Within minutes, our traveling companions were gripped by the same fever. They agreed to our prior claim to the ground adjacent to Moody's. It had already been a long hard day by land and water, but the decision to get moving immediately was a unanimous one.

We launched the skiff and a short pull carried us to an almost naked point of rock directly across the lake from the mining camp. Here Beck and I landed.

"We'll just mosey along the south shore till we see something that's worth a gamble," said White. "How soon do you want us to come back and pick you up?"

"Two days should do it," answered Beck. "We haven't got enough grub to do any serious prospecting, so once we take a quick look we'll start tying on. Come back here in 48 hours."

When our comrades shoved off, their oars dipping in the molten pathway cast by the midnight sun, we had a sense of freedom and the satisfaction any prospector feels when he has a promising piece of ground to himself. But we regretted losing use of the green, mosquito-proof tent.

The terrain back of the rocky finger on which we landed was a clutter of pond-sized lakes, dismal swamps and a forest of tangled undergrowth. There was a great deal of overburden, ideal breeding ground for every vicious form of insect life. The bugs had made the most of it. To brave this jungle we were equipped with one sleeping bag, one flybar and our new-found optimism. They turned out to be dismally inadequate.

We rigged the flybar as close to Contact Lake as possible after locating a spot level enough to make a bed. We hoped for a helpful breeze. The water, however, was still as a mirror. Undisturbed by the slightest current of air, the mosquitoes and flies closed in on us, an arrogant army with unlimited time to harrass its enemy.

A flybar is a tent of sorts – a canvas roof with draped walls of netting, just big enough to be suspended over a single sleeper. It is supposed to be a secondary line of defence, something to guard its owner from the occasional infiltrator which has managed to invade the main protection of tent or cabin. In our case, it faced the massive attack on its own.

It might have offered some serious protection for one man, but with two under it, the situation was hopeless. We lay with the tarp under us on a mattress of spruce boughs and uneven rock. The opened-out sleeping bag was over us. The fringes of the netting lay loosely on top of the sleeping bag, offering numerous tunnels and gateways into our stronghold. The enemy lost no time exploiting them.

Not every attacker got inside the bar. Great, black sheets of bugs were plastered in almost unbroken ranks on the outside of the netting, keening with frustration, or possibly encouraging those who had penetrated our defences.

In darkness the sight would have been bad enough, but in the full light of midnight it was ghastly. Each time a few minutes of fitful slumber ended in feverish wakefulness, the first thing that met the eye was a field of bloated mosquitoes hanging from the inner surface of the flybar's roof. On each awakening, I could see that their numbers had risen. These were the storm troops who had taken all they could of Beck and Watt blood. They hung like clusters of red grapes.

Earlier in the season, we had experimented with fly-dope brought from Outside and found it to be more trouble than it was worth, running off quickly with our perspiration, stinging our eyes and making a general mess that was harder to take than any bites it prevented. We had settled on using a large bandana handkerchief, drawn around the face and up under the hat brim, with only a slit open to see out of. It was a stifling arrangement in hot weather, but it reduced the area of bare skin. Now, under the flybar, we remembered the dope. In this extreme situation, it might be useful after all. Unhappily we also remembered we had left it behind at Cameron Bay.

Beck wearied of taking this punishment lying down and lit a smudge. The utterly still air, however, caused the smoke to rise in a small, neat plume, which failed to spread to where it would do any good. Standing over it was useless. The smoke was so concentrated it made us choke.

When Eric returned inside the bar we launched a blitz. The miniature grapes on the ceiling were bloodily crushed, even though they were too sated to do us further harm, and every active mosquito or blackfly we could locate inside our coffin-like sleeping space was hunted down individually and killed. There were a few minutes in which we knew comparative peace – but only a few. Fresh legions crawled under our walls and the carnage resumed.

The final ordeal was caused by another bug species which up to this time had remained neutral. We felt movement inside our clothes. At first this was only mildly irritating but when we scratched, the new enemy launched sharp assaults on tender portions of the body which had previously escaped attack. The bites had authority. When we threw back the bag to seek out the new enemy we discovered that the parachutists had been joined by ground troops. Ants!

They had come primarily for the corpses of the flying bugs. Most of them were dragging away dead mosquitoes and flies, but the proximity of warm human flesh had obviously been too much for the carnivorous instincts of others. Or perhaps they were just counter-attacking after our attempts to squash them. Whatever their motive, they provided the climax to a night of utter misery. It was a relief to crawl out from the bloody hell beneath the flybar at 6 A.M. Much of our staking that day was in the swamps, and the flies continued to harass us, rising in clouds that at times stifled and blinded us. Their poisons were eating into us.

Somehow the "Silverex" group was completed: 12 claims which used up all my licenses, leaving me with a clear conscience. I was satisfied that the syndicate had a group which would sell quickly, since it tied onto Contact Lake property and was directly across the lake from a strike. As we battled the flies all day, we comforted ourselves with the thought that White would soon be back and that we would either sleep in the tent again or head directly for home. But he didn't show up and we turned in for another ghastly night beneath the bar.

On June 30 we loafed all morning, keeping to the rocky point where the flies weren't so bad, and waiting for the others to arrive. This they did at two o'clock, having staked 15 claims and run out of grub and tobacco.

We rowed home in waves too heavy for safety considering the big load and the inadequate boat. Our run down Contact Lake's eight-mile length was foolhardy. The wind was strong and we had a following wash. It would have taken only one of the long swells, breaking over the stern, to swamp the boat with its infinitesimal freeboard. We did, in fact, take occasional dollops of water but they slopped in amidships as a wave, sliding along the beam like a lazy sea-serpent raising its back, tipping a quart or two inboard in a grimly playful gesture.

The temperature of the lake was still barely above the freezing point. We should have stayed close to shore to have a fighting chance of swimming for it should we be dumped. But our caution was gone. The wind was blowing us home and the oars were required more for steering than propulsion. We drove straight down the middle of the lake, careless of the dwindling shoreline as we chose the shortest distance between two points. Every mile was another mile away from the whining purgatory of flies on the "Silverex" group.

Only when we reached the end of the lake did we realize how steep the waves really were. They charged against the shore in noisy, frothing rollers. The beach was something rare in that country – a stretch of sand over which the water gradually shallowed. Shouting with mingled relief and excitement, we gave the oars everything we had and surged through the breakers until the bottom of the skiff came to rest as softly as if it touched foam rubber.

The flies had one more go at us. The portage from Contact Lake to the Southwest Arm of Echo Bay was a mile long and very steep. The experience of carrying the skiff over it was the worst of its sort I have ever known. When we reached the Arm the exposed part of each man's face – the band between hat brim and bandana mask – was one great welt. Our eyes were sunk in puffed, red pockets, as though they had taken a physical beating. In my own case at least they were also inflamed by tears. Helpless and hand-tied under the skiff, I silently wept in an agony of exhausted nerves.

Our luck returned when we were crossing Echo Bay. The wind dropped and Gossan Island broke the force of the heavy waves. At the end of the three-mile pull, the chimneys of Cameron Bay signaled dinnertime.

There was a letter awaiting me saying that my father was seriously ill.

It was a nasty conclusion to a soul-shaking day. I was numb with weariness, insect bites and a brain that turned over like a motor missing on three cylinders. Wop May came in to visit, but I was barely aware of him.

It seemed only fair that such an investment in blood, sweat and tears should ultimately bring its reward. It did. In August White and McKee found pitchblende on their Contact Lake claims.

14

I had been too tired to wash before turning in and woke to an unpleasant awareness of the dirt, sweat and dried blood all over me. Once I was launched on a cleanup, I had a strong urge to make a job of it. Not only did I take a full scale sponge bath – even the smaller lakes were far too frigid for a dip – but, shifted to clean clothes, I found myself coming to an even more drastic decision. The time had come to shave off my beard.

It was a fine apostolic growth, having had its own way since we had left Fort McMurray in February. There would have been some discomfort in removing it under any circumstances, but the raw flesh resulting from our recent war with the flies was unusually touchy. When the ordeal was over I felt more skinned than shaven.

Looking at myself in a small, steel mirror hung on a tree, I became reacquainted with a face that seemed to belong to the past. But whatever thoughts I might have had were interrupted by the silent arrival of Wop May. He was on his way to the red Bellanca beached below our tent. I braced myself for his sarcastic comment, but none came.

"You look better than you did last night," he said flatly.

Billy Nadin, his slight, plain-spoken engineer, moved past us towards the plane but Wop stayed where he was. He was obviously disturbed. I knew his moods well enough to realize he had more than a balky engine or a laggardly passenger on his mind. There were times when he responded best to patience, and this seemed to be one of them. Finally he spoke abruptly.

"Andy's overdue."

It took time for it to sink in. Then I asked, "How long?"

"This is the third day."

"Where?"

"Between here and Rae. Southbound."

"Anybody with him except Harry?"

"Yes," said Wop. "Hod Torrie."

I could only answer with silence.

"He'd got Frank Barager's plane flying again," the airman went on jerkily. "Didn't have to come in to do it – could have sent someone else – but you know Hod. Worked around the clock and we told him to lay up here for a day or so before he went back to McMurray. But not Hod. He had to get back to his bloody base."

"Three days isn't much in this country," I offered. I was an amateur venturing to tell a professional his business. "Glyn was adrift longer – and he was only 20 miles from a settlement. The McAlpine crowd – well, you know more about it than I do."

"Sure," said Wop. "I know."

"A man's seldom out of gliding distance of a lake if his engine packs up on the Rae run."

"Sure," the flyer repeated woodenly. "Well, I'd better go and find them."

It was difficult to say how many men in Cameron Bay already knew Andy was missing. Wop had told Gerry Murphy, but, apart from Murphy's military preciseness being a bit more marked, he acted no differently than he did on any other day. Tim Ramsey probably knew about it, too. But whatever the number of men who knew, each held his tongue, and for good reason. If the news became generally known it would quickly find its way Outside and upset the families of the missing men. When Wop returned next day, most of Cameron Bay was still ignorant of what was worrying him.

When May's brightly colored monoplane pulled in to the

beach this time, though, the suspicion that something was amiss quickly spread through the settlement. Perhaps it was touched off by Wop's expression, perhaps by the fact that "Tommy" Thompson, Western Canada Airways' superintendent, was with him. In any event, one thing led to another and within half an hour the entire camp was sharing the disquieting news.

May remained no longer than it took to refuel, then swept back to his search along the route to Rae. Only after he had disappeared beyond the Southwest Arm did I realize I was involved in something which touched more than my friendship for the men in "SL". I was also a newspaperman and this was a developing story. Not only was a plane missing, but the pilot's name was already well known to the reading public. Andy had made headlines on many search missions.

I sought out Thompson and pointed out my dilemma. He was brisk but understanding.

"Naturally, it's up to you," he said. "It's news and you're the only reporter on the ground. No one can blame you for wanting to break it." He paused. "What's on your mind?"

"If I thought it would be possible to keep it from leaking Outside," I said, "I'd hold it till there's something more definite to tell. Do you think your people could sit on it?"

"They had succeeded by the time I came North yesterday," said Thompson. "Not a line's appeared anywhere and that was three days after we had the first word he was down."

"Would you wireless them that it's my exclusive the moment you know Andy's safe – or whatever happens?"

"Certainly," Thompson agreed. "I can't give you any guarantee it won't get away from us, of course."

"Do your best," I said. "I'll take a chance."

It rained heavily that night and kept it up the following day. A series of bad-tempered thunderstorms rode the sky, obviously impeding the search to the south and putting further strain on already taut nerves at Cameron Bay. As the evening wore on, a bridge game began in the restaurant. There were excellent players – Robinson and Erickson, the McIntyre-Porcupine mining engineers; Tim Ramsey; Doc Robertson – but it was a desultory contest.

Our game was broken up shortly before midnight when Walter Gilbert and Con Farrell roared in through the rain. There'd been no sign of Andy but Lou Parmenter, who was flying with Con, believed he had seen a wrecked ship near Fabre Lake. Both pilots were dead tired, having been flying on and off since 5 A.M. I thought they were convinced that Andy had cracked up badly, though they refused to admit it – even to themselves.

I turned in at 3 A.M., but couldn't sleep. I remembered what it was like during our nights on Contact Lake. We had a certain amount of protection there and healthy hands with which to slap the flies. What would it be like to be badly injured and at their mercy for five days?

The next morning I was up early to write a story for release in case our worst fears were realized. I also sent a wireless to the Journal warning that the story was liable to break at any moment. The fliers pulled out to check on what Lou Parmenter had seen. Gerry went out with them for a quick trip to Edmonton and offered to cover the story for me if they found anything.

The vigil ended next day. There was no need to ask questions when Wop May taxied into Cameron Bay after droning in from the south. The tight set of his lips was enough. There were none of the customary greetings tossed between ship and shore as the machine slid towards the beach. Bill Nadin, standing on a pontoon with a heaving line in his hand, caught the unspoken question from the waiting knot of men. He simply spread his hands in the "washout" signal of airmen and looked away. A low "damn" was drawn from one of the bystanders. The rest of us remained silent.

Wop had little to offer after he landed and nobody pressed him. For that matter, there was little to tell. Farrell had flown directly back to the place near Fabre Lake where Lou Parmenter had spotted the unpleasantly suggestive break in the landscape while they were dodging rain squalls. "SL" was piled on a rock slope, a complete wreck.

It was obvious that its three occupants had died instantly. There had been no drawn-out suffering. The cause of the crash was never clearly established. It was possible that an eagle or other large bird had exploded through the wind-screen. From the appearance of the wreck and its location, the pilot might have been seeking the safety of a nearby lake for a landing, but had failed to make it by a matter of two or three hundred yards.

Wop was going Outside and flew my story to Edmonton. By that time it had little to convey except local color. The news had broken the day Canadian Airways had word of the wreck's discovery.

Very early on the morning after the blow had fallen I was wakened by the whine of an outboard motor drifting up Echo Bay. It was a common enough sound now but I became inexplicably curious about this one. Though I had slept little I was instantly alert. When the boat rounded the point I was the only man on the beach to greet it.

The pilot was one of the McLaren boys from Smat. As I pulled the bow up on the sand he grinned and asked, "How did you know? Been pacing the floor all night?"

"About what?" I asked sourly.

"About this," he answered. He handed me an envelope from the wireless station.

It had been filed in Edmonton four days earlier but the bad weather had discouraged anyone from boating down The Labrador from Smat. McLaren had brought a number of other delayed messages. It seemed somehow right that mine should have been the first delivered. I had been the father of a new son since July 2. Joy crowded in on my sorrow and I was useless for work that day.

Bill Jewitt flew in to look over our Echo Bay claims and decide if Consolidated would be interested in them. Beck, who had just acquired a 13-foot canoe from a man who was leaving the field, paddled Bill around the shoreline to the property and they were there the greater part of the day. When they returned, the mining engineer was predictably uncommunicative about his impressions.

I was surprisingly free of the tension I had expected to feel over this visit, even though a representative of the colossus of the Canadian mining industry was passing judgment on what we had to offer.

After Jewitt had taken off for Glacier Bay, Beck and I attempted to discuss the day's visit. Beck picked his way carefully through an account of what had happened on the claims, but I had learned little when he finished. This might have been a big day for our syndicate, but its field party was falling apart.

Soon we lapsed into the silence that had become typical of the time we were compelled to spend together. Then I remembered something. From the bottom of my pack I unearthed the cigar box. There were still two Havanas in it, saved ever since the evening on De Melt Cove when I had announced, "After tonight we smoke our pipes. These last two panatellas are going into reserve until there's something to celebrate."

Now I took one out, rolled it between my fingers, smelled it. It had kept well. I offered it to Eric. He accepted it, carefully cut the tip with his hunting knife and lit it. When I had followed suit we lounged on our bags, shoulders resting against the packsacks at the head of each bed. The smoke drifted out the open door, blue and fragrant.

Occasionally our eyes met – baffled, sad, hurt, angry. The newborn child in Edmonton was a powerful influence in Great Bear that night. I found myself thinking, "Something new has begun with the birth of my son. Perhaps something new could start here." The cigars brought back memories of the hard, happy evenings when the box had first been opened. But I could not find words to express these thoughts. The graying cigars slowly fell to ashes. There was nothing left to do but to burrow into our sleeping bags.

The following day, Beck went to the claims to do some tagging and mounding. I turned to the eternal chore of restoring the woodpile. The source of supply had now moved well back from the settlement. Not only were there many stoves drawing on it but Murphy, the unelected mayor, had declared the lovely nearby plateau a park, to be preserved in perpetuity for public events and the aesthetic stimulation of the new metropolis. Woodcutters had agreed to pass it up and go beyond for dry timber.

There was no hardship in the extra trek that day. It was fine, windless weather and the pride of fatherhood was upon me. Even with the long carry back to the tent, the woodpile was in excellent shape by noon.

Just after lunch I heard what seemed to be the sound of a plane roaring over the heights to the west. Machines occasionally appeared from that direction, the noise of their approach subdued by the walls of rock and trees until they were almost above the bay. No one paid much attention to the sound until one man leaped up from his meal, pointed up the hillside and yelled, "Look!"

The sound we had been hearing was combustion, all right. But it wasn't coming from any airplane engine. Flames were leaping in a stand of evergreens a couple of hundred yards from the edge of the town. They were taking a tree at a time, running up each resinous mast in almost rhythmic order. The devil might have been cavorting through the woods touching off a display of great Roman candles. It was a fearsome sound and sight, tearing through the noonday calm.

Cameron Bay had no fire brigade as such, but it was rich in talent. Most of the population were veterans of this too-familiar woodland peril. The shout of *"fire"* was barely out before every man in the place was in motion, grabbing the handiest axe or shovel as he ran.

The speed with which the firefighters reached the threatened holocaust, the skill with which they surrounded it, the deftness with which they isolated it with firebreaks where it would otherwise have run wild, were amazing. Men who were obviously accustomed to command in such situations took charge automatically. Others, new to the drill, responded with discipline. In a matter of minutes the last sparks were being buried in sand or painstakingly extinguished with buckets of water drawn from the lake. Only the blackened skeletons of a few flame-stripped trees stood as reminders of what could have overtaken the settlement.

Several of us had been on the hillside during the morning, all smokers whose pipes might have dropped the hot ashes which probably had given the blaze its start. Before the day was out, however, the culprit had been "identified" beyond any hope of denial. There was no investigation, no verdict brought in by democratic procedure. The circumstantial evidence, someone declared in a loud voice, was clear. The father of a new son had deliberately set the forest ablaze as a beacon to mark the event.

Everybody accepted this good-natured explanation. It was preferable to any serious attempt to fix blame on anyone, though all of us had stood to be wiped out if the fire had swept the settlement. There was need for a safety valve after the close call – and I provided it. Years passed before I heard the last of that one!

15

My responsibilities to the syndicate were now fulfilled, and I assumed I would take on my role of freelance writer. But I hadn't concerned myself much with practical detail. The questions of where I would lay my head and what I would find to fill my stomach were pertinent ones. I had no money, there was none at home to borrow, and no news agency had suggested staking me. And I couldn't just say, "To hell with it all," and head Outside. It dawned on me that it might prove harder to get out than it had been to get in.

Beck and I, the field force, had been in frequent communication with the headquarters of Beck Syndicate since touch had been re-established with the Outside, but reception had been garbled. Eric and I wrote separately to John Sydie and he, the harrassed organizer, became quickly aware of our civil war. He maintained diplomatic relations with us individually.

One point he made perfectly clear was that money was still as hard to find Outside as highgrade ore had been on our claims. The Canadian economy remained prostrate. The hope of quick cash for our snowshoe staking had yet to be realized, and such adventurous capital as did exist tended towards outfits which at least had some modest showings of precious metal.

The state of Beck Syndicate's exchequer was best indicated

by the fact that the overweight supplies we had been compelled to leave at Fort McMurray were still there, doubtless awaiting a guarantee that air freight charges would be paid. If there were no funds to bring the needed supplies in, there would be none to bring me, the prospector's assistant, out.

Beck declared his intention of remaining North for the open season regardless of what happened at the other end.

"There's nothing for me Outside," he said. "I've got a stake in the syndicate and, as long as there's something to eat, I might as well carry on. If I start going hungry I can always get a job with one of the other outfits here. Meanwhile I think I'll go up and look at those islands we staked in Lindsley Bay. I'll leave you enough grub to carry on with for awhile."

There was nothing in his voice to suggest that there might be a place for me on this trip even if I asked to go along. I didn't know whether I was relieved or resentful. I knew it was no longer reasonable for us to go into the bush together. Yet I was haunted by the days when we had worked as one. The thought that those times were finished was almost as punishing as the thought of what it would be like to face them again.

The division of cooking gear gave us the most trouble. We had no more equipment than a single man would normally require. In the end, Beck took the bulk of it, since I would be near other campers, and could scrounge what I needed. He decided against taking the tent when he considered the weight to which he was already committed on the portages.

He asked me to make him a batch of bannock for the trip. You need two frying pans to make bannock properly. One is fitted over the other, creating a sort of oven in which the heat of the open fire can be retained as the dough bakes. I had become handy at bannock-making, and I took special pains with this batch. The thought that it was the last time the two skillets would be working together was a melancholy one.

Eric had the canoe loaded by the time my contribution to his grub-sack was ready. The little 13-foot Peterborough was too small for the outside passage to Lindsley Bay, but light enough for a single man to carry if he went by way of the portage. When he had backwatered from the shore, he pointed the bow towards the great trench between the hills and the three stepping-stone lakes we had explored.

"Well," he said across the widening lane of water, "so long."

"So long," I answered.

It was as casual as that.

July 10 was a Sunday but there was no Sabbath calm on Cameron Bay. Planes arrived and departed almost continuously. Wop May arrived with a big batch of mail which brought me a complete run-down on my new son. There was no information whatever on the state of the syndicate. I decided I might as well be philosophical about that. As the tempo of life at the settlement quickened there was much to write about.

Canada's infant air force was now hard at work resuming the aerial mapping of the territory and servicing federal government parties on the ground. Formed only in 1924, with less than 400 men and some unimpressive equipment, the RCAF had found the North an excellent outlet for spirits chafing under a restricted military program and budget.

Among those spreading their wings in the Great Bear area was a tall, whip-like Flight Lieutenant called Slemon. Still under 30, he had brought an engineering degree with him when he joined the RCAF "originals". The zest, self-discipline and judgment he displayed in air-mapping 10 000 square miles became legendary. No one who knew him was greatly surprised when, in time, he became Air Marshall C.R. Slemon, Chief of Staff of the tremendously expanded air force Canada continued to maintain following the second world war.

(He was, incidentally, still young enough to be the man for the job when his country provided NORAD with its second-in-command. When the time came for him to retire in 1964 as the last RCAF "original", the president of the United States told him, "You have been a tower of strength in moments when split-second decisions were required – decisions that, had they not been adroitly taken, might well have resulted in the most devastating consequences for humanity.")

While the clearing bays were welcoming Slemon and his airborne companions in that summer of 1932, the traditional harbingers of the open season were not far behind. Though the main ice was still solid, the ubiquitous Joe Dillon, Fort Franklin behind him, came talking his way into harbor one morning. He had snaked around the south shore, following the leads of open water as they came to life in the bays. His family was with him in his large canoe and his shy Loucheux wife was the first woman on whom we had set eyes since our glimpse of Princess Galitzine five months before. Even more moving was the sight of his little daughter. I realized that our childless community had been desperately incomplete.

A pair of voyageurs who would have stirred the admiration of Alexander Mackenzie himself steered their 21-foot freight canoe into Cameron Bay on July 7. Fred Peet and Olaf Slaatten were nearly two months out from Fort McMurray and had come by way of the tortuous route from Fort Rae to Conjuror Bay. Even allowing for their strapping physiques and unquestioned spirit, Northern veterans admitted it had been an amazing performance.

The hardest part, the bronzed young men reported, had been crossing Great Slave Lake. They had made a fast start down the already-clear Athabasca and Slave rivers but from Resolution to Rae the still-extensive ice fields had kept them imprisoned for days in the middle of the lake, which is only slightly smaller than Great Bear. Leads would open, then close again quickly. At times, they measured their daily progress in feet instead of miles.

There were other delays once the prospectors had passed Rae, but they were easier to take. Pushing their way up the Marian River they encountered bands of Indians at nearly every portage. All were paddling towards the fort for the annual payment of treaty money – the modest financial acknowledgment the native people received from their white brothers in return for the northern half of the continent.

The farther Peet and Slaatten voyaged, the more impressed were the Indians when they heard how long the journey had been and where it would end. The meetings at the portages became ceremonial occasions, with each member of the band, from patriarch to papoose, lining up to shake hands. Sometimes sign language was the only means of communication and this lengthened the stops. There was one advantage to this, Slaatten explained wryly. They had considerably less tobacco to carry by the time the last of the southbound tribesmen had passed.

Later, on the Camsell, their ton of supplies had been further lightened when the canoe capsized in white water.

"We were lucky not to lose more than we did," said Peet. "The river runs mighty fast most of the way. We counted 51 portages on the two rivers – and took off on a side trip to raise it to 60."

Sixty portages and a ton to be backpacked!

They had covered the 300 miles from Rae to Echo Bay in 22 days and would have done better if their outboard motor hadn't given up just as they reached Conjuror Bay. Continuing by paddle, they were emerging into the open lake at the scene of Beck's accident when they encountered Bill Olmstead and his party returning under power from a prospecting jaunt. Slaatten and Peet got a tow to the mouth of Echo Bay.

To provide contrast for this gristle-and-guts performance, a planeload of tourists arrived from Fort Norman the following day. There were, it appeared, still people in the world with enough money to come to Great Bear out of curiosity. They took a quick boat trip down to Eldorado, were back in Cameron Bay before the day was out, and by evening they were on their way to Fort Norman and points south.

The tourists' chief virtue was that they were ferried in by Paul Calder, another Canadian Airways pilot with whom I had grown up in Edmonton. Though he was a mature flyer – another warbird – and a responsible family man, Paul had the soul of a pixie.

He had been long in the air and had found his passengers an uninspiring lot, but a couple of hours of sleep took the tired wrinkles from around his eyes and restored his normal buoyancy. Few men so rippled with the joy of living and he was excellent for my morale.

On July 14 I went to the claims for a session of tagging and mounding. For the first time in months, I had real shoe leather on my feet. My moccasins and mukluks were completely shot, and I had no choice but to climb into my boots. My feet were tired and sore at the end of the day.

On July 15, I had supper with Doc Robertson. Doc's mind had carried him over great distances and to boldly inquisitive heights and depths. He had been headed for the ministry when the war swept him into the air force. His experience in the war had left him with questions about things he once had taken for granted. The practice of medicine had seemed the most promising way to find answers to those questions. But, after his postwar graduation and a few years as a physician in an Ottawa Valley town, he had again taken to flying. Wings had taken him closest to what he was seeking.

I always felt better for his company. He was not cynical, but he punctured sham with surgical deftness. Sometimes he drew me close to honesty about what had happened at Conjuror Bay. No one else was able to do that.

The boats began to arrive on July 16. Evening brought in the *Speed II*, largest craft on the lake, with Fred Yorke in command. The decks were crawling with men. It was a scene that might have come out of a real old-time gold rush. The faces of the would-be stakers fell when they learned how far they would have to go to find open ground.

As I set about recording the arrival of the main invasion I found myself in temporary possession of a perfect working base. Canadian Airways were in the process of establishing a wireless station at Cameron Bay and the log building was practically complete. It would be empty until the equipment arrived, and was only 50 feet away from my own front door. It became my literary headquarters with the full blessing of its owners.

Working there was a vast improvement over hunching in the tent with my typewriter on my knees. I had hopes of some useful privacy. But once the flood of waterborne humanity fully developed, it swirled in and out of each habitation in the settlement. Everyone was renewing friendships, seeking information, or simply being sociable while waiting around for developments.

My plans for getting in a decent day's work went by the board. Bill Boland arrived with his boat and a scow; he was moving his trading post from Fort Franklin. With all the newcomers in camp, the place was a madhouse.

My existence was due to be further complicated. A canoe appeared at the end of Lindsley Bay portage that evening and into the deceptive calm paddled Beck. His news of the island claims he had been prospecting was not very cheering, but he had picked up a letter from John Sydie which had found its way to Smat. The syndicate, said John, was eager for me to remain for the rest of the open season and was trying hard to raise a salary which would make it worth my while to do so.

Again I was plunged into a turmoil of indecision. My comparative freedom of recent days was complicated by a returning sense of responsibility to the syndicate, and by the primitive instincts of a prospector's assistant, which were aggravated by the swelling rumor of a significant strike at Conjuror Bay.

The word was gold. Jack Borthwick, big, grizzled and businesslike, had found it. Free gold, no less! Not even pitchblende had the excitement of the yellow metal, particularly for the independent prospector. Finding other minerals meant dickering with a large established company capable of financing the massive job of recovery. But free gold was the stuff of the Klondike and other camps where the little man had often been able to bypass the giants and cash in on his own discovery. Gold has been fire in the veins of mineral-seekers throughout history.

A rush to Conjuror Bay was imminent. I was up in the air over the syndicate's offer, but I hoped Beck would go.

There was no discussion of whether I would be accompanying him if he went, though this had been an unspoken issue between us since John's letter had suggested the resumption of our active partnership. Plainly, Beck was determined to reserve comment until I made up my mind.

The quagmire of silence in which we were already so deep closed over us completely during the next two days. Sydie had not only raised the question of my remaining at Great Bear; he had indicated that the syndicate would shortly be able to fly me out if that turned out to be my wish. A mental wrestling match occupied my waking hours and haunted my dreams. It always ended with me pinned down by the ugly truth: I could not return to the bush with Beck. I hated to abandon my hopes of a find at Great Bear. I feared returning to the Outside a failure. But I could no longer work with the man in whose partnership I had once invested such great hope for financial freedom. Still, I couldn't seem to tell him, to make the clean break.

It was Eric who ended the impasse.

At midnight on July 19, he announced he would be pulling out early in the morning for a month and would take the tent with him.

At 5 A.M., Beck and others pulled out for the Conjuror Bay gold rush. I was left like a flood refugee, without a roof over my head and with a limited amount of grub. I worked all day raising my log walls and putting up the tarp from the cache as a roof. My residence was not palatial and, lacking protection against the flies, was no place to work or laze in, but it would suffice until I knew what was coming next.

On July 21, it rained hard in the early morning. My unfinished dwelling wasn't up to the job of keeping me dry. I dashed out to cover the cache and got soaked. It drizzled on and off all day. The camp was dead with so many people headed for Conjuror Bay. My spirits were low and moldy. The sleeping bag was the only warm spot, so I retired to it early.

The next morning brought sun into my open-ended pavilion. The mice and squirrels turned my house into a sort of circus in the early hours, doing acrobatics on top of the mosquito bar, fighting on the ridgepole, and stopping between rounds to refresh themselves from my slender stock of food. One mouse, in his enthusiasm, fell into my pail of boiled raisins and drowned.

This was no ordinary forest tragedy. The mouse was an old friend who had dropped in on many successive mornings to share my breakfast. I was aware he was missing long before I discovered the sad little body at dessert time the following day. If I hadn't been so hard up for food, I doubt if I could have continued eating from that particular pail of boiled raisins.

Another accident, this time involving a human at Smat, brought a hurried call for Doc Robertson. He suggested I might like to go along with him for the ride in his little Fairchild. I hadn't traversed the Lindsley Bay portage by air since McMullen had first flown us in. Seeing it again, this time with the three ice-blue lakes set in the rich fabric of the summer forest, was a bittersweet experience.

There were two wireless signals awaiting me at Smat, both from John Sydie. One announced that the delayed supplies were on their way in from McMurray. The other said that if I should decide to come Outside my passage to Edmonton could be picked up at Canadian Airways as soon as I chose to claim it.

16

I was free to leave, but I realized my involvement in what was happening at Great Bear would make that difficult. Events during the next few days made my dilemma worse.

On July 25, more men pulled out for Conjuror Bay. Charlie LaBine, George Moody and several others came by Cameron Bay and reported three fresh strikes, on which detailed news was being withheld.

On July 26, I visited our Echo Bay claims. It was hot, tricky going on the talus slopes and diabase sill of the east cliffs. The return to the mosquitoes and flies was not pleasant, but it was good to be in the field again. I came across pyrite and some quartz stringers - apparently barren - and that was all.

There was no need for me to be on the cliffs. I had fulfilled my undertaking to the syndicate and the field was pulsing with news that cried to be written. I didn't even have a prospector's pick with which to investigate any mineralization I might encounter. Yet I had been drawn back time and again to the one spot on the claims that had a frankly metallic glint.

It was a long crack in a soft, conglomerate face, heavily laden with iron. When it was attacked, even with the back of an axe-head, a stream of fine pyrites, glistening in the sun like granulated silver, separated from the porous gray and pink rock and cascaded over the horizontal sill on which I stood.

Beck had explained that in itself the stuff was valueless, but that it would probably rate further investigation when there was dynamite with which to blow the fissure open. Perhaps, deeper in the shimmering dust, there was something solid and worthy. This hadn't prevented me from battering away at the cliff with my axe every time I made one of my lone expeditions. Setting the silvery stream waterfalling over the sill to the talus slope below had become almost a ritual.

I probably had a bedraggled hope on the final visit that somewhere in the disintegrating vein of pyrite there might be a sudden collision between the steel of my axe and something more solid than fool's gold. Such things did happen. What a jolt it would hand Beck if my stubborn ignorance were to be justified! But the useless stuff streamed out uninterrupted and the blackflies feasted on. Eventually I gave up, counter-attacked my tormentors and climbed to a less precarious perch to relax and catch my breath.

Below, the inner sweep of Echo Bay was as untenanted as when I first had known it. Old hands like Jack St. Paul and Colin Campbell, who held ground in the vicinity, had joined the rush to Conjuror. Unmarked for the moment by the wake of a single boat, the long arm of Bay 66 reached peacefully into the distant hills.

I thought back to the days when these Beck and Watt claims had first been staked. From this very spot we had glimpsed the only other man who had then shared our interest in the immediate area. It had been many weeks before we finally met him face to face but by then he had become a familiar sight as, black against the snow, he limped resolutely along the edge of the distant shore.

DeMelt had told us we would probably encounter him – a Dutchman called John Herkuleyn who was staying close to the claims he had staked across the bay the previous fall. Wintering alone in a small cabin, he had damaged his big toe, which became frostbitten and then turned gangrenous. But Herkuleyn had seen no need to seek assistance. By the time his first visitor came along, his foot was healing nicely. He had, according to Ed, amputated the toe with a razor blade.

The courage of such men involved so much more than the

ability to work with another man under difficult circumstances. I had found some of their magic – had worked that way, testing myself learning a new freedom – and then lost it again. I was desperate to leave Great Bear because I had failed the ideal. Still, something in me clung to it with desperation, clung to it as I did to the hope that there was something of value behind the waterfall of iron pyrites.

But the romantic in me had been burned out.

I decided to accept the inevitable. I would take the plane back to Edmonton and hope that something of worth would eventually show up on Beck Syndicate property, to at least free me financially.

Rediscovery of the other freedom I had lost might one day come.

I had help in choosing the day of my departure. On August 4 the field would celebrate Great Bear's coming of age. There would be a founding meeting of the Great Bear Lake Prospectors' Association at Cameron Bay. In Edmonton, a planeload of the necessary refreshments was being organized. There was word that distinguished visitors would be coming in for the occasion. They would fly out again the next day.

That evening I told Canadian Airways I would be going Outside on August 5.

As if to confirm my decision, a fresh wave of progress washed me out of my office. Johnny Bythell, another of the Mackenzie air mail veterans, flew in with wireless operators McLaughlin and Rodd and the equipment which would put the Canadian Airways station on the air. Since it was going to handle general traffic as well as Airways business, this was a red letter day for most of the inhabitants. They would no longer be dependent on the government station at Smat.

I was driven back to my log and tarp dwelling.

Inadequate though it might be as a workroom, the primitive home had its attractions. Not only was it the playground of the squirrels, mice, hornets and whisky jacks, it was also the gathering place for many other untrammeled spirits. Its open-air architecture seemed to be conducive to good fellowship. Almost everybody dropped in.

July 24 was a typical day. There was no mail, although the

camp was full of men expecting it. My makeshift house was full and busy with half the Contact Lake gang in for lunch and supper. It was fun repaying their past hospitality in my crude quarters. Earl Harcourt and Billy Graham arrived that night, with 2100 miles of canoe travel between them and Edmonton.

Harcourt in later years commanded a transportation system which reached out to all the navigable waters of the upper third of Canada. Ships of his Yellowknife Transportation Company sailed from Pacific coast ports to Point Barrow and found their way to the Mackenzie River system from the Arctic Ocean. He built others on the shores of the waterway itself. Earl was already thinking in generous dimensions on the evening he paddled into Cameron Bay as a 21-year old University of Alberta student making energetic use of his summer holidays.

When the college term ended in May, Harcourt and Graham had transported their 16-foot canoe and essential supplies to the headwaters of the Nelson River. They followed its spring flood down through the Rockies to the Liard, mightiest of the Mackenzie's tributaries. At Fort Simpson they picked up the main stream, which quickly carried them to the mouth of the Bear.

"Things went fine as we pushed up the Bear," Earl recounted, "until we were within three miles of the lake. We had to pause there – for 10 solid days. I never expected to see so much ice in that fast a river."

Once the raging stream had carried the floes clear and opened the gate to the lake, the young men crossed the open water at a time when the schooners were reporting heavy weather.

They saw nothing remarkable in what they had done nor in the way they had done it. Cameron Bay was simply a stop for news – to discover where the action was. Two days later they were paddling down the coast to Conjuror Bay.

Law and order reached the settlement on July 25. The *Speed II* , completing her second voyage from Fort Franklin, landed a couple of stalwart Mounties. This was no passing patrol. They had come to set up a permanent detachment. Hard on their heels the Hudson's Bay Company schooner *North Star* put ashore a tall, broad-shouldered figure in moccasins, overalls and militant red windbreaker. The voice that boomed from the depths of a magnificent beard belonged to Father Gaethy, recently of the Oblate mission at Fort Norman – and now of Cameron Bay.

The policemen found themselves in a community notably short of crime. This could, to some extent, be credited to their colleagues farther south. At McMurray, Smith and other check points, the RCMP kept an eye on the northward flow of humanity. It had been their long-established practice to discourage the unfit from proceeding deeper into the Territories. If a man lacked the necessary supplies or the means of getting them, or appeared to be unsuited for any other reason, it was recommended that he return south.

As a result the only outlaws around Echo Bay so far were four-footed villains such as the Barren Lands grizzly that had attempted to scalp Spud Arsenault, and the black bear Jack Carey had surprised stealing jam from his tent. The shaggy looter had been a sneak thief, not a killer, and frantically clawed its way out through the side of the tent rather than face the infuriated Carey as he blocked the doorway.

Father Gaethy had many more men in need of his services than the police did, and he seemed well pleased with his new parish. Great Bear had been part of his territory before Echo Bay had any particular significance, so he was already at home. He was as uncomplicated mentally as he was powerful physically and the approach he used with his Indian charges was transferred to the white saints and sinners now within range of his rugged ministry.

"Meet Father Gaethy," said the Fort Norman trapper who introduced us. "If you need a cabin built, a canoe paddled, a dog team driven or a good bannock baked, he's your man. Just one thing, though – don't get into a poker game with him. His beard is full of aces."

This was confirmed when I walked into the restaurant that evening and found the big Oblate holding a crowd spellbound with a superb display of sleight-of-hand. What he could do with a deck of cards was frightening. It would be sinful – and wrong – to infer that the devotion of his Indian congregation had been influenced by the magic of his nimble fingers, but there was no mistaking the delight with which Joe Dillon and his friends watched various objects disappearing and reappearing in thin air.

The same day the church and the law brought their orderly influence ashore another equally powerful one slid into the bay on board one of two gas-engined scows.

Each boxlike craft had a crew of two overalled figures, typical Northern rivermen judging by the deft way they handled the cumbersome boats. When they had tied up, we found that they had had plenty of opportunity for developing their navigational skills.

They had ridden the scows 2000 miles, starting far up the Peace River. For two months they had followed that majestic stream until it joined the Slave, moved with the Slave to the Mackenzie, ridden the brown back of the main stream to the Bear, then fought their way up that brawling flood to the lake.

All were from Berwyn, Alberta, frontiersmen who were quickly at home in Cameron Bay. The last one to come ashore was slighter than the others and had unusually fine features.

We realized we had a white woman in our midst!

Quiet, mature and clear-eyed, Mrs. Joe Gerhart had a face that was weathered as saddle-brown as her big, stockily-built husband's. But the coloring accentuated her femininity, which became even more marked when, after settling in, she emerged from her tent wearing a gingham dress, her fair hair done up in a neat bun.

Mrs. Gerhart's arrival did not cause revolutionary changes in our everyday habits or activities, but something subtle did happen to the camp, something deep and decent. It was a tribute to a courageous, unpretentious woman, who reminded us of the other women we had been close to, in other days and places.

An endless chain of aircraft had been swinging in and out of Great Bear without incident since the early-season disaster with "SL", but we suddenly began to have a series of reminders that bush flying still had its hazards.

Squadron Leader McLeod, gliding his Air Force Fairchild into the harbor at Smat, was suddenly jerked out of the air by a treacherous downdraft. His floats hit the water hard and the aircraft somersaulted. Lockie Burwash and his men were watching from the beach, and they reacted with the speed of a trained lifeboat crew. Their canoes were alongside the upturned machine before the icy waters could kill the injured pilot and his engineer.

The flyers were barely brought ashore before Roy Slemon, already in Smat, was airborne to fetch Doc Robertson. Slemon located Doc at Conjuror Bay, and by evening the casualties had their wounds dressed and were being flown south for hospitalization. I remembered how long it had taken to get Beck within reach of medical attention after his accident. What a difference it would have made to have had airplanes on call!

The second crackup that week was 60 miles in from Echo Bay. Cal Mews found himself with his AX Syndicate Fairchild crippled on a lonely lakeshore. A prospector carried his SOS across the maze of lakes and hills to Lindsley Bay.

The third accident happened right on our own doorstep. A Consolidated Smelters Moth, gliding serenely down in front of the settlement, encountered water as smooth as steel plate. Floatborne pilots dislike this as much as the winter whiteout. The Moth hit while the man at the controls was still under the impression he had plenty of air in which to flatten out.

He was lucky. Not only were he and his passengers uninjured when the light plane flipped on its back, but they were immediately surrounded by so many boats that it was possible to beach the machine itself before it could sink.

Having struck out there, Great Bear gave up on its caprices for that summer. There were no more plane accidents.

The buildup for the picnic began on August 1. Punch Dickins and Wop May each flew in a passenger list of notables – some special guests, some future residents. In the first category Courtney Riley Cooper, the American author, was the undoubted star. A regular contributor to Saturday Evening Post, at that time the most widely read magazine in Canada, he already had written an article on Great Bear from a distance. It had done much for public awareness of the field. With Cooper actually on the ground, there was much potential for further publicity.

Among the future residents was the third partner of Murphy Services, Vic Ingraham. Gerry and Tim Ramsey had spun so many yarns about Ingraham that he was already a legend as far as I was concerned. Before he died he was a legend to the entire North.

Ingraham had a broad, well-balanced frame, and rigorous physical activity had made the most of it. A darkly handsome man of 40 or so, he had strong convictions and a quick tongue to express them. Brutally frank if the occasion called for it, he was equally capable of sensitivity. Like Gerry, he had once had a Territories-wide reputation as a heller with a bottle of whiskey, and like Gerry, he had decided he was better on the wagon. Vic had what it took to make the decision stick.

As an organizer he was tough and tireless and the dispatch with which Murphy Services' supplies had become available at Cameron Bay was due to Ingraham's energy along the water route with the *Speed II*. The schooner was almost the death of him two years later, however, when it exploded and burned in an autumn storm between Franklin and Echo Bay. Vic, one of the two survivors, was terribly frostbitten and suffered a series of amputations.

He still had plenty to go on with, though, when the time came to turn Yellowknife into the metropolis of the North. His hotel became its social center. When he died, a large planeload of Edmontonians flew in to Yellowknife to join in the ceremonial scattering of his ashes over Great Slave Lake.

Although he was done with booze himself, Ingraham's packsacks had a gurgling sound the evening he landed at Cameron Bay. Refreshments were on the house. The restaurant was crowded for a memorable party.

Courtney Cooper was its sparkplug. He talked as well as he wrote – and he was a first-rate writer. His own life was patterned in bold and garish colors. To his global wanderings as a war correspondent and freelance reporter, he had brought his basic training as press agent for a big American circus. The cat man, the fat lady, the snake charmer, the roustabout and the local rube invariably became involved in his reminiscences regardless of where his untrammeled mind carried him. He didn't hog the stage that night, but the skill with which he set it aroused the latent yarn-spinner in almost every man in the room. There were wonderful tales and most of them were true.

Though our friendship was brief, I became acquainted with both sides of Cooper's contradictory nature. He and Wop May were dedicated fishermen and during that week they slipped away several times in the quiet hours to commune with the great lake trout in the lee of Gossan Island. I was invited along to handle the canoe.

Fishing is a sport for quiet men and ours was carried on in the accentuated stillness of the Arctic night. The midnight sun was now below the horizon but there was still a strong, pearly light and, on the windless lake, you could see the bottom at extreme depth. Approaching Gossan Island it was possible to follow its shelving underwater bulk far out from the shoreline and, as the canoe slipped closer to the island and the bottom rose steeply, there was the uncanny sense of paddling uphill. Far below, the lakers – some of them 40-pounders or better – drifted lazily and gracefully, the occupants of an oversized aquarium.

I don't recall how many fish were boated, how big they were, whether they fought well or poorly. But I can remember, between the strikes, the quietness of Gossan Island and of the lake and of those who fished it. The men's faces were at once intense and relaxed, and on the rare occasions when they spoke it was gently, so as not to alert the trout.

The mood gave Cooper's features new strength, yet disarmed them too. The cynicism faded and melancholy took over. The world, he remarked as we paddled back to Cameron Bay one night, was a mighty indigestible place. It was good to be far enough away from it to get most of it out of your system.

I asked what you did when you had to re-absorb it.

"You just hold your nose and swallow, I suppose," he said.

The days before the picnic provided a perfect opportunity for my last survey of the field. Conducted tours were laid on for the visitors and invariably there was room for me to stow away. The activity was impressive. Across from Eldorado, one of LaBine's parties was opening up good-looking showings on the Bonanza. Up by the Southwest Arm, Seiberg and Cragg had a fair silver strike. At Contact Lake, men were confidently following the vein that had "kicked" and, down the shore, Bernhard Day of the Bear Exploration and Radium company was tunneling into a 14-inch break of pitchblende.

There was word, too, that Borthwick hadn't been the only one to score in the Conjuror Bay and Camsell River areas. A new flurry had broken out at White Eagle Falls.

The main show, of course, was still Eldorado and the two big operations around the corner in Glacier Bay – Consolidated and Great Bear Lake Mines. J.J. Byrne, president of the latter, had flown in with the visitors and now, on board the company's new schooner, the *Charles E. Sloan,* we were taken on a luxury cruise to all three camps.

The voyage would have been perfect under canvas and even the prosaic thump of the diesel engine, knocking some of the music out of the breeze, couldn't spoil the lift of the swell and the jeweled bursts of spray at the bow when we negotiated the broader reaches of Echo Bay.

The man standing at Byrne's side on the quarterdeck was Charlie Sloan, whose name had for 20 years marked the stakes of uncounted claims lapsing around Hunter Bay. He had at last come into his own. Not only did his name grace the bow of the new schooner; it was now permanently on the map, attached to the spirited river that comes down from the Barrens to the northwest corner of Great Bear.

In proud isolation, Charlie had combined two decades of trapping and prospecting on the Sloan River. When Byrne, the Eastern promoter, first cast an eye on such claims as Charlie still retained in his previously unchallenged kingdom, he was not only drawn to the property but to the man himself. A big, quietly forceful fellow, equally at home in the hinterland or in the Toronto Mining Exchange, "J.J." made gaunt, weathered Charlie Sloan the symbol of his Great Bear Lake Mines operations.

When the promising-looking stuff at Hunter Bay had been overshadowed by LaBine's galvanic discovery farther down the coast, Sloan had been among the first to reach the new territory. On the peninsula between Glacier Bay and the open lake, Eldorado, Consolidated and Great Bear Lake Mines faced each other across an appropriately named body of water, Common Lake.

An engineer, Cy Stewart, was now in charge of Byrne's development program. The *Charles E. Sloan* – specially built for the lake – was attending to heavy transportation, and chartered planes were whisking prospecting parties in minutes to remote places which had once cost Charlie weeks of footslogging.

There was a big campfire on the point at Cameron Bay that night. The eyes of the newcomers were large from having gazed on the Midas-lode of Eldorado. What Great Bear had given and was promising to give had lifted everybody's spirits.

Beyond the glow of the fire a canoe rounded the point and slipped in to the beach. It might have been any one of the many craft which had brought visitors that night, but when two tall figures stepped ashore their silhouettes, sharp against the luminous harbor, conveyed an enormous weariness.

As they approached the fire, several of us realized we had welcomed this pair once before at the end of a canoe trip. We recognized Peet and Slaatten, the young voyagers who had made the remarkable 2000-mile passage via Fort Rae. When we had last seen them, they had shown some of the signs of hard going, but they were fresh and confident then, compared to the half-bearded, bleary-eyed men we were watching now. The lines of each face were deeply etched by smoke and grime.

Gerry Murphy rose to greet them. "You must have found something good to have made it worthwhile going at it *that* hard," he said.

"I hope so," answered Slaatten simply. "Otherwise we're cleaned."

"We haven't eaten for three days," added Peet.

"Come over to the restaurant," invited Gerry. "We can at least do something about that."

Later they joined us by the fire. Their need for sleep was cruelly obvious but their need for human company appeared to be even greater. They were the center of curiosity and concern but when, at first, they offered no information, the conversation already underway picked up again. There was a rare sensitivity in this circle, even among those fresh from the

Outside. In due time, Peet began to talk.

"We had just finished staking some good-looking stuff down in Conjuror," he explained. "Three days ago we went into the bush to prospect more thoroughly and when we came back there was a big fire where our camp had been. Everything was burning except the canoe. It was well out on the beach – away from those damned, flaming woods. That was our one good break. The canoe was still there when the fire moved on. Of course, we still had our axes. That was a break, too. We needed them. The paddles had been left in the camp and we had to shape a couple of birches before we had anything to push ourselves back here with."

Slaatten took up the tale. "Losing our films is what really hurt. We'd shot some mighty good stuff on the trip from Rae. Didn't want to chance it out of our hands when we cached our outboard motor and some dynamite here before we started for Conjuror. So we took it along with us." He laughed mirthlessly. "I guess we're going to have to live on dynamite for awhile."

"And it took you three days to make it back?" someone interjected.

"Hell, no," said Slaatten. "There was nothing wrong with those paddles we cut. We made good time."

"But three days – "

"There was a bush fire burning," said Peet brusquely. "We stayed as long as we could, to see if we could stop it from spreading. It was too big, though, and on the second day we started to get hungry."

Here were two men miles in the bush, without a shred of canvas for shelter at night, without flybars in country where insect pests were at their worst, without food to bolster their exhausted bodies. The fire had already reduced to ashes everything they owned. Yet their first instinct, and the instinct they followed until their endurance reached its limit, was to thrust themselves between the flames and the forest.

17

The picnic was the biggest day, said someone, "since Gilbert LaBine started pecking rock on Echo Bay." The settlement was full the night before but by morning the largest gathering of white men in the history of the Northwest Territories had converged on the place from Hunter to Conjuror bays. From Outside came two Canadian Airways planes, heavy with pleasantly mixed cargoes – fresh fruit and vegetables for the feast, an impressive supply of liquid refreshment, prizes for the competitions, and several passengers. Among them was Colonel R.H. "Red" Mulock, legendary wartime pilot and assistant to the president of the airways. His company was flying in the supplies as its contribution to the picnic.

Only one element was missing. John Michaels, the driving force behind the Outside arrangements, couldn't make it. Organizing – for profit, for the public good or just for the fun of it – was his never-ending enthusiasm, and the Great Bear celebration was his masterpiece.

By noon of the big day it required every yard of beach to accommodate the lineup of planes and schooners. Small craft had been pulled well above the waterline to make room for them. Under a smiling sky, Cameron Bay's habitations and open spaces swarmed with life. The buzz and the roar of it carried deep into the forest.

Beck had reappeared the previous night, having jumped

aboard one of the schooners coming up from Conjuror Bay. It had been an impulsive decision and he arrived in the clothes he stood in, lacking even his sleeping bag. We co-hosted a lunch for friends who dropped in on my air-conditioned quarters. However deep our differences might be, Eric and I shared a common indebtedness to our guests.

With lunch over, the sports were on. First came the schooner race. This was more like a workhorse derby than a contest of greyhounds but, if the boats lacked grace as they came chugging up the bay, their decks were thick with eager competitors. What the race might lack in dash was made up for in the sheer noise of shouted encouragement and salty insult.

The canoe competitions were taken more seriously. Muscle, sinew and skill were involved here, men in the peak of condition moving in craft as close to them as their skins. The teamwork of each pair of racers was a legacy of uncounted miles of wide and narrow water, on stormy lakes and rapids, where stern-man and bowman had become one in every physical and mental reaction. Grace and power rippled in their movements, which were keenly appreciated by the watchers on shore, most of whom were themselves intimately attuned to the bite and flash of the paddle.

"The Park" came into its own. The lovely area back of the settlement, so jealously preserved by Gerry Murphy and others, had its first public gathering. It was perfect for land sports – tug-of-war, shot-put (utilizing an eight-pound rock), and foot races. The event for men over 60 drew a remarkable entry list. Arthur Bird, who was 70 (and who vanished on the ice of the main lake two winters later), asked no handicap, but several suspected ringers had to be grilled. Those judged guilty of falsifying their ages were carried off to summary punishment by self-elected disciplinary committees.

The crew from Eldorado had arrived with two secret weapons – a college yell, and massive Charlie LaBine as anchorman of their tug-of-war team. Despite this, Cameron Bay team No. 2 pulled the Eldoradans sprawling through the moss and sand in the final heave. Murphy claimed the meals he served made all the difference. The visitors' team, early favorites as a result of Courtney Cooper's advance press-agenting and the enlistment of several mercenaries like myself, collapsed badly under the pressure of the unpublicized hard-rock miners.

When the sports were finished, the bar opened. A new log storehouse, with a barn-type half-door as the one breach in its solid defences, had been chosen as the strategic operational center. In the aperture above the closed lower half of the door appeared the welcoming faces of the camp's most distinguished teetotalers – Murphy and Ingraham. Punch Dickins, the master of ceremonies, invited anyone interested to form a line to the right.

If the athletic events had produced skilled coordination and endurance, the performance of the bartenders topped everything. The line formed, passed the open half-door and moved on in a state of satisfaction with impressive ease.

Appetites were whetted, and the bar was closed – assurance being given it would reopen later. Dinner was served in the open. It was a magnificent spread of fresh meat, fresh vegetables, fresh everything that a man dreamed of when he had been on a bacon-and-beans diet for months.

Then came the presentation of prizes. Bold or bashful men were made bolder or more bashful by the vocal encouragement they received as they stepped forward for their rewards.

Finally Punch said quietly, ''There's just one more thing and I'm through. There was no difficulty in financing this picnic. The outfits that wanted to be a part of it, both Outside and in here, were generous. In fact, the committee found itself with twice as much money as it needed. The decision it reached was that the surplus should go to the widows of Andy Cruickshank and Harry King. They've both asked me to thank you.''

Silence had fallen as he spoke. Heads turned towards the beach where ''SL'' had nudged the sand with its pontoons a month before to break the in-between. Then, without signal, men arose, drifted together into spontaneous groups and began to light campfires along the slope above the landing or in the pleasant reaches of ''The Park''.

The bar reopened and the line reformed. This time there was no regulated closing. Gerry and Vic had their stamina fully tested before the night was out. From one fire-lit circle rose a melancholy tenor voice that pleaded, *Bury Me Out On The Lone Prairie*. Lynch Conroy, the singer, had punched cattle in the Alberta foothills before turning prospector and he gave an authentic version of the old cowboy ballad. Lynch's audience grew in proportion to the demands for encores. Refreshed by couriers from the bar, he responded generously, so that by midnight, he had to be gently laid out on such prairie as Cameron Bay offered.

For those who liked their verse without music, Jack Carey had become established in the flush of another campfire. Someone had recalled that as "Porcupine Jack" in his younger days he had been a notable exponent of Robert W. Service's goldfields ballads. Once Jack was established on an oil-drum stage, *Dangerous Dan McGrew* came to snarling, passionate life and remained in fine voice until the early hours.

Towards morning the ranks began to thin and so did some tempers among the survivors. A few old grudges, real or imagined, found expression. Most of the roundhouse swings were wild, though, and the moss and sand gently received the falling bodies. There were always good-natured spectators to act as seconds, and they were quick to restrain any over-zealous combatants.

The possibility that the newly arrived Mountie or Father Gaethy might be called on for professional services arose when journeys home had to be organized. Many returning celebrants were either too lively or too limp for safety. This was bad enough where boats were involved, but hair-raising in the case of the planes. Only sober hands were at the controls, but with passengers already at a high altitude before climbing or being lugged on board, too little respect was paid to the hazards of flight.

Doc Robertson had a particularly bad moment after he had taxied out into the bay to fly a cargo of miners back to Contact Lake. There was something I wanted to say to Doc and I went down to the beach as he was in the final stages of revving up his engine. Doc was occupied with his controls and dials, so I stepped out on the pontoon to catch his ear.

I woozily decided he hadn't noticed me, for he gunned the

motor and slid out into the bay. It occurred to me that he would be pretty busy for the next few minutes, but that I could tell him what was on my mind after he was airborne. So I sat down on the pontoon, my arm around a strut, to wait.

There was a good deal of shouting and waving of arms on the shore by now and Doc throttled down to see what it was all about. This seemed like a good opportunity to speak to him, so I hauled myself up and addressed him through the open cockpit window. When Doc found us nose-to-nose, his expression was beyond description.

Even in my woolly condition, I sensed that our friendship was in serious jeopardy when he deposited me back on the beach. His language, at least, was hardly that of a one-time divinity student.

The next day was my time for leaving. Luckily for me, some of the visitors from Outside had asked Punch Dickins to fly them across the Barrens to where the Coppermine River meets the Arctic Ocean, to see a small trading post and an Eskimo settlement. It meant that the flight south, on which I was scheduled, would be delayed until afternoon. I was spared an early-morning rising.

Even with the added sleep it was a dismal awakening. There were three of us under the sleeping bag. Colin Campbell had joined Beck and me after two unsuccessful attempts the previous night to make it back to his camp on the other side of the bay. Each time, his canoe had capsized within a few feet of his takeoff point and bystanders had to pull him from the water. He was thoroughly saturated. He had crawled in, fully clothed, between us and his sodden condition was perfectly in keeping with my state of mind when I awoke.

Charlie Maydwell and some of the other prospectors who were returning to Conjuror mercifully came to collect Beck, and there was time only for the briefest of partings. Suffering my first hangover in half a year, I was incapable of anything else.

With Eric gone, I struck camp. There was little to do. My packsack was ready. There were a few utensils to stow on the cache, the tarp to strip from the ridgepole and to return to its proper place protecting the platform. I felt as empty as the roofless log walls of the dwelling I was dismantling.

Punch returned from Coppermine anxious to get underway in time to push through to McMurray before the end of the day – for, far to the south, there would be darkness at the end of steel by evening. Again the time for partings was blessedly short. My head ached and I was miserably grateful when we were airborne.

There were eight men and their gear on board, a maximum payload, and the redoubtable "SK" took her time lifting from the bay. She was still laboring as we climbed over Gossan Island's ruddy heights. Through a starboard window I followed the silver flood of Echo Bay flowing into the infinity of lake, so alive with breeze and sunlight it might have been a coursing river rather than a fiord.

The other passengers except Cooper, who sat opposite me, were soon asleep. Open-eyed but unusually quiet, the writer studied the volcanic turbulence below or stared straight ahead into his own thoughts. As we approached the area where Andy Cruikshank had crashed I scanned the hard terrain and, with Billy Nadin's help, probably located the torn, golden wings in a tangle of rock and tree. But I couldn't be sure.

We put down at Rae and gassed up. Lake Marian was silken smooth, without a breath of moving air. Punch's first attempt to take off was futile, the suction of the still waters holding his pontoons no matter how strenuously the plane's motor strained. The pilot retraced his path and used all the wiles of his long experience with float planes. He stirred the waters in one direction, then doubled sharply back to take advantage of the rippled course he had drawn. It was useless, though. There would have to be at least some assistance from the wind to lift the heavily loaded craft.

When we drew up to the dock at the Fort again and Punch announced we would have to remain overnight, I seethed with anger. It became terribly important that I get home. Every minute counted. If Punch would only take one more run at it I was certain he would manage a takeoff. Wasn't there a little burst of breeze ruffling Lake Marian over on its far reach even now? Wouldn't it freshen if we gave it a chance?

But the hot, heavy calm persisted and my burst of feeling

settled into it, much as the pontoons had abandoned their struggle to escape the spiritless waters. We straggled up to the Hudson's Bay post, had something to eat and rolled in.

Sleep was difficult. The makeshift dormitory was overheated and close. This didn't seem to bother my companions, who snored peacefully, oblivious to the strangeness of having a wooden roof overhead.

Perhaps I was only reacting to the mattress and the steel bed-springs that creaked each time I moved. The comfort, so different from the hard lying of the past 164 nights, was strange to me. But the longer I lay awake, the more sharply I was aware of the truth. I was feeling the insecurity of a man torn from the sweetest bed he had ever known – the firm, certain embrace of the earth itself.

18

The Outside was unchanged. All the financial pressures I had dreaded at a distance were there, hard and immediate. There was a period of three months in which our income totalled $85. The creditor's knock by day was amplified in restless dreams at night.

Extra money had been scraped up by the syndicate to keep Beck in the field and he had staked some ground on the Camsell that sounded promising, but the Great Bear hopes to which I had clung for so long became threadbare. They no longer compensated for stories that wouldn't sell, bill collectors who wouldn't understand, colds that wouldn't stop recurring in the sporadically heated old house.

I seemed to feel the cold more in civilization than in the bush. The upper part of the house was uninhabitable. I tried to work in the dining room but family life revolved there and in the kitchen, destroying my concentration.

When the worst had passed Ernestine and my parents acknowledged how worried they had been during the first days of my return. It had started immediately. I was taken to see our new son, blissfully sprawled in his afternoon sleep. Everyone waited for my delighted exclamation but I surveyed him silently, then turned away.

It wasn't that I was untouched; it was simply that any comment demanded more of me than I could muster. Already the verbal clamor attending my arrival had left me exhausted and my tongue, failing to find the right words, gave up the attempt. For more than a week lengthy conversation was beyond me. The one relieving element of the Outside was the fact that evening brought darkness and, with it, the sanctuary of sleep.

Ernie was understanding and patient, as gradual readjustment to the ways and moods of civilization returned my power of speech. But worst of all, the steady attrition had extended to our last citadel – the determination to see things through together. Old, deep hurts in two strong-willed people, by silent agreement pronounced healed in better times, were throbbing again. The agony of their return responded to nothing except a deadening fatalism about life itself. My reaction to the suicide on a single day of two friends who had been successful, prominent men before the Depression, was that of envying them their decisiveness.

My resentment towards Beck intensified during the black months after my retreat from the lake. Every disappointment, every setback seemed rooted in the breakup of our venture, for which I held him responsible.

Whatever discouragement John Sydie had experienced over that falling-out, he had offered no criticism on my return. His office remained a source of news and, when a business deal went through, of liquid warmth and momentary optimism. I had a drink in mind when I visited him on December 23 but, despite the nearness of Christmas, there was no bottle in his filing cabinet. There was news, though. He eyed me speculatively.

"Eric's coming out on the 26th. When he's briefed us on how things are going at the lake he'll be taking the train East to visit his folks. How would you feel about sitting in with us when he's here?"

An answer was beyond me at first. Finally I said, "You know how I feel about him."

John nodded.

"But you'd still like to have me at the meeting?"

"If you'd like to be there," he answered.

What happened in those moments was in its essence, similar to the experience on the rotten ice of Conjuror. There was the same sense of time having stopped – of emotion being

rechannelled from its normal course. Something more powerful than my bitterness broke through. I experienced a sudden
anticipation of reunion with the Beck of Lindsley Bay, the
Beck with whom I'd shared the greatest freedom I'd ever
known.

"Thanks, John," I heard myself saying. "I'll be there."

The meeting was on December 27. Eric was already with
John when I arrived. He was freshly barbered, dressed in the
conservative suit he had once worn as a stockbroker and, apart
from his windburned features and calloused hands, might have
been just another businessman who had dropped in from
Jasper Avenue.

Even in the North, among the colorful fraternity of the
bush, he had been neutral-shaded and now, against the flat
background of the Outside, his appearance was even less
remarkable. I was momentarily ashamed that I was aware of
this. When he rose and held out his hand, though, I was conscious only of my once-familiar response to a basically simple,
naturally generous man – the response that had once made our
partnership fruitful and which had helped to lift me clear of
many limitations.

Our eyes met and remained steady. The handclasp was
honest.

"Good to see you, Eric," I said.

"You look all right, too," he grinned.

We talked syndicate business the rest of the afternoon. Eric
described the new claims on the Camsell and his hopes of interesting some new capital in the East. He showed his
customary restraint – a restraint just short of pessimism – but
today it made me more reassured than impatient. It was a part
of the realism that marked the meeting.

When John's hospitality began to encourage more extravagant visions I went home. The couple of Scotches I had
downed were as many as I wanted.

That evening I had a sane discussion with my wife. The
high point came during my description of the afternoon with
Eric.

"It was as though we were back on Lindsley Bay," I recounted, "in the days when every card was face up – when

there was nothing that happened that went too deep to be talked out.''

As I spoke a long-buried memory quietly surfaced and silenced me. Ernie, more than usually sensitive, waited me out as I struggled with embarrassment.

Finally I ventured, "You're wondering why, if I was so all-fired straightforward, I never referred to your note in my sewing kit?''

She nodded.

The incident of the sewing kit had happened about three weeks after Beck and I had first camped on Lindsley Bay. I had torn my parka on a snag and opened the package of needles and thread Ernie had put together for me. Inside was a piece of white cardboard, with Ernie's handwriting on it. I read: *"For He shall give His angels charge over thee, to keep thee in all thy ways. They shall bear thee up in their hands lest thou dash thy foot against a stone."*

We had an understanding about this sort of thing, reached in the earlier stages of the Depression when Ernie had tended to fall back on the religious indoctrination of her childhood. My reaction was violent enough that she had finally seemed as relieved as I to avoid the subject.

"Were you angry when you found the note in the kit?'' she asked now.

"No,'' I answered, honestly anxious to remember the moment as it actually had happened. "I think I was moved – sentimentally that is.'' After a time I added, "There was more to it than that, though – more than I knew. More than I know. Let me tell you something that happened on Conjuror Bay.''

Two or three times since my return, I had come close to giving my wife a forthright account of the Conjuror Bay episode, in an attempt to explain the falling-out with Beck. But our lack of intimacy had somehow prevented me from speaking about it. Now I found the words.

I told her of my bewilderment at my own behavior and about the phenomenon of being "bushed'', when two men, stretched thin by savage pressures, had turned on one another.

I tried to explain what had happened – the spiritual awakening I had been unable to communicate to Beck, the strange calm which had come over me when it seemed certain I was about to plunge through Conjuror's ice.

Much later that night Ernie asked, "Where has it left you – truthfully?"

"I'm not sure," I answered. "It's not as simple for me as it obviously is for you, with your good Baptist upbringing. God – whoever He is, whatever He is – is mixed up in this. I've been protected when I didn't rate it, didn't even ask it. Something has made it possible to have Beck as a friend again. But I had a job saying the word 'God' out loud just now. I'm certain I couldn't do it with anyone but you. It shouldn't be that way – unless there's something phony about it all."

Ernie suggested there was a good deal I wasn't going to learn overnight, but that enough had happened in one day to suggest that the next night might be even better.

Eric joined us on New Year's Eve and we headed for a party thrown by some of the Northern crowd. Ernie had the time of her life and I was soberly conscious, for the first time in my adult life, of the new year being born.

I wrote in my diary that night:

"As the year has ended, Beck has again come into my life. He is as sound as he was in the first days of our adventure, and in no way resembles the man who almost drove me out of my mind. It makes me wonder what manner of man I was myself when loneliness, disaster and disappointment reduced us to a couple of snarling animals."

The wondering became painful. Any illusions I had left about my previous ability to take an honest look at myself fell apart as I seriously attempted to see, through Beck's eyes, the companion he had been saddled with at the blackest hour of his life. I could not take an easy course of self-justification. The understanding and the honest words I was searching for were still slow in coming.

Beck had left for the East. I thought that I would be able to tell him of my inward discoveries at some later time, when I was ready to do so. It seemed, then, that the words could take their time without further imperiling our friendship.

At length, the energy I was using in wandering through dark labyrinths of introspection and self-pity began to be spent on dealing with things as they actually were. Not that reality became any more accommodating. The Outside was still unsparing in its hostility towards a freelance writer. Then, abruptly, a series of hammer blows came from the North.

On January 13, 1933, operating north of The Pas, Bill Spence crashed on Oxford Lake. His passenger survived but Bill died at the controls. At De Melt Cove I had developed an impression that this seemingly tireless airman was indestructible.

Then, three weeks later, we had more shocking news from the North. Paul Calder and Billy Nadin had been killed at Grouard Lake, 70 miles south of Cameron Bay, on January 31. Wop May found them on February 5. The machine had burned. I remembered Paul boasting of his four boys while sprawled in my tent at Cameron Bay, and Billy pointing out the wreck of "SL" as we flew over it on the way out last August. Their deaths hit me hard. The work I was trying to do seemed trivial.

The third crash came just one week later.

This time it was Wop. Taking off from Fort Chipewyan, he hit a drift and, with his throttle wide open, tore off one of his skis. Fortunately, he had just reached flying speed and managed to yank the machine into the air. Circling above Lake Athabaska he methodically glided back to the most promising-looking ice and put the Bellanca down on the single ski. Balancing evenly as long as he could, he had reduced its speed to the minimum when it crashed. Not only did he walk away, but the plane was repairable. It had been a day for skilled and panic-proof hands on the stick, however.

Ernie and I talked late the night we got the news, made thoughtful by Wop's close call, and still sobered by the fatal accidents that had preceded it.

"Your angels were with Wop, all right," I said. "I wonder where they were, though, when Paul and Billy needed them."

"They were there, too," said Ernie firmly.

"They didn't change anything," I reminded her.

The warning flags of a futile theological discussion shot up and I added hurriedly, "I'm not saying that it's impossible to sometimes beat the bad breaks. We did it in the first months at

Great Bear. I think I could stay on top if I were back there now, knowing what I do."

"You'd like to live there permanently?"

"Why not?"

"I only wanted to be sure what you meant."

"What else could I mean? That I ought to be able to stay on top of the breaks no matter where I find myself?"

This time it was she who asked, "Why not?"

Next day I wrote Beck, the words forming as naturally as they had done with Ernie, as naturally as they had once done on Lindsley Bay. I offered my gratitude for everything he had given, my apology for anything I had withheld after allowing the lifeline to break between us. It seemed tremendously important that he should understand every detail of what had happened on Conjuror's rotten ice.

To this day I don't know whether he ever received my letter. It was my last direct touch with him. Thereafter any word I had was through John, himself puzzled by the absence of communication that developed after Eric reached Toronto.

Until John's death we never met without one or the other enquiring, "Ever hear of what happened to Eric?" Neither of us ever did.

My feeling that Great Bear might yet hold the answer to my financial insecurity had been growing ever since the reunion with Beck. It hung partly on the freshened hope that a strike on our property would give value to my syndicate shares. I now accepted that the odds against this happening were long. I knew I had to do something more practical than simply clinging to a possibility. Writing had failed to ease our marginal existence and I canvassed several of the established mining outfits for a pick and shovel job. I was told every time to apply again after the open season.

I went back to my typewriter with new determination. As June brought the promise of leads opening on the ice of Cameron Bay, I again went looking for work, but this time – as a writer. Within the week, I was packing my bush gear again. I had been promised a flight to Great Bear. The Edmonton Journal was not only interested in what I could file from there, but a modest expense account went with the offer.

During my interviews with the Journal editors, I was confident. The gut-tugging tensions, the half-expectation of failure were gone. I wasn't pleading for a break. I was offering something of value I was confident I could deliver.

Leigh Brintnell was the man who agreed to provide the transportation. Earlier that spring he had resigned as general manager of Canadian Airways to form his own company. It was to be known as Mackenzie Air Services and Eldorado was to be its principal customer. Not only would supplies be flown in to the mine; there would soon be concentrates to be rushed to the railhead. Brintnell had lined up Stan MacMillan and Matt Berry as pilots, but planned to do a good deal of flying himself while the company was becoming established.

I knew Leigh only slightly. When I managed to catch him in his Edmonton office and suggest he might like to fly me deadhead to Great Bear, he was beleaguered by myriad details of getting his new airline in operation. I had to remind myself that this hard-driving business executive was also an outstanding bush pilot.

Formidable as he appeared on first sight, Brintnell responded to my proposition.

"You may have to adjust to the paying traffic," he said. "But find your way to Fort McMurray next week and you'll have your ride North."

This was not all. Before I boarded the Muskeg Express on June 27 there was further word from the Journal. If I could be back in Edmonton by mid-July they'd be needing a man to relieve on the editorial page for several weeks.

The day I reached McMurray, Brintnell and MacMillan both boomed into the snye, the bright new lettering of "Mackenzie Air Services" gleaming on their green and gold Fokkers. They paused only briefly to refuel before heading North.

"It's going to be night and day flying with capacity loads if we're to keep up with our charters," Leigh explained. "I'll get you in all right, though. Harry Hayter's joining our company and he'll be taking his Curtis-Robin into Great Bear later this week. You should be able to squeeze in with him. Until he arrives, spread your bag in the cabin I've rented for our pilots."

It was a haunted house. Accommodation had always been scarce at McMurray, with frequent movement of families, and in succession this had been home to Harry King, Hod Torrie and Billy Nadin. The ghosts of the dead airmen seemed to linger particularly after evening fell.

My return to Great Bear on July 1 reminded me that Northern flying was still no game for amateurs. But Harry Hayter was a brisk young professional. His personality was as reassuring as his touch on the sensitive controls of the Curtis-Robin.

The quick-handling machine was unusually well adapted to our first landing, the fast-running stretch of the Slave River before Fort Fitzgerald. The stream was dotted with barely visible deadheads, waterlogged trees swept into the larger river by the flooding Peace. Just around the bend downstream, too close for comfort, roared the Rapids of the Drowned.

Harry put the plane down like a trained athlete running an obstacle course. A few months later, he saved Vic Ingraham's life with the same aircraft and the same skill. His Great Bear search and rescue, made during the freezeup season when flying was normally out of the question, was an epic achievement.

For all the confidence Harry inspired, I would have settled for a less intimate plane with a longer range, in the hours that followed our Fitzgerald takeoff.

A headwind slowed us as we followed the Slave River and, although the air was clear until we were halfway across Great Slave Lake, the reach from Fort Resolution to Fort Rae seemed immeasurably longer in the little Curtis-Robin than it had in larger aircraft. It became even more so, when fog slid in below us from opposite directions, like the closing doors of an automatic elevator. Great Slave is only slightly smaller than Great Bear, but the speed with which we mislaid it was breathtaking.

The long spearhead of Rae Arm, thrusting to the north, had been dead ahead when we lost visibility. Harry began to let down gradually on as accurate a compass course as the highly magnetized shores permitted. When we picked up the ground, it was at the western corner of the Arm, exactly where it opened out into the vast lake. The altitude by this time was uncomfortable – something under 1000 feet. There was a spiked bed of spruce trees to the left. The cold, impersonal waters of the Arm lay to the right.

Once in touch with the coastline, Harry hung on for dear life. It was the one guide on which he could depend, for it was now evident that the fog was widespread. If we drifted to the left, it meant encountering dangerous higher ground – terrain that lacked any aids to visual navigation. Drifting too far to the right meant the possibility of becoming lost over the featureless sweep of the Arm. As long as the shoreline remained below we knew where we were, but following the indentations of the coast was hard on our gas supply. The gauge needle was slumping wearily. The fog had become thicker, and we could only guess how far it was to the tip of the Arm, the readily identified narrows, and Fort Rae.

Dipping so low at times that the trees seemed about to brush the fuselage, Harry continued to hug the shore. The fuel-gauge sank dangerously. Then we saw a smudge in the misty rain, and the buildings of the fort appeared. Five grounded planes were at the dock. When we landed, we found that there had been fuel to spare. We might have flown for another 15 minutes, said Harry.

Three hours later, the air cleared and word came from Cameron Bay that the weather was good. The radioed meteorological reports that were now available on this run were a great advance over the by-guess-and-by-God methods of the previous year. Again we took to the air.

Small, savage storms were ranging in the North that day despite the general report. In the region where Andy Cruikshank had gone down, we again found ourselves out of visual touch with the ground.

Once more we scraped the tree tops, but there was no coastline to follow. We caught only fleeting glimpses of the trench which cradled the tortuous waterways between the lakes. Even though we could not see them, the high, rough walls to either side were a haunting, dangerous presence.

Twice we were captured by the smother, and broke out again. Our second escape was into magnificently free air. Sunlight glinted on the winding rivers and lakes ahead, and on the horizon were the battlements of the lower Camsell and the unforgettable basin of Conjuror.

I turned to Harry and shouted, "We're almost home."

He looked puzzled briefly, then grinned and nodded.

Great Bear rose up to meet us, serene and softly shining. As we approached Echo Bay nothing seemed changed. To the west the still-undisturbed ice of the main lake was impassive except for the subtle play of mirages near the horizon. Between the corded arms of the mountains the open water of the early-thawing fiords was quicksilver. Until we were well down the length of the Southwest Arm even the jaws of Cameron Bay were a firm, unaltered green. As we glided closer, freshly sawn lumber and newly peeled logs picked up the sunlight.

I was not prepared for the changes the settlement had undergone. Last year it was a sprawling tent city with a store and wireless cabin its only permanent structures. Now there were 25 buildings ranged along the streets of the townsite and the walls of several more were rapidly rising.

The disorderly makeshift of the previous season had vanished. McKay Meikle had surveyed the beautiful point with an eye to retaining as much as possible of its original loveliness. The streets conformed to the graceful curves of the shoreline. Dr. Thomas Byrnes, the new medical health officer, had seen to it that each resident maintained his property with care. The result was a community that fitted harmoniously into its magnificent setting.

Along the waterfront were the most marked signs of change. Where the planes had tied up hit-and-miss fashion, the bank had now been cut away to form a natural landing stage to shelter half a dozen airships. The rocks that had dotted the sandy beach had been blasted and the unsightly litter of open gas caches had disappeared into storehouses set in the bank.

Along the shore, the *Speed II* was being made ready for the open water (which came 10 days later than the previous year). A big scow, under construction, spread its naked ribs up the entire width of the bank, like the skeleton of a prehistoric animal. Smaller craft were being built and at the tip of the point a sawmill was turning Bear Lake spruce into lumber. A second mill, I learned, was being set up in McIvar Arm, on the southern shore of the lake, where the timber was larger. It was a far cry from Jack Wiley's whipsaw operation.

There were several stores and stopping places in town now. The original trading building of Murphy Services, which had looked like the Woolworth Tower to those of us who had seen it rise, was now only a section of a much larger structure. Two wireless stations connected the place to the outside world. A Mounted Police barracks was rising, the ground had been chosen for the Hudson's Bay Company post, and Bishop Breynat, vicar of the Mackenzie River district, was in town to decide on the location of a hospital.

Cameron Bay had become a typical mining camp town, with a strong touch of the fur-trading North thrown in for good measure. During the week there was a steady procession of prospecting parties moving in and out by air and water. Even with the improved accommodation, it was a rare night when there was an empty bed in the place.

During the winter, close to 200 Indians had been in the district, following the caribou and trapping. This, along with the unexpected number of whites who wintered there, had temporarily emptied the shelves of the stores. While several loads of supplies were being rushed in by air, there would still be a severe shortage of many less essential commodities until the boats arrived with the opening of the lake.

The most pleasant difference from the community of the previous year was the greater population of women. There were now six, five of them wives of residents, and the sixth the daughter of Henry Swanson, who was spending the summer with her father. There were also half a dozen children. They had worked a profound change in the atmosphere of unrelieved adult masculinity.

In one portion of the townsite the scene was unchanged. "The Park", the beautiful spot on the point, was still as it had been when Beck and I had camped on its edge. A couple of acres of moss-carpeted forest had been preserved and a large sign requested that the beauty of the place be respected.

One detail of the scene made me thoughtful. I approached the site of the first residence that had ever risen here. Under the naked radio mast, which had been a bushy spruce tree when Beck and I originally camped there, the log walls of my rabbit-hutch were still standing and the place had been neatly maintained. It was still occupied – by old tin cans and other refuse. Our camp site was now a trash dump.

19

It was well after midnight before I unrolled my sleeping bag in space Gerry Murphy had offered. I was barely asleep before Walter Gilbert was shaking me by the shoulders.

"If you want to be the first man into LaBine Bay this season, you've got just five minutes to make it," he announced.

Unshaven and still half awake, I managed to board the Junkers monoplane Walter was flying. George Drew, lawyer, magazine writer and later leader of the Conservative Party of Canada, was already in the cabin.

Though the bay inside LaBine Point was open, the thick ice still pressed close to its entrance. It had been exactly like this when, the previous year, I had flown into Eldorado on the first pontoon landing of the season.

There were marked changes ashore. Charlie LaBine led us into a 1000-foot tunnel that now pierced the rock wall back of several new buildings. A hot sun beat on the hillside but stepping into the black maw was like moving from July to December. The permafrost goes deep in Great Bear. Ceiling and walls were white with rime and there were little mounds of ice between the rails of the tunnel's narrow-gauge track. This was seepage from the lake far above our heads, Charlie explained.

It was a journey into an Alladin's cave. The rich promise of the surface pits was more than fulfilled. The walls of mineral, both precious and base, were highly glazed by the dampness and the sub-zero temperature. The rays from our miner's lamps brought out a riot of metallic and oxidized coloring – orange, pink, yellow, green, coal black, silver, copper – in a brilliant tapestry.

An ore chute opened in the roof and a square of daylight was visible 100 feet above. The sound of drills came down hollowly. Charlie explained that work was being concentrated along the massive 1400-foot surface break while the open weather held. Highgrade ore was being blasted from its 18-foot width and would shortly be roaring down the chute into the waiting cars.

The miners surveyed wth impatient eyes the ice beyond the bay – the locked gate that barred the arrival of the heavy machinery still to come in by water. Only then, when the new mill went into operation, would it be possible to ship concentrates to the refinery Eldorado had built in Port Hope, 3000 miles away in the heart of industrial Ontario. Until then, highgrade ore would have to be laboriously hand-cobbed.

Not only were cargos for Eldorado approaching from Outside; they were coming from the northern Mackenzie as well. The Imperial Oil installation beyond Fort Norman, which had produced only a thimbleful of high-test spirit since the discovery there a dozen years before, was now settling down to the serious business of servicing a mining field. Fuel and lubricating oils would be winched over the Bear River rapids in ever-increasing quantities before the summer was out, to find their way to the silvery tanks rising on Great Bear's eastern shore.

LaBine excused himself to attend to something up by the enginehouse, inviting us to join him at lunch when the shift changed. Walter Gilbert, well acquainted with the camp, took Drew off to show him other details. This left me free for a sentimental walk across the point, only a matter of a few hundred yards, to a place where the throb of the diesel engines and the machine-gun rattle of the drills died away. I found myself a smooth slab of rock where there was an unobstructed view of the lake, stretched out in the sun, and let my eyes move over the unbroken ice.

I remembered the first time I had seen this spot, on the

early morning when Pete Baker and I had moved out through the narrow entrance between the little island and LaBine Point. We had paused in the half-light to adjust the harness of one of the dogs before the long haul up The Labrador and, for a few seconds, the hugeness of the lake and the intensity of its winter silence had been awesome.

In those moments, 18 months before, I had an uncanny experience. Half a world away from the nearest steam whistle, I heard a long, commanding wail drifting along the coast. It sounded exactly like the voice of the weekly train at McMurray, echoing across the three miles between the Waterways railhead and the old fur post.

Now, as I watched the shimmer of the sleepless sun raising mirages on the ice shield, the sound of the whistle came back. It was real this time, a long, commanding hoot that set echoes rebounding from the steep shore and charging out through the channel until they faded in the void of ice and sky.

Suddenly, I realized I was hearing the noonday whistle from Eldorado's new enginehouse as it called the workers in from the hill to lunch.

Anyone wishing to go to Contact Lake, Hunter Bay or the Camsell now could do so with relative ease. Air and water transport was plentiful. I was able to cover the field thoroughly in the next two weeks. I found a succession of volunteered free lifts, and, wherever I landed, there was generous hospitality and an invitation to stay as long as I liked.

These were perfect days, strongly reminiscent of those when Beck and I had followed the spring in to Eagle Nest Lake. I roamed the proud terrain freely. And this time there was no cringing when I remembered that eventually I would return Outside.

I had instead, a sense of optimism: no physical setting, no economic handicap, no human relationship need ever again exert final control over my life. The main thrust behind my return to Great Bear was, I suspected, the desire to match truths I was beginning to find Outside with those that had originally set me searching.

There was a luminous quality about everything I felt and did. I knew the feeling wouldn't last forever – but when the fragile emotion had faded, my life had taken on a new simplicity.

There was never a shortage of grist for my journalistic mill, whether I was on the move or in Cameron Bay, and my free hours were rich with comradeship.

One evening I flew with Wop May to a camp beyond Echo Bay where he had decided to anchor a mooring buoy rather than continue the risk of damaged pontoons. He frequently serviced this place. The prevailing wind and a shoreline spiked with rocks had given him some bad times.

The buoy, a sealed gas drum with a heavy rock for an anchor, was moved out by skiff to the point Wop indicated. The entire contraption was resting on planks laid across the thwarts and, when it was dumped over the side, the sudden weight on the outboard end of the timbers created a natural catapult. Wop, on the projectile end, shot into the air, then plunged headlong in the lake. It was like a movie gag. The two of us still in the skiff roared with laughter. But not for long. When Wop surfaced, the look on his face reminded us sharply that men who perished in these waters did not have time to drown. Canoeists had been pulled out with lungs still clear of water, but dead anyway. Their hearts had been stopped by the cold.

Thoroughly sobered, we hauled Wop inboard almost as quickly as he reappeared. For a long time he lay in the bottom of the boat, blue in the face and incapable of speech. But eventually his natural color and his voice returned.

"That was a damn fool thing to do," he groaned. "Row me ashore before I get pneumonia. I need to bum some dry clothes."

When he was re-equipped he addressed me brusquely.

"Get aboard."

I told him that while he had been changing his clothes I had been invited to stay at the camp for a day or so and there was some good material here.

"Get aboard," he repeated. "I've a call to make at Bay 66, I'll drop you back here before I go on to Cameron Bay."

So, at one o'clock in the morning, we took off, paused briefly at the camp on Bay 66 while Wop did his business, then headed back towards my destination. The first half of the round trip was accomplished in complete silence except for the drone of the motor. Wop gave no indication of what was on his mind and it seemed like one of those times when it was unwise to probe. On the return flight, however, he spoke. "Father Gaethy was telling me you spilled your guts in the restaurant the other night."

"About what?"

"About what happened to you and Beck last year on Conjuror Bay."

"Oh, that?" I laughed. "You know how things go when you get sucked into one of those religious arguments Gerry Murphy likes to start. Doc Robertson, McKay Meikle and a few other fellows were there. It was quite an evening."

"Well, what *did* happen to you?" demanded Wop.

I told him, including my reunion with Eric in Edmonton. When I was finished he asked, "Is that why you've quit boozing the way you used to?"

"There's a relationship, I suppose."

"Did you figure you had to?"

"No, somewhere along the line I found I didn't have to."

"Didn't have to what? Quit?"

"No. Didn't have to booze the way I used to."

Wop chuckled. "I think I get it. I'm not a heathen, you know."

"Amen, brother. I'll back you in that."

"What do you mean?"

"You were responsible for getting me North in the first place. That put you on the side of the angels."

"Some angel!" barked Wop.

When we came down at the camp we tied up to the new buoy for awhile. Wop said it was as good a time as any to make sure it was well anchored. We were able to finish our talk without competing against the roar of the motor.

The next day Wop left, taking several of my stories out with him. I went over to the Beck Syndicate claims in the afternoon and found a new quartz vein. The flies, appearing in hordes, plagued me. One leg was so badly bitten, I felt as though it had been poisoned.

I didn't know it then, but I had made my last pilgrimage to

the cliffs and my last gesture as a prospector.

As the time grew near for me to return to the Outside I was a little worried over my eagerness to go. My work seemed far from complete.

I spent my remaining time gathering material and basking in the sun, which had made a welcome reappearance. The possibility that Leigh Brintnell might fly in made it unwise to go far afield. With the weather uncertain, and Mackenzie Air Services planes infrequent, it had become important that I move south at the first opportunity if I was to be sure of catching that weekend's train out of Fort McMurray.

On July 11, Leigh breezed in, looking desperately tired, and announced he was going south in 10 minutes. There was a wild rush to pack, with little opportunity for goodbyes. On the flight south, we made a couple of stops on the Camsell to pick up and drop a prospector, then flew on to Rae in heavy rain. The post was crowded with Treaty Indians – 600 of them – and the night was wild with the howling of their dogs.

On July 12, we were up at 3 A.M. and took off immediately with a Captain Atkinson as a passenger. We were to land him on a lonely lake east of the Yellowknife River, where he planned to prospect for the rest of the open season.

Atkinson was a powerfully built man with a thick moustache, a restrained presence and a military bearing. The small lake where he landed is still unknown to me, for I adhered to the unwritten law that where a man landed on a prospecting charter flight was between himself and his pilot.

It was, however, as unattractive a body of water as any prospector had ever had to face on his own. There was no beach. The shoreline bristled with deadfalls and tangled brush that thrust out into the water like obstacles planted to repel an invasion. Atkinson, taking off from the toe of the pontoon, fought his way along one of the projecting fallen trees and landed his outfit on the dank shore. The insects swirled about him in a gray mist. He was a desolate figure, standing on the mosquito-infested shore as we took off.

Once we were out of the melancholy sink-hole, the world beneath us looked almost pleasant. Even the lake we had departed winked back at the early morning sun. Not far away, the Yellowknife was a molten stream flowing down the ancient rock of the Precambrian Shield and broadening gradually as it joined the glowing mass of Great Slave Lake.

Below, near the lonely prospector hacking himself a campsite beside his cheerless lake, the unknown bounty of the earth lay waiting beneath the Shield. Within the year the word "Yellowknife" would have the same magical ring as Echo Bay. With it would be coupled the single word "Gold!"

But I never heard of Captain Atkinson again.

To the bay where the Yellowknife clouded Great Slave's waters Vic Ingraham and Gerry Murphy were drawn to build anew. With them came Bill Jewitt, Lockie Burwash, J.J. Byrne, the LaBines and others with the means to raise shaft heads on the spruce-spiked, heavily scarred face of the Shield. Pete Baker, Spud Arsenault – in fact, most of the celebrants at the first Great Bear Lake Prospectors' picnic – arrived sooner or later.

On the bay where the settlement of Yellowknife was born, the waters boiled to the arrivals and departures of Punch Dickins, Wop May, Leigh Brintnell, and the other flying legends. As the years passed, the bush pilots continued to follow the Marian and the Camsell to Great Bear. But inexorably, the air traffic lessened.

Not that the glossy black mineral at LaBine Point failed to live up to its early promise. But there would be only one Eldorado. Other mines with potential, lacking such fabulous highgrade ore, would ultimately close, killed by the prohibitive cost of transportation and development at that time. Prospects waned, wildcats lapsed and the lifeblood of Great Bear thinned – syphoned south by new strikes at Yellowknife, Pine Point and Lake Athabaska's Goldfields.

Beck Syndicate's Great Bear claims cancelled themselves. They had not returned a dollar to the investors or the field party. The indefatigable John Sydie reorganized and, with Punch Dickins added to the shareholders, made a bid for a waterpower site to serve the new Lake Athabaska field. When this too, failed, the last trace of the syndicate vanished.

The Alladin's cave of Eldorado, however, continued deeper and deeper into the fateful lode and the settlement at its mouth was named Port Radium. The electric lights shone and the whistle blew and the precious concentrates were moved by air, water and rail to the refinery thousands of miles away.

In 1943, the Canadian government suddenly took over the mine. The second world war was raging and few noticed the change of ownership. Even the fact that unauthorized visitors were no longer allowed ashore at LaBine Point attracted scant attention. As far as the Outside was concerned, Great Bear had returned to the loneliness and mystery in which it had always been shrouded.

But there was an ironic footnote to those who first sought the black pitchblende because, as radium, it had an enormous value to medicine. The trove at Great Bear yielded yet another technological advance – nuclear fission. And in 1945, its power, unleashed in the first atomic bomb fired in anger, devastated Hiroshima in a single horrifying blast. As in man himself, the elements of both healing and holocaust had lain in Great Bear's treasure.

Epilogue – September, 1980

Great Bear today is still a silent, brooding monster, glacial and forbidding even in high summer as light winds buffet its shores and toss leaves of yellowing aspens along the glowering cliffs. It is still rarely visited, except by fishermen and mining men.

There is a busy settlement at Port Radium, on the site of LaBine's Eldorado, where highgrade silver ores are dug from Echo Bay's crags. It is regularly serviced by air, and I took an opportunity to go into Great Bear once more. It had been 47 years since I last saw the giant's face, and I looked forward to the experience with a jumble of emotions.

We took off, in a Convair operated by Echo Bay Mines, from Yellowknife. When I had last seen the bay, there was no visible sign of habitation on its shores. Now the highrise towers of a city of 10 000 lifted there and the sails of late-summer pleasure craft dotted Great Slave Lake far below.

The Convair slanted steeply towards its 12 000 foot cruising altitude. The twin engine turbo-prop craft was three times faster than Harry Hayter's tiny low-flying Curtis-Robin.

Ahead of me, the cabin was stuffed with provisions: crates of asparagus, California cauliflowers, B.C. peaches and machine parts were strapped to the Convair's steel floorplates. A couple of dozen other passengers – engineers, miners, young mothers with their children – chattered in rows of regulation airliner seats. A businesslike hostess in clean brown coveralls matching those of the pilot and co-pilot, served coffee.

Great Bear was a couple of hours away. Well before we reached it, pilot Don Siddle invited me to the cockpit. The remembered shapes of Echo Bay – Southwest Arm, Bay 66, Cameron Bay, Gossan Island, LaBine Point – readily identified themselves. Around the corner which shelters Eldorado lay the indentation of Glacier Bay. Optimistically, I reminded myself that the company's vast-bellied, four-engine Hercules aircraft regularly flew in and out fully loaded. But as I remembered them, Echo Bay's crags left no place to land. Then the landing strip was ahead of us, blasted out of sheer rock in one wall of Glacier Lake.

We pulled into a wide, flattened area alongside rows of neatly baled concentrates. Mine manager Peter Parashyniak was waiting in a truck to take me two roller-coaster miles to the site. We passed a pair of decaying log shacks that made me momentarily feel my age. Finally, the road dropped steeply down to the cove where Gilbert LaBine and Charlie St. Paul had camped in 1930.

Treasure was still being mined from the depths back of the hanging wall – no longer pitchblende, but silver, now at peak world value. Peter told me of other activity – Contact Lake had come back into production and field parties had returned to other places abandoned in less encouraging days. The company had a new gold prospect, at Contwoyto Lake, some 200 miles away, being readied for production.

There was barely opportunity to take in the exterior detail of the mine buildings – the gymnasium, the curling rink and the marina lined with trim private launches.

I managed one thoughtful, lake-level glance at Great Bear itself. There it stretched between the foreland and the sheltering island – glacial, uncompromising – and it stirred emotions I had cautiously anticipated. I had little opportunity to brood. Almost at once, Peter headed back to the landing-strip, for the return flight would not wait.

On the outward climb, low-scudding overcast and bursts of rain blotted out the familiar coastline. "Well, it's down there, somewhere," I thought sourly.

Then, suddenly, it was.

An explosion of evening sun suddenly scattered the overcast in fiery shards. To the west stretched Great Bear. Directly below lay Conjuror – the hook of cliffs where Beck had fallen, the long channel I had trudged in desolation, the treacherous narrows. The break in the gold-rimmed clouds seemed a confirmation, somehow, that this indeed was where my life's journey had begun.